CRITICAL STUDIES ON CORPORATE RESPONSIBILITY,
GOVERNANCE AND SUSTAINABILITY   VOLUME 9

THE HUMAN FACTOR IN SOCIAL CAPITAL MANAGEMENT: THE OWNER-MANAGER PERSPECTIVE

BY

PAUL C. MANNING
The University of Chester, Chester, UK

Emerald

United Kingdom – North America – Japan
India – Malaysia – China

Emerald Group Publishing Limited
Howard House, Wagon Lane, Bingley BD16 1WA, UK

First edition 2015

Copyright © 2015 Emerald Group Publishing Limited

Reprints and permissions service
Contact: permissions@emeraldinsight.com

British Library Cataloguing in Publication Data
A catalogue record for this book is available from the British Library

ISBN: 978-1-78441-584-6
ISSN: 2043-9059 (Series)

ISOQAR certified
Management System,
awarded to Emerald
for adherence to
Environmental
standard
ISO 14001:2004.

Certificate Number 1985
ISO 14001

INVESTOR IN PEOPLE

THE HUMAN FACTOR IN SOCIAL CAPITAL MANAGEMENT: THE OWNER-MANAGER PERSPECTIVE

CRITICAL STUDIES ON CORPORATE RESPONSIBILITY, GOVERNANCE AND SUSTAINABILITY

Series Editor: William Sun

Recent Volumes:

CONTENTS

LIST OF TABLES

LIST OF APPENDICES

EDITORIAL ADVISORY AND REVIEW BOARD

ABOUT THE AUTHOR

Paul C. Manning attended school in Liverpool then studied history at the University of Birmingham. After graduation he was self-employed for 10 years and built-up and sold a number of enterprises. He subsequently embarked on a career in education and his first position in HE was as a lecturer at Liverpool University's LIPAM (Liverpool Institute of Public Administration and Management). His next two appointments were as a lecturer at Northumbria University, which he left to become a senior lecturer at Leeds Metropolitan University. His next appointment was as the Director of MSc Programmes at the University of Liverpool's Management School (ULMS). He is currently Professor in Business History and Ethics at the University of Chester.

Paul is an active researcher and regularly presents conference papers and publishes in leading journals. His research interests include socio-economics with a focus on social capital and social network theory. He also researches business ethics, knowledge management and various aspects of small business and enterprise.

ACKNOWLEDGEMENTS

I would like to thank all those that have engaged with and contributed to this volume.

I would especially like to thank Professor Laura Spence and her colleagues at Royal Holloway, the University of London, for their constructive criticisms and unflagging support during the writing of this book.

I would also like to thank Professor Keith Dickson of Brunel University who offered me much needed encouragement and perceptive advice.

In addition, I am grateful for the constructive advice offered by Professor Simon Robinson and Dr William Sun.

This book was also made possible by the understanding nature of my wife Rachel, who was prepared to put up with my musing on social capital, and by my children Alexandra and Paul who inspired me to conduct this research. I am also indebted to my mother Mary and to Joseph, Anthony, Marie and Clare who offered me much needed words of encouragement to complete this research.

PREFACE

This book investigates the management of social capital processes as they are accomplished-understood, experienced and shaped-by owner-managers. The aim of the book is to develop a deeper understanding of the management of social capital processes, to achieve a greater congruence between real-life perspectives and experiences and social capital literature.

The book argues that social capital is situational, and in the economic situation the theory has been bounded by rational choice framing assumptions. The research problem is that claims for the universality of the economic way of looking at life, and for looking at social capital processes are over-stated. Predicated on this insight the research investigates economic notions of rationality, and low and non-rationality, as well as their interdependence in the management of social capital processes.

The research follows a qualitative approach for data collection, with flexible pre-coding to guide the research where to look, while retaining an inductive openness to emergent data.

The research population is drawn from SME owner-managers in the service and retail sectors, who were researched over two years using semi-structured interviews, observation, and by researcher participant observation.

The research presents a number of contributions to knowledge. First, the research offers an in-depth, single source review explicating the meaning of the economic form of social capital, with reference to its intellectual antecedents, conceptual debates and key theoretical authors.

The second (emergent research) contribution is to identify the significance of ethics and autodidactic reading for managing social capital processes.

The third (theoretical) contribution argues for an expanded social capital perspective, beyond the prevailing and over-confident rational framing assumptions, and also for a new holistic ontological understanding.

The fourth contribution is to identify a number of generic processes that can guide the management of social capital processes.

Paul C. Manning

CHAPTER 1

INTRODUCTION

1.1. OVERVIEW OF RESEARCH

The aim of this research is to develop understanding of the management of social capital processes, as they are accomplished – interpreted, experienced and shaped – by owner-managers in the small business sector. This research also aims to contribute to a greater congruence between theoretical literature and the viewpoints and experiences of economic actors (owner-managers) in the management of social capital, which will be achieved by investigating the validity of social capital's rational choice framing assumptions.

This research understands social capital as being 'situational', with different forms in different contexts (Coleman, 1990, p. 302; Woolcock, 2001, p. 194), and will argue that in its economic form social capital has been framed by background assumptions originating in James Coleman's rational utility optimisation modelling (1990, 2000). Coleman pioneered the application of economic concepts in sociology, and his theoretical legacy is evident in the prevalence of rational choice suppositions in social capital literature. For example, Fine and Green (2000), Fine (2001), Lin (2001), Ahn and Ostrom (2008) and Commin (2008) have all discussed the significance of rational choice theory in framing social capital. However, 'The Economic Way of Looking at Life' with its method of analysis which assumes individuals 'maximize welfare as they conceive it', as well as displaying a consistency in forward looking behaviour (Becker, 1992), has been subject to intense criticism (see Sections 1.7 and 1.8). It is also worth emphasising that criticisms of rational choice theory, which is based on a paradigm of self-interest and arguably posits a gloomy view of the human personality, are more acute when the utility maximising method is extended beyond its established field of economics. Thus, it is problematic to apply the economic understanding of rationality as a method of analysis to sociological/humanistic phenomena that have not hitherto fallen within the cost/benefit optimisation approach.[1] Moreover, the book will argue that economic rationality is just one of many social constructions and consequently rational choice assumptions do not offer a comprehensive analytical or explanatory framework for understanding the management of social capital.

The research in the book is qualitative and grounded in ethnography in the tradition of Herbert Blumer's symbolic interaction which, '... may be envisioned as the study of the ways in which people make sense of their life situations and the ways in which they go about their activities' (Prus, 1996, p. 10). This is an interpretivist perspective, '... centrally concerned with the meaning people attach to their situations and the ways in which they go about constructing their activities in conjunction with others' (*ibid.*, p. 9). This approach acknowledges the significance of human agency and emphasises the social construction of meaning. This approach can also be termed, 'phenomenological symbolic interaction', which is '... typified by its emphasis on the emergent properties of interaction, through which individuals create their social world rather than merely reacting to it' (Burrell & Morgan, 1979, p. 251). Further, in this approach, human group life is also understood as inter-subjective, '... that takes its shape as people interact with one another' (Prus, 1996, p. 15), and processual; that is, '... experiences are viewed as emergent or on-going social constructions or productions' (*ibid.*, p. 17). In sum, the research will ethnographically investigate the mental states and the lived experience of the management of social capital.

Social capital ontology is understood as integrative and processual, being organic and self-generating, and therefore resistant to a linear chain cause and effect explanatory analysis, which is consistent with the views of an author often cited as a founding theoretical scholar, Jane Jacobs (Castiglione, 2008, p. 178; Putnam, 2000, pp. 19, 308). Jacobs argued that ecosystems had to be understood in terms of complex, varied and interdependent components that developed over time in a constant and dynamic state of flux (1961/1993, pp. xvi–xvii). Jacob's view was that there must be an underlying continuity of people to maintain networks that constituted a '... city's irreplaceable social capital' (*ibid.*, p. 180). This processual understanding also accords with a symbolic interaction approach to 'process' (see Chapter 3) and also with Heraclitus philosophy of constant change or flow, which contends that it's impossible to step twice into the same river, as neither the river nor the individual will be the same. In sum, in this processual understanding, social capital will be researched synoptically, to examine its interwoven management processes of generation, maintenance and enhancement.

Social capital is also taken to reside in individual level interactions and social relations and is therefore taken as an individual level endowment in the sociological egocentric tradition (Appendix B). However, while the egocentric sociological interpretation is taken as the most convenient label for the research focus, social capital is also understood to interact at different levels. In Lin's words:

> Most scholars agree that it is both a collective and individual good; that is, institutionalized social relations with embedded resources are expected to benefit both the collective and the individual in the collective. (2001, p. 26)

For example, a firm's social capital is an aggregation of the interactions and social structures of its individual stakeholders, which at the same time are also influenced by this firm level social capital. Coleman described this process as an 'individual-level theory of action' in terms of fluid macro-to-micro and micro-to-macro transitions (1990, pp. 19−23). The book therefore rejects the stark division between external and internal classifications of social capital as proposed by Adler and Kwon (2002), in favour of a viewpoint that understands the levels as being intertwined and inseparable, which is also consistent with the book's holistic ontological understanding.

The book's focus will be at the micro level of individual owner-managers and will investigate how they negotiate the social contexts in which they find themselves; that is, how they made sense and order their interactions and environment in terms of their management of social capital. Thus the book will investigate how the owner-managers accomplish − interpret, experience and shape − the management of social capital. The book therefore aims to develop understanding of the management of social capital by investigating the inter-subjective perspectives and experiences of owner-managers.

Owner-managers in the service and retail sectors were selected as the most appropriate focus for investigating social capital processes for a number of reasons. First, extant literature suggests that they are engaged in a socio-economic process (Anderson, Park, & Jack, 2007; Granovetter, 1985, 2005), and further that they intensely self-identified with their organisations, in many cases personifying or reflecting themselves in their form of their firms (Brenkert, 2002, p. 30). Second, it can be argued that owner-managers are closer to free agents, or rugged individualist and thus able to describe their real views, as opposed to bureaucratically constrained corporate employees, though market conditions impose constraints on all economic actors. In consequence, owner-managers' perspectives on their way of life, and its processes of constant refinement and pragmatic development were taken as appropriate for research into the management of social capital. The research population was also exclusively selected from the service and retail sectors, in part because they rely significantly on the quality of their network and relational interactions to market their services and retail goods, arguably more so than other sectors, for instance manufacturers' products are tangible and storable and therefore open to more considered objective assessment. Thus the service sector, with its reliance on intangibles, such as knowledge and reputation management, is appropriate for social capital research (see Chapter 2 for a discussion of the relationship between intangibles and social capital).

To achieve familiarity and insight into the world of the owner-manager the research relied on three sources of data collection collected over a two-year period, which all involved interaction between the owner-managers and the researcher. In order of importance, the first of these sources of data were semi-structured, open ended, face-to-face, rapport interviews (based on an interaction of mutual understanding and agreed trust). These interviews were approached as interactions in which the interviewer actively probed and developed the dialogue to gain greater detail and understanding of social capital processes. Collectively these interviews offer a multi-voiced narrative examining (in the owner-managers' own words) their perspectives and experiences of the management of social capital. Second, the research relied on data from observation that, '... encompasses not only things that one witnesses through one's visual and audio senses, but also includes any documents, diaries, records, frequency counts, maps, and the like that one may be able to obtain in particular settings' (Prus, 1996). For this research, 'observation' material included owner-managers' power point presentations, induction and training documents, websites and various internal and external texts. The third source of data was participant-observation, with the researcher in a number of cases directly advising and participating with the owner-managers with reference to operational and training matters.

To conclude, the book aims to inductively develop understanding of social capital management by conducting an ethnographic, qualitative investigation into owner-manager's activities on a day-to-day basis, considering their perspectives, practices, dilemmas and interpretations of the management of social capital. The research questions (detailed in Section 1.6) guided the research, by considering the significance and interplay of rationality and low non-rationality in this managerial process. Further the research investigated the management of social capital from the owner-managers' viewpoints, on the (symbolic) interactionist understanding that owner-managers do not merely respond to structural constraints and environmental stimuli, but are actively engaged in a dynamic process of responding, shaping and learning from their social interactions.

1.2. REFLECTIONS ON RESEARCH CHOICE

The idea for this research first took root from my time as a retail owner-manager in a small and medium sized enterprise (SME) in the 1990s. My abiding memory was that owner-management was a deeply social activity, which required the cultivation of collaborative connections: in my case with customers, suppliers, partners and employees; but also with any number of other stakeholders, depending on the day-to-day situational variables of social interaction. In my experience as far as economic activity is concerned, most people are attuned and predisposed to be wary of self-interested, instrumental behaviour and consequently trying to build relations from this egoistic perspective was usually ineffective. Conversely, I found that the optimum approach for cultivating work-based relations was to develop a consistent character or reputation for integrity and trustworthiness among key stakeholders. The efficacy of this latter approach was apparent in my observation that owner-managers who focussed exclusively on utility maximisation; that is on calculative, opportunistic transactional interactions tended to be less financially successful than owner-managers who attempted to build enduring relational ties. In my view the latter approach was more successful as it engendered a level of commitment and facilitated trust-based relations, which constituted vital intangible assets. In synopsis, I would characterise owner-management às predicated on an ever-shifting fluidity of competition and cooperation. For illustration, the most poignant illustration of owner-management as a social activity occurred at the marriage of a relative, a successful retailer, when a number of his customers, suppliers, partners, bankers, solicitors and rivals attended the wedding, to offer their congratulations and I also noticed to 'talk shop'. Their presence struck a chord, as I had never heard my uncle describe them as friends, yet their attendance at the service attested to these connections being more than narrow transactional relations. Reflecting on that happy occasion, it struck me that owner-managers didn't just live by egoistic, ends-means calculations; they were also embedded in collaborative social relations, as evinced by these guests at the nuptials.

The more immediate motivation for this research developed from working in a business school teaching theories of management that emphasised assumptions of rational forward planning and self-interestedness, in my view to the exclusion of other methods of analyses.[2] It has always struck me that these theories were not consistent with my experiences of owner-management, which emphasised social interaction as a complicated and unpredictable process, subject to infinite situational subtleties of interaction. In consequence, I could not describe or explain my SME knowledge with reference to the pre-eminent strategic theoretical frameworks. For example, in my experience rather than being driven by rational calculation to pursue (financial self-interest), owner-management was frequently a process activity (pursued for its intrinsic pleasure), for instance in terms of the inherent delight of striking deals. The business school orthodoxy of management as a 'positivistic' science, with an inclination to generate generic mechanistic tools also appeared to me as misguided, at least in terms of owner-management which is characterised by unpredictability, that is by, '... inductive process{es} in conditions of uncertainty' (Anderson & Jack, 2002). Thus, my experiences were at odds with the management orthodoxy that is characterised by scientism (physics envy) and an overemphasis on formulating rigorous models. Further the management tendency to follow the (Newtonian) scientific method of disaggregating business phenomena into discrete constituent sub-components, in order to build up a supposedly more accurate analysis, also clashed with my experiences over the unity and interdependence of human life, and hence the unity and interdependence of being an owner-manager. For illustration, in my experience most owner-managers did not separate work from the rest of their lives, rather they regarded themselves as being or as personifying their businesses.

I was further emboldened to embark on this research by the observations of leading academics who have recently questioned the universal application of rational theoretical orthodoxies (prompted by business scandals). For example: 'Excessive truth claims, based on extreme assumptions and partial analysis of complex phenomena can be bad even when they are not altogether wrong' (Ghoshal, 2005, p. 87).

My interest in the importance of relations and the socially embedded nature of being an owner-manager was further heightened while managing Leeds Metropolitan's Business Incubator. During this year-long placement in 1997 I worked closely with a number of start-ups and was struck by the effort owner-managers placed on establishing connections. For illustration, I vividly remember planning a series of workshops, and (to ensure that they would be relevant) sending out a mass e-mail to over 500 start-ups with connections to the incubator, requesting a response in terms of preferences for training sessions. I expected the most popular request to relate to an SME management function, such as business planning, financial management or marketing. However, by far the most popular request was for a networking training session, which surprised me and also indicated the premium placed by owner-managers on establishing networks and relational connections.

Given that my research interest was peaked by the significance of networks and relations for owner-managers, and also by the dissonance between management theory and my owner-manager experiences, the choice of research site was self-selecting. The next step was to fix on the most apposite theoretical literature to examine the enduring social realities of owner-management, and after some musing I decided upon social capital theory. I chose this field of literature as social capital's core nostrums, stressing the importance of connections, tallied with my experiences of owner-management. Further, this theory is, 'wonderfully elastic' (Lappe & Du Bois, 1997, p. 119), and I also agreed with the conclusion that, '... the major strength of the social capital idea has probably been its capacity to re-energise a series of lines of research in social theory that cut across different disciplines in the social sciences' (Castiglione, 2008, p. 193). In consequence, social capital has a trans-disciplinary, integrating quality that permits a broad perspective, which is necessary to capture the fuzzy, non-linear nature of owner-managers' interaction and relationships. I opted on social capital theory therefore as it offers a board sweep method of analysis, with a federating and fresh contemporary perspective on social interaction, which incidentally refutes the logic of much theoretical criticism, including Ahn and Ostram's evaluation that: 'From a traditional economics perspective social capital is a fancy term used to refer to the cooperation-enhancing effects of repeated interaction and networks' (2008, p. 71).

It is also worth mentioning that another reason for selecting social capital theory is that it is an established neo-capital theory replete with a 'capitalisation' syntax, which blends the language of rational economics and sociology. The assumption of the researcher is that this syntax would be more readily understood by owner-managers than more abstract social science theories, and thus would have the potential to ease communication with the research population.

Conversely, I also acknowledge from the outset that social capital literature is bedevilled with flaws. For instance there is a theoretical orthodoxy that splits interactions into narrow categories of relationships that are particular to social capital and social network analysis, resulting in a very flat characterisation of social interaction. In part to address the limitations of extant social capital literature, and also to offer a more rounded characterisation of interaction, I decided to expand the theoretical perspective to include insights from the distinct, but complementary socio-economics literature, which embeds economic action in its social context (Wallis & Killerby, 2004, pp. 239–258). The embedded perspective also rejects 'Economics' individualist bias, with its emphasis on mathematical rigour that also holds sway over much management pedagogy.

It is also worth stating that the book refers to its research population as owner-managers. The owner-managers in the research vary enormously, but exhibited continuity in that they all self-defined themselves as entrepreneurs, which they took as synonymous with owner-management. Further, the author's view is that academic debates over the meaning of entrepreneurs and entrepreneurship are sterile, semantic intellectual exercises, the management studies equivalent of the medieval theoretical obsession over how many angels could dance on the point of a needle. Further, the prospect of any resolution of these debates is also distant, as indicated by Jack and Anderson's contention over the complicated nature of entrepreneurship in that it is enigmatic, and combines both science and art involving the 'crystallisation of complex and contingent variables' (1999, p. 111). In consequence, as entrepreneurship definitional agreement is likely to remain elusive, the following observation from a standard work on philosophical analysis is apt:

> What, then, are we doing when we 'indicate what a word means'? We are doing one of two things: either (1) we are stating what we are going to mean by it, or (2) we are reporting what people in general, more specifically those who use the language we are speaking, or some segment of those who use that language, already mean by it. In the first case we are stipulating a meaning, and we have a stipulative definition. In the second case we are reporting the usage of others, and we have a reportive, or lexical definition ... As a rule we stipulate only when (1) a word is ambiguous, and we want to stipulate which sense we mean – even here we do not usually stipulate a new meaning, but only point out which of several meanings that are already attached to the word we are using on this occasion. (Hospers, 1956, pp. 32–33)

Thus given the lack of consensus over the meaning of entrepreneurship this research will offer a stipulative meaning, which is to understand entrepreneurship at its essence as being concerned with creating and extracting value from a situation (Anderson, 1998). Further this broad understanding takes entrepreneurship and owner-management as being so closely related to be synonymous. In my view a synoptic perspective, which melds different understandings of entrepreneurship also has the best chance of representing the experience of being an entrepreneur or owner-manager, which is consistent with Chell's (2010) interdisciplinary approach to understanding 'The Entrepreneurial Personality'.[3]

1.3. INTRODUCTION TO SOCIAL CAPITAL

Critics of the extensions of social capital contend that the theory has developed into a less than rigorous, fashionable, a-theoretical catch-all term for describing the positive outcomes of sociability. For illustration:

> Divorced from its roots in individual interactions and networking, social capital becomes merely another trendy term to employ, or deploy in the broad context of building social integration and solidarity. (Lin, 2001, p. 26)

In overview, social capital can be characterised as lacking agreement, which can be gauged by considering the diversity of introductions to this contested and elusive theory. For example, one way to introduce the social capital is with a literary quotation and Prusak and Cohen (2001) and Flapp (1994, p. 29) preface their different treatments of social capital with the same couplet from John Donne:

> No man is an island, entire of itself: every man is a piece of a continent, a part of man.

Another approach is to argue that social capital is so well understood as to require no general definition (Hooghe & Stolle, 2003, p. 1). As Partha Dasgupta notes: 'The literature on the idea of social capital is now enormous' (2005, p. 2). Ronald Burt has also identified, with a touch of hyperbole, the voluminous extent of theoretical literature:

> Social capital is the Wild West of academic work. There are no skills or academic barriers to entry. Contributions vary from rigorous research to devotional opinion, from carefully considered to bromide blather. (2005, p. 5)

Thus, it also has been contended that the sheer volume of social capital literature has left readers aware of the theory's meaning through its ubiquity, which according to Hooghe and Stolle can be thought of as the benefits of dense networks and norms of generalised trust and reciprocity (2003, p. 1).

Yet another approach is to discuss the causal factors motivating interest in social capital, reflecting Wittgenstein's conclusion that the meaning of a word derives from its use (1968). What then is the use of social capital? One answer is as part of a communitarian critique and call for action to counter the perceived atomisation of contemporary society, as associated with Robert Putnam.[4] This approach to social capital usually references Putnam's seminal publications on civicness and Italian regional democracy (1973) and America's contemporary proclivity for 'Bowling Alone' (2000). Further, in this 'declentionist narrative' (see Chapter 2) America is analysed as being increasingly denuded of social connections, and consequently of social cohesion. For illustration, from team sport participation in the immediate post-war years, to bowling alone in the 1990s, to the contemporary lone jogger wearing an IPOD, who is isolated socially and aurally. These insights, incidentally also 'rescued' Putnam, in his own words from being an 'obscure academic' (2000, p. 506).

Another, understanding of the uses of social capital suggests its meaning can be explicated by investigating the political context of the concept's multidisciplinary intellectual success (Baron, Field, & Schuller, 2000). For example, Halpern contends that social capital captured the political zeitgeist for the centre left, which wanted to refute the charge that 'there was no such thing as society' with an alternative view that challenged this reductive, asocial understanding of behaviour (2005). Thus in this interpretation social capital met a political need as a successor for the then unfashionable and widely perceived failed socialist model, while extenuating against the more extreme excesses of neo-liberal markets. Social capital was taken to offer the prospect of marrying market efficiency with centre left objectives, such as promoting 'inclusion' and 'social justice' (see Chapter 2).

In sum social capital is a contemporary theory whose prominence has been achieved from the last quarter of the twentieth century, stimulated most by Putnam's scholarship dating to 1973. Social capital's prominence has also been driven by a number of theoretical authors who have created overlapping but distinct literature streams that continue to frame the social capital discourse (see Chapter 2). Of course, the phenomena social capital examines have been discussed under different terms in the past, which has led to questions over whether the theory offers anything new or merely dresses up earlier insights in trendy language (Portes, 1998). These earlier and/or related theories, which in certain instances are also less fashionable and therefore undervalued are given in Table 1.1.

To conclude, the current social capital discourse is 'probably less than twenty or so years old' (Castiglione, 2008, p. 1), and it is unsurprising therefore that such a recently prominent theory has yet to settle disagreements over theoretical definition, application and quantification. Nevertheless, the novelty and value of social capital is to examine previously studied phenomena within one broad approach, while at the same time re-invigorating a number of neglected areas of socio-economic research.

Table 1.1. Related Theories.

Earlier and/or Related Theory	Key Scholars
Transaction cost theory and exchange economics	Williamson (1985, 1993) (Nobel economics prize winner 2009)
Communities of practice	Lave and Wenger (1991) and Wenger, McDermott, and Snyder (2002)
Absorptive capacity	Cohen & Levinthal (1990)
2nd generation theories of collective action	Elinor Ostrom (1990) (Nobel prize economics winner 2009)
Trust	Simmel (1950), Soule (1998) and Tonkiss & Passey (2000)
Reputation theory	Bromley (1993)
Tacit knowledge	Polanyi (1958)
Embeddedness	Polanyi (1944/2001)
Mutual aid	Peter Kropotkin: Mutual aid: A factor in evolution (1902)
Social exchange theories	Homans (1958), Blau (1964) and Emerson (1976). The influence of these authors on Coleman is reviewed by Fine (2001, pp. 66−72)
Communitarianism	De Tocqueville (1835/1956) and Etzioni (1988)
Humanist understanding of the workplace	Maslow (1954)

Source: This author.
Note: For a more derailed reflection of the connections of these earlier theories to social capital see Appendix A.

1.4. STATEMENT OF RESEARCH PROBLEM: SOCIAL CAPITAL AND ECONOMIC NOTIONS OF RATIONALITY

The book's view is that self-interested, opportunistic, ends-means rationality offers a penetrating but narrow lens for understanding purposive economic action. Thus rational choice theory with its utility maximisation has the potential to explain, and to an extent predict certain aspects of reality. However, rational choice theory is not a comprehensive method of analysis or a universal theory of motivation and action (see Sections 1.7 and 1.8). In consequence, the research problem is that the universal claims for the rational method of analysis inhibit the development of insights that more accurately depict and explain the management of social capital processes. Further, this understanding is consistent with recent literature into second-generation theories of collective knowledge which argue that: 'Unlike first generation theories of collective action that presuppose universal selfishness, second generation collective action theories acknowledge the existence of multiple types of individuals as a core principle of modelling human behaviour' (Ostrom, 1990).

1.5. RESEARCH AIM AND QUESTIONS

The research aim is to develop understanding of the management of social capital processes as they are accomplished (interpreted, experienced and shaped) by owner-managers. Thus, to research owner-manager's perspectives and experiences on how they make sense and go about the management of social capital processes.

The view of the research is that existing social capital literature that examines economic behaviour is framed by rational choice representations, which are limited as discussed in Sections 1.7. and 1.8.

The research will be guided by the following research questions:

1. How significant are rational notions of utility maximisation in the management of social capital processes?

   This question will investigate ends-means economic rationality in social capital management, an approach that puts an economic value on social connections, levels of sociability, attitudes and values. This rational understanding takes the view that business interactions are a marketplace of social exchanges in which individuals are continually making utilitarian calculations to rationally pursue their self-interested goals.

   This question will also research a broader understanding of rationality in the management of social capital. For example, Lin takes a broad view of rationality arguing that social capital is a theory about the access and benefit of resources for the benefit of individuals. Thus in Lin's treatment it is rational to pursue resources, which he describes as valued goods that correspond to wealth, reputation and power (2001, pp. 55−77). Granovetter also describes these non-economic notions of rationality as aiming at 'sociability, approval, status and power' goals, which he labels in historical terms as 'passions' as opposed to 'interests' (1985, p. 506).

2. How significant are low and non-rationality in the management of social capital processes?

This question will research phenomena that fall outside a rational/ reason-based analysis, including for example the significance of risk taking, ambition and emotions in the management of social capital. Further, low rationality is understood as relating to motivations that are driven more by emotion than reason, though retaining characteristics of both: for example risk taking or gambling, and pride in doing a job to a good standard. Non-rationality relates to motivations and actions driven by emotions and the sub-conscious: for example in terms of instinctively preferring to associate with certain individuals over others without being able to offer a rational explanation for the selection.

3. How significant is the interplay or interdependence of rational motivations (including rational economic optimisation) with low or non-rational motivations and behaviour in the management of social capital processes?

1.6. THE ECONOMIC UNDERSTANDING OF SOCIAL CAPITAL: A RATIONAL CHOICE THEORY

This section will introduce rational choice sociology, with reference to Coleman, who as already stated is widely acknowledged as one of the initiating scholars of social capital. The contention of this book is that Coleman's influence is critical in development of the economic form of social capital, which is also understood as a distinct form of the theory.[5] In overview, Coleman's theoretical contribution has been to establish rational choice framing assumptions for the economic form of social capital, which have been conceptualised as the research problem.

Moreover, pinning down the meaning of rationality is difficult as: 'There are almost as many definitions of rationality as there are people who have written on the subject' (Frank, 1988, p. 2). In broad terms rationalist believe that human reason is the primary source of knowledge of the world. In consequence, the theory or more accurately, 'body of ideas' (Kelly, 1995, pp. 96–97), origins are diverse, stretching from the Ancient Epicureans, to the French Enlightenment (often called the 'Age of Reason') and later to the utilitarian philosophy of Jeremy Bentham. In synopsis, rational choice theory belongs to a set of theories that emphasise the reason-based character of the human personality. Further, given its multiple origins together with its claims to be a grand or meta-theory, it is best to consider rational choice as a term for a family of sometimes conflicting theories, which nevertheless share a common assumption on the importance of reason.[6]

1.6.1. Coleman, Rational Choice and Social Capital

Rational choice sociology assumes that actors act rationally (based on reason) in terms of calculating the costs and benefits of actions (Coleman & Fararo, 1992; Friedman, 1973; Green, 2002; Hedstrom & Stern, 2008; Scott, 2000). Rational choice theory (termed the neo-classical paradigm in Economics) is also based on the materialist assumption that individuals are self-interested and deliberate utility maximisers. Further, according to Lin while rational choice has multiple motives regarding valued resources, two are fundamental: 'the minimization of loss and the maximisation of gain' (2001, p. 128).

In sociology the pioneers of the rational approach were Blau (1964) — associated with contract theory — and Homas (1961), who contended that sociological theories should be grounded in behavioural psychology. It also has been argued that Coleman's rational choice sociology should also be viewed as a direct extension of the Homas framework of exchange theory (Scott, 2000). In this interpretation, Coleman developed his rational choice sociology, from an understanding that social interaction was a form of trade (1972, 1973): the core assumption of social exchange theory is that individuals are engaged in a market of social exchanges (Fine, 2001, p. 72). In sum, in this interpretation Coleman developed his conceptualisation of interactions as a marketplace (driven by self-interested, cost/benefit notions of maximisation), as an extension of social exchange theory. Therefore one interpretation is that Coleman's social capital is a variant of social exchange theory in terms of emphasising self-interestedness, opportunism and bounded rationality.

However, to take Coleman in his words: 'If we begin with a theory of rational action, in which each actor has control over certain resources and interests and events, then social capital constitutes a particular type of resource available to an actor' (2000, p. 20). The key features of Coleman's rational approach can be listed as follows:

- Macro phenomena can be explained with reference to micro behaviour.
- Optimisation, utility maximisation motivate and explain all purposeful action.

- All action is rational from the perspective of the individual, who examine their environment, weigh possible courses of action and choose what they view as the most expedient path to their preferences.
- Macro-level norms (accepted and standardised ways of accomplishing goals) are also significant in making certain choices more likely while restricting other choices.

It has also been noted that Coleman worked closely with fellow Chicago University Professor Gary Becker, winner of the Nobel Economics Prize in 1962 for his human capital theories[7] and Coleman stated he understood social capital as, '... paralleling the concepts of financial capital, physical capital and human capital, but embodied in relations among persons' (2000, p. 38). Therefore, it is reasonable to assume that Coleman's social capital was grounded in a rational/materialist view of social interaction, an approach with universal claims that it could be applied to any social interaction. For illustration of the breadth of this economic approach to rationality, Becker's 'A Treatise on the Family' examines the efficiencies in a marriage market in which, '... people with stable well-defined preferences act in purposeful ways to choose a mate that best promoted their material interests' (Frank, 1988, p. 185).

In summary, for Coleman the purpose of social capital was as an explanatory theory of cooperative behaviour and group level behaviour within the framework of rational choice theory. Coleman's social capital was also an attempt to explain systematic cooperative behaviour within a metatheory of 'methodological individualism', in which the interaction of the individual level rational pursuit of utility, leads to 'emergent phenomena at the system level' (1990, pp. 1–23). For example, Coleman's contended that by forgoing immediate advantage individual actors could gain greater utility by being part of a collective structure/network.[8]

The influence of Coleman in the rise of this rational choice sociology has also been acknowledged by a number of authors. For example, he has been described as:

> ... the single most important person to influence rational-choice sociology ... In Foundations, he shows how a range of traditional sociological concerns such as norms, authority systems, trust and collective action can be addressed from a rational choice perspective. (Hedstrom & Stern, 2008, pp. 4–5)

Further, in Ben Fine's impassioned evaluation Coleman was the 'initiating contributor' to social capital and in this scholar's chronology the theory developed in an unbroken lineage from Coleman's earlier interest in social exchange theory. In this critical optic: 'Social capital represents a remarkable triumph within social theory both for methodological individualism and for economics' (Fine, 2001, pp. 65–81). Fine also views the development of social capital as a, '… colonisation of the social sciences' in which areas of the social sciences are claimed for economics' 'individualistic traditions' (Fine & Green, 2000, pp. 78–93). Swedberg agrees with Fine's interpretation of Coleman's influence, which he claims is responsible for, '… trying to recast sociology on the basis of rational choice' (1990, p. 6). In sum there are a number of scholars who have identified Coleman's social capital treatment as the moving force in the rise of rational choice theory in the social sciences (Field, 2003, p. 21).

Furthermore, this book's contention is that Coleman's rational approach has framed the economic form of social capital, which can be gauged by the 'rationalist' views of leading theoretical scholars detailed in Appendix B.

In summary, the rational choice understanding of social capital focuses on greater productivity returns. Accordingly, it is taken as desirable to nurture interactions and to develop a collective social structure, as these will lead to positive utility outcomes. From this rational choice theoretical perspective it also follows that it is rational to develop social capital for maximising returns on utility: an understanding which is consistent with the utility maximising 'Homo Economicus' of the 'Formalist School'.

1.7. THE LIMITATIONS OF THE RATIONAL CHOICE UNDERSTANDING OF SOCIAL CAPITAL

There are numerous alternatives to the rational choice paradigm, including the Austrian, Post-Keynesian, Marxist and behavioural constructions of reality: rational choice sociology therefore has competing theoretical paradigms. Further, Coleman was acutely aware of the alternatives to rational choice theory and sought to delineate and defend the rational vantage in a co-edited book (with Thomas J. Fararo) entitled: *Rational Choice Theory: Advocacy and Critique*, with chapters arguing for and against the merits of 'using optimization as a criterion at all points' (1972). However, for the sake of brevity this section will limit its discussion to a number of the key limitations of rational choice theory as relevant for this research into the management of social capital processes.

The first limitation of Coleman's understanding of social capital is the broad conclusion that rational choice assumptions do not offer a comprehensive (and consequently accurate) method of analysis for understanding the viewpoints and inter-subjective experience of managing social capital. For example, the accuracy of economic rationality's consistency of self-interestedness can be questioned for positing an overly materialist and perhaps misanthropic (driven by greed) understanding of motivations and behaviour. Further, beyond economics the inherent flaws of economic rationality's assumptions are long held and not controversial. For example, ancient scholars such as Cleon noted the lack of rationality that people, '... despise those who treat them well and look up to those who make no concession', and philosophers such as Thomas Hobbes, John Locke, Spinoza and John Hume have also noted that impulses make people choose irrationally, being led by passions and desires instead of by the dictates of reason (Frank, 1988, pp. 84–85). Further well-known examples of irrationality in the economy are detailed in Charles Mackey's the 'Extraordinary Popular Delusions and the Madness of Crowds' which gives a convincing account of irrational, 'National Delusions', 'Peculiar Follies' and 'Philosophical Delusions' (1841/1980). For instance during the 'South Sea Bubble' of 1720 investors clamoured to pour money into various strangely titled schemes, the strangest being: 'A Company for carrying on an Undertaking of Great Advantage, but nobody to Know what it is'. Market-based booms, such as 'Tulipmania' in seventeenth-century Holland, are further recurring examples of the non-rational side of market behaviour. In synopsis, there are numerous examples of low or non-rational behaviour in the economy and it follows that rational choice theory can be questioned for its claims to be a comprehensive method of analysis for describing and explaining behaviour and motivation.

Second, it can be contended that the rational approach has been over-extended from its still contentious, but arguably more natural domain in economics. Thus the marketplace is the area of activity where rational materialist, instrumental behaviour is acceptable (at least in the West), whereas in other spheres of activity or social interaction a cost/benefit optimisation approach would not hitherto have been taken as legitimate. For example, in law notions of justice will often override a strictly cost/benefit approach, and in medicine rationality is tempered by views on the intrinsic worth of individuals, against rational utilitarian or eugenic approaches that exclusively focus on the costs and potential outcomes of treatment. Further, even within the market sphere rational choice theory is controversial: Lane for instance offers a succinct summary of the rational choice as an inadequate theory of behaviour in the market (1995, pp. 108–114). For this research the rational approach to social capital key limitation is that though the focus is on economic activity, the theory also examines humanistic phenomena that are not readily reduced to a rational analysis. For example, approaching social relations from a cost/benefit angle ignores the intuitive aspect of social interaction: people possess instincts that make them recoil from such (charm-less) self-serving networking and excessive instrumentalism of social connections. In sum, the rational/economic approach can lead to insights that are at variance with conclusions from other disciplines, as well as being at odds from conventional non-economic wisdom and observed behaviour. For illustration, it is not rational to rely on gut instincts or take high risks; but no market has ever functioned without these low or non-rational forces.

Third, Coleman took a very broad interpretation of rationality (1990, p. 18), which is arguably tautological. For example, according to Coleman any action can be termed rational as the manifestation of the individual's preferences. Accordingly, drug addiction can be interpreted as rational behaviour as the expression of the addict's preferences.[9] Thus, '... the essentially tautological nature of the wide version' (Dunham, 2009, p. 102), is that it defines rationality too broadly, so that any action is deemed rational, if understood from the individual's perspective. Etzioni's comments are therefore apt; 'Once a concept is defined so that it encompasses all that incidents that are members of a given category (in the case at hand, the motives for all human activities) it ceases to enhance one's ability to explain' (1988, p. 27). In sum the rational approach can be criticised for overextension and claims for universalism.

Fourth, Granovetter has questioned rational choice theory, in terms of the assumption that:

> ... one's economic interest is pursued only by comparatively gentlemanly means. The Hobbesian question − how can it be that those who pursue their own interests do not do so mainly by force and fraud − is finessed by this conception. Yet as Hobbes saw so clearly there is nothing in the intrinsic meaning of 'self-interest' that excludes force of fraud. (1985, p. 488)

It can be argued therefore that there is no reason for a rationalist to exclude force or fraud, other than the risk of being apprehended and punished. However, in economic behaviour there are many instances when individuals could use force or fraud with little chance of being caught, but choose not to: hence the 'policing mechanism' does not explain their actions.[10] An alternative understanding is that the markets need shared values to function, Fukuyama for example stresses the importance of trust and 'ingrained ethical habit' (1995a) for 'lubricating' market-based transactions. Further it could also be argued that the most transparent examples of rationalists in the marketplace are criminals and fraudsters who pursue a Machiavellian 'realpolitik', self-interested approach: Bernie Madoff for example, can be understood as an extreme rationalist who ruthlessly worked at promoting his own interests (self-interested utility optimisation) without regard to any non-rational (moral) frameworks (Manning, 2010c).

1.7.1. Concluding Comments: Las Vegas Wouldn't Exist in a Rational Economy

The rational perspective on social relations in social capital has flourished, driven by the view that this method of analysis has extensive explanatory and predictive power. Coleman's variant of methodological individualism can also be interpreted as a 'wide version' of rational choice that aims to expand rational assumptions within neo-classical economics, to include beliefs, altruisms norms and social sanctions in explaining behaviour (Dunham, 2009, p. 101). However, this section has discussed a number of key limitations of the rational understanding of motivations and behaviour. For instance social cooperation may be based on emotional motivations, as Coleman acknowledges when he attempts to elucidate the 'rationality of free-riding and zeal' (1990, pp. 273–276): an impossible task because zeal is not rational. Further, rational choice theory cannot fully explain outcomes that are by-products of other activities, or the result of addictive or moral imperatives. The 'selfish' utility maximisation understanding of individual motivation and method of analysis can also result in an idealised emotionless, 'rational fool', who does not acknowledge the importance of humanistic factors, such as cultural constraints and 'moral sentiments' in social interactions.

It is also worth noting the view of Paul Samuelson, who has been credited with the rise to prominence of economics, based on his promotion of the rational consistency approach to mathematical optimisation, with maximisation equalling consistency (Kay, 2010, p. 157; Taleb, 2007, pp. 184–185). Samuelson is much quoted as asserting that, '... many economists would separate economics from sociology upon the basis of rational or irrational behaviour' (quoted in Granovetter, 1985, p. 506). This is the nub of this investigation, as Coleman attempted to approach both economic and sociological phenomena from a rational choice perspective, which as already discussed is an approach replete with considerable limitations.

1.8. INTRODUCTION TO RESEARCH APPROACH: SYMBOLIC INTERACTION ETHNOGRAPHY

The research will follow an interpretative sociology that attempts to understand and explain the social world primarily from the view of the actors involved in social processes. The research also will be conducted in an ethnography in the Blumer tradition of symbolic interaction, sensitive to the emergent properties of interaction.

As the research examines interpretative meanings that underlay social capital process of interaction, a qualitative and interpretivist approach was chosen as most appropriate. This approach allows for research sensitivity to context, and also to the participants' individual level frames of reference. The research further emphasises the significance of the quotidian, taken for granted assumptions that owner-managers share in the day-to-day social interactions. As social capital is understood as 'situational' (Coleman, 1990, p. 302), the research accordingly will be conducted with reference to contingency factors, to offer, 'contextual understanding of social behaviour' (Bryman & Bell, 2003, p. 295). In overview, the research ambition will be to investigate, 'the details of the situation to understand the reality or perhaps a reality working behind them' (Remenyi, Williams, Money, & Swartz. 1998, p. 35).

This research approach is also consistent with Dudwick et al.'s conclusions that:

> Good qualitative research is in many respects the art and science of making legible certain processes (and the relationships between them) that are generally hidden or unfamiliar. Social capital, which is something at once intimately familiar and possible subconscious to the insider and foreign to the outsider, is thus eminently suited to detailed qualitative analysis. (2006, p. 36)

1.9. OUTLINE OF SUBSEQUENT CHAPTERS

The subsequent chapters will be organised as follows. Chapter 2 aims to elucidate the meaning of social capital in its economic context with a focus on its relevance for owner-managers. This aim will be achieved by analysing this fluid concept that has seeped into most academic disciplines, and will consider the broader context that has facilitated the contemporary rise to prominence of social capital in economic activity.

To facilitate a deeper understanding of social capital, Chapter 3 will review the leading theoretical authors and present a synthesis of the various conceptual treatments to demonstrate that this research is grounded in, as well as complementing existing theoretical literature. This chapter argues that the predominant economic understanding of social capital is drawn from the rational choice sociology of Coleman (1990, 2000), and his follower Putnam (1973, 1993, 1995a, 2000). The literature review also demonstrates the connections between this research and the work of the most significant theoretical scholars. In addition, the chapter makes the case for the inclusion of the socio-economic approach, originating in Polanyi (1944/2001), and developed most notably by Granovetter (1973, 1985, 1992, 2005), for expanding the social capital perspective. The chapter also evaluates the significance of Burt (1990, 2000a, 2004, 2005, 2006) and Lin's (1999, 2001) network approach to social capital. In sum, the chapter offers an in-depth single source review of the origins and conceptual literature pertaining to economic activity and social capital. From this thorough review of social capital literature this chapter will also discuss the conceptual and practical areas that the research will investigate.

Chapter 4 details and explains the research approach, stressing the benefits of qualitative research for social capital investigations, both in terms of complementing existing literature, and in terms of offering the flexibility needed to examine the humanistic/sociological essences of network and relational interactions. The interpretive research philosophy will be discussed, as will be the relevance of the 'symbolic interactionist' perspective, which is based on a pragmatic epistemology. The micro research focus on individual entrepreneurs will also be justified.

Chapter 5 presents and analyses the research data with direct reference to the book's aims and guiding questions in the network sub-dimension. Social capital is taken as situational and idiographic, however, generic social processes that may have applications across individual instances are identified and analysed (Prus, 1996, pp. 141–172). Chapter 6 follows the same structure as Chapter 5 with a focus on the relational dimension of social capital. Chapter 7 discusses the extent to which the research questions have been addressed, as well as discussing two emergent themes. Chapter 8 presents a summary of the research-generated conclusions, and details their implications. The chapter also identifies areas for future research, before concluding on the significance of book.

CHAPTER 2

THE ECONOMIC MEANING OF SOCIAL CAPITAL

2.1. INTRODUCTION

This chapter will address the concept's ambiguity and lack of theoretical and definitional agreement by explicating a social capital understanding that is directly relevant for guiding this research into the economic form of the concept. This chapter will also present a single source of the key social capital literature as it relates to economic activity.

The first part of the chapter will detail the lack of conceptual agreement and will respond by defining the terms of the research. The chapter will also argue for integrating the distinct, but complementary socio-economic literature into an expanded social capital perspective. Furthermore, the chapter will review research that has examined social capital processes in the SME and owner-manager milieus, before discussing social capital's economic meaning with reference to its returns in the marketplace. To add depth to the book's review the chapter will elucidate interpretations over the provenance and rise to prominence of social capital. The chapter will then conclude by arguing that social capital has been cast to be supportive of the socio-economic status-quo, and therefore belongs to the 'sociology of regulation', concerned with emphasising unity and cohesiveness (Burrell & Morgan, 1979, pp. 10–20).

In summary, the ambition of this review is to offer a distinctive contribution to theoretical literature by focussing exclusively on the economic meaning of social capital and accordingly will present an integrative and holistic review from this perspective.

2.2. SOCIAL CAPITAL: A PRE-PARADIGMIC CONCEPT

This section will review social capital debates to set the context for the subsequent sections. Moreover, though there is no gainsaying that social capital has developed into one of the most significant social science theories, nonetheless: 'Intellectual and academic success does not come without some controversy' (Castiglione, Van Deth, & Wolleb, 2008, p. 1). In social capital's case these controversies include questions over the legitimacy of the concept in terms of its definition, quantification and operationalisation. For instance it is commonplace in social capital literature for scholars to address the concept's ambiguity by coining their own definition, usually with reference to a classic social capital understanding from one of the seminal theoretical scholars, understood as James Coleman, Pierre Bourdieu or Robert Putnam, as noted by Baron et al. (2000, pp. 2−3) and Fields (2003, p. 13).[1] For illustration of this approach, Bourdieu defined social capital as, 'the aggregate of the actual or potential resources that are linked to possession of a durable network of more or less institutionalised relationships of mutual acquaintance or recognition' (1985, p. 248). And inspired by this definition Portes and Sensenbrenner developed their social capital treatment with reference, '… to what sociology could say about economic life' in a consideration of migrant economics, as follows: 'Those expectations for action within a collectivity that affect the economic goals and goal-seeking behaviour of its members, even if these expectations are not orientated toward the economic sphere' (1993, p. 1328). These authors then proceeded to argue that one source of social capital is in the creation and consolidation of small businesses: 'A solidarity ethnic community represents, simultaneously, a market for culturally defined goods, a pool of reliable and cheap labour, and a potential source of start-up capital' (*ibid.*, p. 1329).

Moreover, according to Foley and Edwards (1997) and Adler and Kwon (2000) social capital tends to be understood from the author's particular area of expertise. In consequence, there are numerous interpretations of social capital, which is appropriate, reflecting the fuzzy and multi-dimensional nature of phenomena that the concept examines. This is one facet's of social capital's 'stagflation' (Adam & Roncevic, 2003, p. 157), which has resulted in a 'plethora of definitions' (*ibid.*, p. 158) that in turn has generated a sub-set of theoretical literature offering reviews and syntheses of social capital's definitional diversity (Adler & Kwon, 2002; Fields, 2003; Foley & Edwards, 1997; Paldam, 2000; Portes, 1998).

Nevertheless, these efforts at settling social capital's meaning and usefulness have yet to convince a considerable body of sceptics of the validity of the concept. For example, according to economists such as Arrow (2000) and Solow (1999), social capital lacks the qualities necessary to be deemed a capital; while for sociologist Ben Fine it is neither social nor capital and the term itself is oxymoronic (2001, p. 26). Fine also criticises the concept for its chaotic nature as, 'a sack of analytical potatoes' (2001, p. 190) and the contested nature of social capital can be gauged in this quote for social capital being, '... a confused and ill specified concept based, furthermore, on empirically unsound research' (Bebbington, Guggenheim, Olson, & Woolcock 2004, p. 36). To give a further tenor of these criticisms, Portes contends that the concept has been overextended to the point that it is in danger of losing any distinct meaning (1998). It could also be argued that a good deal of contemporary social capital literature is no more than a re-labelling of social network analysis as part of an intellectual fad. Therefore given this lack of social capital concord there is a need to set the terms for this research.

2.3. DEFINING THE TERMS OF THE RESEARCH

One interpretation of social capital that is consistent with the research approach is as aspects of social structure that facilitate action for those within the structure. This definitional understanding is taken from Coleman's view of social capital that it, '... inheres in the structure of relations between persons and among persons' (1990, p. 302). Further, social capital examines patterns of embedded relations, built over time in repeated interaction. Social capital is also concerned with examining the dis-utilities of these embedded patterns of relations. Thus: 'Since the value of a form of social capital can range from positive to negative depending on the goal in question, it may be said to have valence' (Sandefur & Luamann, 1988).

This research defines social capital with reference to the following observations:

1. Social capital is a pre-paradigmic, federating concept. This means that the research will be open to emergent findings that can be incorporated under this theoretical umbrella or meeting place.

   First, developing the view that there is limited agreement in social capital this book will stipulate an understanding of social capital as, '... a genotype having various phenotypic applications' (Adam & Roncevic, 2003, p. 170). In consequence, social capital is taken as a federating or 'umbrella construct' (Hirsch & Levin, 1999), which facilitates trans-disciplinary research to examine social phenomena from a multitude of perspectives. Implicit in this interpretation is the rejection of one holistic definition for social capital, based on the understanding that most social capital literature is recent and consequently the concept is in an early, pre-paradigmic stage of development. For instance, social capital literature is yet to settle core conceptual questions such as: is social capital an asset of the individual (Burt, 2005), the group or country (Fukuyama, 1995a); or is it a 'club good' belonging to a firm cluster or network group, but not to wider society (Coleman, 1990)? Adopting a broad understanding of social capital this book will take the view that these interpretations all possess validity.

2. Social capital is situational and this research is only concerned with the economic form of social capital. Thus any findings from this research are not generalisable to non-economic contexts.

In Coleman's words: 'A given form of social capital that is valuable in facilitating certain actions may be useless or even harmful for others' (1990, p. 302). It follows that there are different forms of social capital, which Woolcock contends have, '... coalesced around studies in (at least) seven fields: (1) families and youth behaviour problems; (2) schooling and education; (3) community life ("virtual and civic"); (4) work and organisations; (5) democracy and governance; (6) general case of collective action problems; and (7) economic development' (2001, p. 194). This understanding is also consistent with Sandefur and Laumann's view, that: 'Different types of social capital are useful for attaining different goals' (1988, p. 69).

3. Social capital's ontology is processual, organic and self-reinforcing and therefore resistant to a simple linear cause and effect analysis. Further, social capital must be viewed as integrated, that is from a perspective that acknowledges its unity. The implication of this holistic understanding is that the theoretical orthodoxy of dis-aggregation or tearing apart of social capital has resulted in a fragmented understanding of the concept.

Third, social capital will be understood in processual terms (Chapter 3), in that its sources, antecedents and consequences are understood as integrated, which is consistent with the view that it is, 'organic and self-reinforcing' (Cohen & Prusak, 2001, p. 9). Further, social capital is, '... not unilinear but circular and multilinear' (Adam & Roncevic, 2003, p. 178). This conclusion is also consistent with Cooke and Willis's understanding that social capital can be viewed as the, 'origin and expression of successful network interaction' (1999); and also with Coleman's functional theoretical treatment (1990, p. 302). In consequence, criticisms that this theoretical understanding is tautological, because, '... causal factors and effectual factors are folded into a single function' (Lin, 2001, pp. 27–28) are misplaced. Moreover, the frequent criticisms of Coleman and Putnam for logical circularity, merging cause and effect (Portes, 1998) are misplaced, as social capital's antecedent and consequents are mutually reinforcing and inseparable. Cohen and Prusak sum up the case for taking a non-linear view of social capital: 'Many of the elements of social capital are both cause and effect, simultaneously its underlying conditions, indicators of its presence, and its chief benefits ... (the) lack of rigorous distinctions between social capital causes, indicators, and effects reflects the organic and self-reinforcing nature of social capital and not (in this instance, at least) the sloppy thinking of the authors' (2001, p. 9).

2.4. DEFINING THE RESEARCH SITE: OWNER-MANAGERS

The research selection of owner-managers was justified in Section 1.2 of the introductory chapter. However, there are additional reasons for researching owner-managers, including their pre-eminent influence over their enterprises, which also can be thought of as a defining characteristic of SMEs. For example, Spence has noted that the ethical climate in SMEs reflects the morality of the owner-manager (1999). The dominant position of owner-managers in their organisations therefore renders them a relevant focus for social capital research. Further, paralleling conclusions from social capital literature it has been argued that research into entrepreneurship (which is understood as synonymous with owner-management in this research) tends to be framed in, '... rational action concept that continues to subtly but significantly influence much of the scholarly work in the field of entrepreneurship' (Dunham, 2009, p. 2).

Entrepreneurship literature also parallels social capital as an academic focus that has recently grown in prominence, but has yet to settle to reach a theoretical consensus[1]: akin to social capital it has also been described as being in its infancy (Cope, Jack, & Rose, 2007, p. 213). For example, there is an extensive literature concerned with defining the essential qualities of an entrepreneur (Chell, 2008). It is also notable that the negatives associated with entrepreneurship have been underplayed in recent literature (also reflecting the optimistic understanding of social capital), though one dissenting voice Brenkert has noted the, '... common motivational roots shared by entrepreneurs, criminals and juvenile delinquents. Deception, manipulation, and authoritarianism are often said to be behaviours exhibited by entrepreneurs' (2002, p. 6).[2]

Further, in this research owner-management and entrepreneurship are viewed from a socio-economic perspective. Thus, '... entrepreneurship must be understood contextually. It must be viewed within individual and social circumstances, since entrepreneurship is not simply an individualist pursuit but also a social phenomenon' (Brenkert, 2002, p. 10). This research approach is therefore consistent with Brenkert's (2002) broad interpretation of entrepreneurship,[3] which contends that to pursue profit opportunities and growth entrepreneurs have to emphasise the social aspects of their behaviour. Chell's understanding is that the entrepreneurial personality has to be considered synoptically, within an 'interdisciplinary and multi-level approach to analysis', which acknowledges economic and sociological approaches (2008), is also consistent with this viewpoint.

In this research therefore the owner-managers are understood as engaged in a process that requires optimising relational ties. The most influential discussion of these ties is in Granovetter's seminal social network article on, 'The Strength of Weak Ties' (1973), later developed by Burt in his structural holes analysis (2005). Burt also drew on an, '... analogy between the social capital of structural holes and the market metaphor in the Austrian school of economics, represented by Schumpeter's work on entrepreneurs and Hayek's work on market's as "telecommunication systems"' (2005, p. 227). Thus Burt's social capital understanding of entrepreneurship complements Austrian economic concept: in his view entrepreneurs have a 'vision advantage' to 'bridge structural holes' via the 'information arbitrage' (*ibid.*, p. 2005).

The intersection of social capital and entrepreneurship literature is also an emerging field of research.[4] For example, Anderson, Park and Jack have also recently argued that entrepreneurship in SME is a socio-economic process as follows: '... it is through social relations, social interaction and social networks that entrepreneurship is actually carried out' (2007, p. 256). They also define social capital as, '... a social relational artefact, produced in interactions but that it resides in a network' (2007, p. 249).

Furthermore, Bowey and Easton in a recent paper have also concluded that the use of reciprocity, particularly the trading of reciprocal favours, was the most prominent activity for building social capital relationships among entrepreneurs (2007, p. 294). This conclusion also accords with the findings of Davidsson and Honig (2003), who researched social capital and human capital among nascent entrepreneurs to identify that business networks were a significant social resource for start-ups. Moreover, it is also worth noting that Jenssen and Greve have concluded that social network redundancy influenced the success of start-ups: dense networks avoided information overload and reduced uncertainties as well as establishing much needed operational consensus (2002, p. 264). Thus research suggests that network literature's 'close ties' are a valuable resource to be cultivated in the start-up phase of a firm.

In addition, Cooke and Clifton have written extensively on social capital and SMEs (2002, 2004). For instance, in 'Social Capital and the Knowledge of Economy' (2002), they investigated the relationship between social capital and SME performance over a three-year timeframe. This research was subsequently described in detail in 'Spatial Variation in Social Capital Among Small and Medium-Sized Enterprises' (2004). Their hypothesis was that social capital was situational and would operate in distinctive ways in different settings. This research moreover operationalised SME performance, in terms of standards accounting metrics, including turnover, profitability and employment, as well as in terms of engagement in professional, social, cultural or political networks that had a bearing on business performance.[5] The findings of this research included social capital being ubiquitous, for instance SMEs were found to understand the importance of building networks and developing social capital by 'paying on the nail' or 'selling at cost' to build relations with new customers (*ibid.*, p. 128). Another relevant finding was the observation that SMEs constantly displayed traded interdependencies, which were predominantly financial interactions, and it was only after considerable prompting that they could offer any examples, usually to do with advice that were not financially based (*ibid.*, p. 112). These findings reiterate earlier research which noted the 'rugged individual' character trait of owner-managers, in the sense of maintaining their independence or 'locus of control' (Chell, 2008, pp. 98–101).

More general accounts of social capital and SMEs can be found in *Responsibility and Social Capital* (Spence, Habisch, & Schmidpeter, 2004, pp. 25–34), which concluded that there were limits on the extent that social capital could be imposed, 'top-down' by governments, which reflects Fukuyama view that the state is more adept at destroying than creating social capital. In Fukuyama's analysis the state can create social capital through education provision, but it can more easily destroy 'spontaneous sociability' by intruding into private sphere with regulations (2000, pp. 257–59).

In summary therefore there is a considerable body of research confirming the benefits of social capital for owner-managers. However, it is worth noting that social capital is not an unalloyed resource in the SME sector. For example, Thorpe, Holt, Macpherson, and Pittaway have highlighted that a risk of developing social capital with a larger firm is that an SME, '... becomes, almost by osmosis, an echo of its larger partner, losing both its individuality and flexibility' (2006, p. 56). This research also comments on the dangers of being over-embedded and thus reducing the opportunities for brokerage. For instance, Thorpe et al. also note that social capital concentrated in a closed network can expose the firm to leveraging from a dominant stakeholder (ibid., p. 54). Further, these findings reflect earlier research by Burt's on the dangers of network closure (2005), as well as Cohen and Prusak's conclusions that being over-embedded can result in firms losing their entrepreneurial 'creative abrasion' (2001, p. 11), which is also consistent with Uzzi's cautions on the dangers of being over-embedded (1996).

In addition, Blanchard and Horan (1998) have analysed 'Virtual Communities and Social Capital', arguing that social capital will be most facilitated if these communities can 'foster additional communities of interest', such as education or political participation. Baron and Markman (2003) have further identified the influence of social competence and entrepreneurial success in the high-tech and cosmetic sectors. Their conclusion is that high levels of social capital assist entrepreneurs in gaining access to persons important to their success. Further, Liao and Welsch (2005) have concluded that IT entrepreneurs 'are probably more capable of utilizing one form of social capital to amplify other forms of social capital'. They also stressed the importance of relational social capital, which they defined as, '... trustfulness in the relationship and the accessibility of information and knowledge made possible by such relationships' (2005, p. 359).

To conclude, there is a developing research stream that examines social capital processes in SMEs and among owner-managers and entrepreneurs. However, it can be argued that there is no current consensus in this field of research, though there is an emphasis on the significance of ties for owner-managers, as well as an over-reliance on operationalising social capital with reference to Nahapiet's and Ghoshal's three sub-dimensions (1998).[6]

2.5. THE ECONOMIC RETURNS OF SOCIAL CAPITAL FOR OWNER-MANAGERS

This section will develop the understanding of the economic form of social capital with reference to owner-managers by elucidating the benefits or returns of social capital. These returns will be conceptualised with reference to the management of intangible assets (knowledge and reputation), which significantly contribute to economic success. For example, according to Martin and Hartley:

> Intangible assets provide the basis of superior profits and enterprise value beyond that determined by competitive market conditions ... Intangible assets were indirect sources of value for most SMEs in ways that reflected the particular business model underlying each category. Specifically, they:
>
> • underpinned sales and maintainable income
> • supported price premiums
> • provided cost advantages. (2006)

2.5.1. Social Capital and Managing Identity Intangibles

The economic form of social capital provides economic returns in terms of facilitating the creation and enhancement of commercially valuable identity intangibles. These intangible assets can be termed, credibility, prestige, social standing, goodwill and integrity, however the most common appellation for identity intangibles in social capital literature is reputation.

Moreover, reputation's status in social capital literature is much commented upon and varied. For example, according to Coleman reputation is a consequence of social capital and its closure mechanism (1990); Lin interprets reputation as a social capital reflection (2001); Fukuyama equates it with recognition (1995, p. 359); Burt sees it as relational asset (2005, pp. 100–101); Nahapiet and Ghoshal view it as deriving from relational factors (1998, p. 252); and Putnam understands reputation as a result of dense social networks (2000, p. 136). Therefore though there are a number of different perspectives on the relationship between social capital and reputation, there is also an extensive literature that acknowledges a connection.

Further, given Coleman's centrality to this research it is worth considering his viewpoint on reputation in terms of network closure mechanisms:

> When there is closure ... norms and reputations can develop that keep the actors in the system from imposing externalities on one another. When closure is not present ... those norms and reputations cannot develop. (1990, p. 320)

Coleman also noted that: 'A rational, self interested person may attempt to prevent others from doing favours for him or may attempt to relieve himself of an obligation at a time when he chooses (that is when repaying the favour cost him little)' (see below). Thus according to Coleman it can be rational to avoid favours in order to avoid 'tit for tat' obligations (*ibid.*, p. 310). In Coleman's conception, '... creating obligations by doing favours can constitute a kind of insurance policy' (Coleman, 1990, p. 306).

Lin also developed the idea of relational rationality, with reference to Coleman's notion of social credits; that is, 'credit slips' on which an actor in a network can draw if necessary. For instance: 'The critical element in maintaining relationships between partners is social credits (and social debts)' (Lin, 2001, p. 151). And: 'Transactions are means to maintain and promote social relations, create social credits and social debts, and accumulate social recognition' (*ibid.*, p. 152). Lin's conclusion is that reputation, '... is the aggregate asset of recognitions received' (*ibid.*, p. 153). Recognition is described in terms of the debtors' willingness to acknowledge the asymmetrical relationship in their network and the ability of the network to relay and spread this information. Thus unequal transactions create credits and debts and result in different social standing, which according to Lin this equates to reputation.

In Burt's view reputation is also a relational asset that he defines as, 'behaviour expected of you'. He also notes that: 'Where reputation is an asset, people can be expected to behave in a prescribed ways to protect their reputation' (2005, p. 100). Further, Burt considers the question of identity and its connections to Granovetter's relational embeddedness. In his view opportunism is avoided to protect a reputation and social relationship: malfeasance would be detrimental to a reputation and discourage future cooperation in a relationship. However, opportunism is also avoided to protect the ego's identity, which is partly constructed from embedded emotional and relational ties in social relations. In sum, exploiting these ties will detrimentally affect self-identity. Moreover, patterns of behaviour tend to become self-replicating. 'The repetition of cooperative exchange promotes trust' (*ibid.*, p. 100). And 'If people have an erratic history of cooperation, they will distrust one another, avoiding collaborative endeavours without guarantees on the other's behaviour' (*ibid.*, p. 101). Thus according to Burt reputation has contemporary and path dependency dimensions. For example trust, which Burt along with Fukuyama (1995), uses as synonymous with social capital, is built in a cumulative process over the long term (*ibid.*, p. 104).

It is also worth considering Burt's identity formation hypothesis which contends that there is a perception that people within a social network are more trustworthy than strangers: the social and emotional costs of opportunism within the network deter opportunism, resulting in a proclivity for 'comfort in interaction'. Burt views this as self-reinforcing process that creates relational embedding that in turn 'lowers coordination risk and cost' (*ibid.*, p. 138). Thus industry structure will not usually be driven by pure market competition because there are social relations built over time that lead individuals to make choices based on social networks criteria. For instance, (ethnic) minority firms will often trade within a network based on the trust of a shared social network (Portes & Sensenbrenner, 1993).

Burt also considers that network closure's reputation mechanism creates economic value by decreasing labour costs: 'The more closed the network, the higher the quality and quantity of labor available at a given price within the network' (*ibid.*, p. 148). This is due to deeply shared goals and peer pressure ensuring guilt-induced conformity. Burt illustrates this observation quoting approvingly of Steve Jobs (Apple's CEO) on work teams: 'The greatest people are self-managing. They don't need to be managed. Once they know what to do, they'll go out and figure how to do it' (2005, p. 149). Moreover, Burt argues that peers create more routine work; that is, less uncertainty because their behaviour, '... is a frame of reference for how to proceed' (*ibid.*, p. 157). Legitimacy is established therefore through network closures' capacity to align actors to the conventions of work. However, the converse is also true; that is for less routine work:

> There is no competitive frame of reference: no peers for informal guidance, and it would be inefficient for the firm to define job specificity to only a few employees. The manager has to figure out for herself how to best to perform the job. Further, legitimacy does not come with the job; it has to be established. (*Ibid.*, p. 157)

Pastoriza, Arino, and Ricart (2008) have also considered the extent that social capital and reputation processes are under the influence of individual firms. Their view is that there is limited research into how managers can create social capital. To begin to remedy this research problem they discussed relational closeness and identification as the key elements of developing organisational social capital (OSC). They also identified the significance of intrinsic and transcendent motives in developing OSC. Intrinsic motivation, they averred is based on identification, which develops from the benefits accruing to the individual from the firm's actions. In contrast transcendental motivation occurred when the individual moves away from self-interestedness, and is concerned with external factors to themselves, 'to other's well-being' (*ibid.*, p. 334). This intrinsic/transcendental insight into motivation is important as it suggests that reputation cannot be imposed. In sum, sentient stakeholders with free will cannot have a particular reputation imposed.

Further, recent research by Maak (2007) has concluded that the consequences of developing social capital among a web of sustainable stakeholder relations include higher levels of trust in the firm and, '... ultimately a reputation as a concerned, responsible, caring and thus authentic organisation'. However, Maak cautions that social capital can only emerge if, 'stakeholders believe that they are not being instrumentalized for the purpose of maximizing profits but engaged instead to contribute to balanced value creation' (2007, p. 338).

To conclude, there is a significant literature stream that examines the relationship between social capital and reputation, for instance according to Lin: 'Reputation can be defined as the extent of favourable/unfavourable opinions about an individual in a collective' (2001, p. 244). And that reputation indicates social standing, including status and prestige and is the 'relational aspect of exchange' (*ibid.*, p. 144). Burt also contends that: 'Reputation is behaviour expected of you. Over the course of repeated exchanges, two people build a sense of who they are in the relationship, a sense of what to expect from the other person as well as themselves' (2005, p. 100). And: 'Social obligation and identity are defined with reputation' (*ibid.*, p. 107). In Burt's view reputation is integral to social identity and social obligations (2005, pp. 173–174). Another relevant conclusion is that the extent of income or power disparity will influence social capital processes and accumulation. For illustration, it has been argued that the poor tend to avoid ties of reciprocity as a survival strategy and consequently display lower levels of trust (Hutchinson & Vidal, 2004, pp. 168–174). Coleman also reaches the same conclusion:

> A rational, self interested person may prevent others doing him favours for him or may attempt to relieve himself of an obligation at a time when he chooses (that is, when repaying the favour costs him little), rather than when the donor is in need because the call for his services may come at an inconvenient time (when repaying the obligation would be costly). Thus in principal there can be a struggle between a person wanting to do a favor for another the other not wanting to have the favour done for him or a struggle between a person attempting to repay a favor and his creditor attempting to prevent repayment. (1990, p. 310)

This view is also consistent with a Sicilian maxim quoted in an expose of financial shenanigans: 'I don't do favours, I collect debts' (1989, p. 92). In summary, a significant number of theoretical scholars have identified that the willingness of actors to maintain relations (with social credits which relate to social capital) is integral to the reputation processes of creating and paying obligations.

2.5.2. Social Capital and Knowledge Intangibles

The second intangible return of social capital relates to the management of knowledge intangibles. Moreover, there is a developing inter-disciplinary literature examining the connection between social capital and knowledge management, which includes Lesser (2000), Tymon and Stumpf (2003), Widen-Wulff and Ginman (2004), Hoffman, Hoelscher, and Sherif (2005), McElroy, Jorna, and Engelen (2006), Smedlund (2008) and Manning (2010a). Further, according to Lesser: 'One of the primary drivers behind interest in social capital is the rise of the knowledge based organisation' (2000, p. 9). Organisational theorists including Nahapiet and Ghoshal (1998) and Inkpen and Tsang (2005) have also analysed the link between social capital, intellectual capital and knowledge management. In aggregate these scholars claim that competitive advantage in the 'post-industrial' globalised economy is characterised by the importance of intangible resources, which they contend can be understood within a social capital framework. For instance, social capital resources embedded in the social fabric of organisations provide firms with the key social assets, including solidarity and norms of cooperation that are essential for the creation, sharing and management of knowledge. Bueno, Salmador and Rodriguez also argue that social capital is becoming increasingly important to knowledge-based economies, as social activities, '... enable the creation of essential competences' (2004, p. 557). These authors, in addition link social capital to intellectual capital for its, '... action stirring role in improving the organisation' (*ibid.*, p. 560).

It is also worth noting that the contemporary economy has been characterised by Cohen and Prusak as being an, 'age of interdependence' in which: 'The increasing complexity of tasks make connections and cooperation — social capital — increasingly important' (2001, p. 16). These authors understand firms as organisms subject to the 'persistent social realities of work'. Their analysis also responds to the 'challenges of virtuality' from a perspective that acknowledges that technology does not exist in a social vacuum. Fukuyama (2000, pp. 194—211) has also discussed the vital role social capital plays in technology development, as well as noting the importance of informality in technological information exchange in this sector

(1995). Further, Baron and Markman (2003) have researched the influence of social competence and entrepreneurial success in the high-tech and cosmetic sectors. Their conclusion is that high levels of social capital assist entrepreneurs in gaining access to individuals important to their venture's success. Liao and Welsch (2005) have also researched high-tech entrepreneurs to conclude that entrepreneurs in this sector, '... are probably more capable of utilizing one form of social capital to amplify other forms of social capital'. They also stressed the importance of relational social capital, which they defined as 'trustfulness in the relationship ands and the accessibility of information and knowledge made possible by such relationships' (*ibid.*, p. 359).

A further example of social capital relevance in the 'new economy' (which is especially reliant on knowledge management) includes Anderson, Park and Jack research into 'Entrepreneurial Social Capital: Conceptualising Social Capital in New High-tech firms', that focussed on Aberdeen's oil-based technology cluster. These authors maintain that this sector is ideal to study social capital because: 'New high-tech ventures are rarely started by individuals acting in isolation. They generally involve teams of highly skilled individuals acting with a complementary mix of technological and commercial management skills that have been effectively combined' (2007, p. 250).

Thus these authors emphasise the significance of social capital in the high-tech enterprises.

To conclude, there is a growing theoretical literature that examines the relationship between optimising knowledge and social capital processes. Further, the interest in this social capital and knowledge management trans-disciplinary connection is intensifying, motivated by the increasing importance of the technology-driven knowledge or virtual economy. However, claims of a decisive technologically generated cleavage with the recent industrial past are overstated: social capital matters for the new economy just as it mattered in the old economy. For example, long established lean manufacturing techniques, '... often lead to great gains in efficiency, but are totally dependent on the social capital of the workforce' (Fukuyama, 2001, p. 10). Thus, social capital has always been central to economic activity and therefore knowledge management, an observation that reflects Maslow's humanist understanding of the workplace, which stressed the significance of social interaction (1954). For this research the significance of this literature stream is that cultivating social capital has the potential to optimise knowledge management, which is understood as a key competitive intangible asset.

2.6. EXPANDING THE THEORETICAL PERSPECTIVE: SOCIO-ECONOMICS AND THE EMBEDDED VIEW OF THE ECONOMY

The literature associated with the economic form of social capital is stymied by its rational choice framing assumptions, and to offer a more comprehensive method of analysis this section will propose an expanded theoretical understanding. The contention is that the inclusion of socio-economics with social capital will facilitate the research by framing the concept, not only with economic notions of rationality but also with more humanistic and sociological/culturalist assumptions, which contend that all economic activity is 'embedded' in sociological phenomena and broader society. According to Portes and Sensenbrenner, this understanding has its origins in classical sociology, including Weber who argued for the moral character of economic transactions (1993, pp. 1322—1327).

However, the most salient antecedent of the socio-economic perspective of the economy can be traced to the social theory of embeddedness, first coined by Karl Polanyi (probably influenced by his research into Britain's mining heritage). Polanyi is associated with the 'Substantivist' School' in anthropology, and the embedded theory was first explicated in this much quoted passage:

> Ultimately, that is why the control of the economic system by the market is of overwhelming consequence for the running to the whole organization of society: it means no less than the running of society as an adjunct to the market, Instead of the economy being embedded in social relations, social relations are embedded in the economic system. (1943/2001, p. 60)

Polanyi argued that, '… previously to our time no economy has ever existed that, even in principle, was controlled by the markets, '… never before our time were markets more than accessories of economic life' (*ibid.*, p. 71). Therefore Adam Smith's view of the, 'propensity to barter, truck and exchange one thing for another', according to Polanyi is a, '… misreading of the past' (*ibid.*, p. 60). Further Polanyi contended that:

> … man's economy, as a rule is submerged in social relationships. He does not act to safeguard his individual interests in the possession of material goods; he acts so as to safeguard his social standing, his social claim, his social assets. He values material goods so far as they serve this end.

He continued by illustrating this insight with reference to a tribal society, observing that in that context social ties are critical: 'First because disregarding the accepted code of honor or generosity, the individual cuts himself off from the community and becomes an outcast; second, because, in the long run, all social obligations are reciprocal, and their fulfilment serves the individual's give and take interest' (*ibid.*, p. 48).

Polanyi's embedded understanding of the economy aimed to reinstate the 'human and natural substance of society' (1943/2001, p. 60). This approach was subsequently developed by the social network theorist Granovetter (1973, 1985, 1992, 2005), who emphasised the socially embedded reality of the market. It is also significant that Granovetter has never claimed allegiance with the burgeoning social capital discourse, which suggests that he regards his social network concept as separate and belonging to a different, one could speculate, 'embedded' literature.[7]

Polanyi's 'embeddedness' insight is his most influential contribution to social theory and has two main strands. First, in Polanyi's view classical economics made a radical break with every previous society in that the market instead of being embedded in wider society would dominate and be the organising principal for wider society. However, the second part of Polanyi's embedded argument (which is less commented upon) is that the dis-embedding of markets, for example the self-regulating, laissez-faire markets, are an impossibility or chimera. Thus, markets always have been, and always will be embedded in broader society. For example, in Polanyi's view markets have to be expensively rescued by civil society (government) at crisis points, which are unpredictable, but nevertheless recurring. For this research the significance of the second strand of Polanyi's embedded argument is Polanyi's emphasis on the significance of embedded social relations in the market.

Polanyi's insights were subsequently developed in socio-economic literature, most notably by Granovetter in an article entitled: 'Economic Action and Social Structure: The Problem of Embeddedness' (1985). It is also significant that Coleman makes reference to Granovetter's 'under-socialised concept of man' and his notion of 'embeddedness'. He states that he wants to: '... incorporate this general set of ideas into the framework presented in earlier chapters. I will conceive of these social-structured resources as a capital asset for the individual, that is, as social capital' (1992). Coleman also notes that Lin had built on Granovetter's work to show how people, '... use social resources to accomplish their goals, particularly in occupational attainment' (*ibid.*). Thus there is a connection between Coleman and Granovetter (and thus to Polanyi), albeit slight, as these references take less than half a page in 'Foundations' 995 pages.

In summary Polanyi based his analysis on a reading of economic history, with a core book that self-regulating markets required extensive state intervention to function, and in any case were always doomed to fail in the long run. Further, in Polanyi's analysis markets were not organic but rather 'laissez-fare' was planned and imposed on society by state-power. Thus, '... the market has been the outcome of a conscious and often violent intervention on the part of the government' (*ibid.*, p. 258). For example, Polanyi argued the free market needed a mobile workforce and this required the state, '... to liquidate organic society that refused to let the individual starve' (*ibid.*, p. 173).

To conclude, Polanyi can be understood as offering an idiosyncratic reading of economic history, in part Marxist; in part Christian-socialist; in part-environmentalist; and in part as a reactionary idealisation for a golden pre-market age. It has also been argued that Polanyi, '... provides the most powerful critique yet produced of market liberalism' (Bloch, 1961).

2.6.1. Granovetter and Embeddedness

Polanyi's embedded understanding of the economy was subsequently developed in socio-economic literature by Granovetter (1973, 1985, 1992, 1995). In Granovetter's view the embedded view of the economy is associated with, 'the "substantivist" school in anthropology, identified especially with the afore-mentioned Karl Polanyi ... and the idea of moral economy in history and political science' (1985, p. 482). Thus Granovetter built on Polanyi's 'fictitious commodities' and hankering after a pre-capitalist age that valued social cohesiveness and the social contract, in his social network analysis. For illustration Granovetter (1992, p. 27), and incidentally Coleman (1990, pp. 300–301), identify the Scottish Enlightenment's market liberalism (and its organising principal of subordinating society to the economy) as the origin of the under-socialised view of the market. However, reflecting the deep disagreements in social capital it is also worth noting that conversely a number of authors reach a contrary conclusion and consider that the notion of the self-serving, self-interested, calculating individual to be a misreading of Adam Smith's morality and commitment to mutual obligation (Fukuyama, 1995b; Patterson, 2000, pp. 39–55).

Granovetter also examined: 'Economic Action and Social Structure: The Problem of Embeddedness'. In this article Granovetter examined the origins of the under and over socialised conceptions of action to contend that '... purposive actions are embedded in concrete, on-going systems of social relations' (1985, p. 487). In Granovetter's embedded logic of exchange market performance can be enhanced via intra-firm resource pooling and commercial cooperation, as well as by social connections coordinating adaptation processes. Conversely, social and structural over-embeddedness can undermine economic performance by locking firms into downward levelling networks that seal firms from non-redundant information, thereby reducing the opportunities for brokerage. Over-embeddedness can thus create inertia that undermines the firm's 'creative abrasion' that creates entrepreneurial risk taking necessary for survival in competitive markets. For example, Uzzi has concluded, from a study of New York garment manufacturers, that both over and under-embeddedness has a negative effect on economic performance; that is, very weak and very strong embeddedness were detrimental to firm survival (1996). A conclusion confirmed in recent research into the effects of 'network redundancy' for start-ups (Westerlund & Savhn, 2008, pp. 492–501).

For an additional illustration of the embedded view of the economy, Granovetter has noted that supplier relationships are not driven both by economic motives and also by embedded personal relationships (business friendships). He reached this conclusion by observing that purely economic motives would cause firms to switch suppliers far more commonly than is the case: he also notes that firms required a shock to jolt them out of their buying patterns (1985, p. 496). Moreover, his comments on personal embeddedness limiting opportunism and encouraging expectations of trust are relevant:

> That is, I may deal fairly with you because it is in my interest, or because I have assimilated your interest to my own (the approach of interdependent utility functions) but because we have been close for so long that we expect this of one another, and I would be mortified and distressed to have cheated on you even if you did not find out (though all the more so if you did). (1990, p. 42)

In overview Granovetter's social network approach subscribes to the embedded understanding of the economy in which individuals do not act individually, gaols are not independently arrived at and interests are not wholly selfish. This understanding of the economy has been summarised as follows, '... the economy should not be identified with the market ("the economist fallacy") and that, indeed the market itself is a system embedded in society' (Smelser & Swedberg, 2005). Moreover, Granovetter's 'embedded' understanding also accords with Polanyi's insight that: 'Co-operation for a joint material advantage is the predominant feature of society as an economic system' (1958, p. 212). Thus Granovetter's embedded view argues that the economy is one branch of human activity alongside many others: it is not a semi-detached area of activity where society's rules and mores do not apply: thus in the embedded perspective there are limits to markets and not everything of value can be captured in the pricing mechanism.

In sum, the economic form of social capital is understood from a socio-economic perspective that takes the market as being embedded in the broader economy, which in turn is embedded in broader society. In addition, an essential aspect of the embedded, socio-economic perspective of the economy is that it offers a sociological and humanistic view of market activity, and rejects the 'obsolete market mentality', with its 'crass materialism' and 'motive of gain' as an inaccurate lens for viewing business interactions (Polanyi, 1944/2001, p. 31). The implication of this literature is that this research will be sensitive to the significance of sociological and humanistic factors in the data.

2.7. FOUNDATIONS: THE PROVENANCE OF SOCIAL CAPITAL

This section will examine the intellectual history of social capital, focussing on its economic meaning, with the aim of adding depth to the book's understanding of the concept. Moreover, according to Portes: 'Tracing the intellectual background of the concept into classical times would be tantamount to revisiting sociology's major nineteenth century sources' (1998, p. 2). And, '... the processes encouraged by the concept are not new and have been studied under other labels in the past' (*ibid.*, p. 21). For example, Durlauf and Blume, begin a review of social capital with a lengthy quote from Aristotle's *Nicomachean Ethics* (2004). Aristotle's view was that people are essentially social and need to be in a community to be fully human. Further examples include theories of 'civic virtue', being re-invigorated and re-labelled as Putnam's notion of social capital (1973). Simon Szreter has also noted social capital precursors in, 'social capability in development economics, or the idea of civic virtue that Machiavelli derived from the Greeks' (2000, p. 5).

In the sense that social capital refers to the importance of community and trustworthiness it is also possible to discern the concept's characteristic features in the sacred texts of ancient civilisations, which often stress connectedness, for instance in being your brother's keeper. Ridley (1996) traces related concepts further into the past, to prehistory with its evolutionary and biological imperatives: 'Human beings have social instincts. They come into the world equipped with a predisposition to learn how to cooperate, to discriminate the trustworthy from the treacherous, to earn good reputations, to exchange foods and information, and to divide labour' (1996, p. 249). Thus it is possible to connect social capital to primeval and biological imperatives to form social connections that constituted an evolutionary advantage (Midgley, 2010).

However, social capital's more immediate and transparent theoretical antecedents have been identified by Patterson who argues that, '… Scottish philosophers of the Enlightenment had a well-developed sense of mutual human obligation that is quite close to the ideas on social capital that have become popular again in academic circles recently' (2000, p. 39). These Scottish philosophers, she continues, had a core belief that, '… society depends on human beings mutual dependence' (*ibid.*, p. 41). Patterson's argument is that the Irish philosopher, Francis Hutcheson, who was professor of moral philosophy at Glasgow University in the early eighteenth century, developed the idea of instinctive 'benevolence'. Moreover, Hutcheson's most illustrious pupil, Adam Smith, noted the importance of 'kin and friendship', and then refined this 'Enlightenment' insight, suggesting that the public spirit could be created. Thus, a sense of justice could and should be created by education. Smith advanced these views in, 'The Concept of Moral Sentiments' (1759), developing the argument that sympathy was an innate characteristic that provided a moral compass for society: in Smith's evaluation people possess an instinctive sense of reciprocity and fair play. However, it is also worth noting that in his later and more famous *The Wealth of Nations* (1776/1999) Smith asserts: 'It is not from the benevolence of the butcher, the brewer, or the baker, that we expect our dinner, but from their regard of their own interest'.

Thus there is a contradiction, which the Germans have labelled, 'Das Adam Smith Problem', in that Smith's first book argues that people are driven by moral sentiments, while his second argues that successful economies depend on rational self-interest (Ridley, 1996, p. 146). One answer to this dilemma lays in the advantages derived from reciprocity and group cohesion. Thus, self-interests can favour: 'Norms and networks of civic engagement [which can] contribute to economic prosperity and in turn are reinforced by that prosperity' (Putnam, 1993, p. 180). In Ridley's words: 'The virtuous are virtuous for no other reason than it enables them to join forces with others who are virtuous, to mutual benefit' (1996, p. 147).

Smith's hidden hand can therefore be understood as a metaphor for the actions of individuals producing unintended macro-level outcomes. The historian E. H. Carr also reached a similar conclusion:

> The Christian believes that the individual acting consciously for his own selfish ends, is the unconscious instrument of God's purpose. Mandeville's 'private public benefits' was an early and deliberately paradoxical expression of this discovery. Adam Smith's hidden hand and Hegel's cunning of reason, which sets individuals to work for it and serve its purposes, though the individuals believe themselves to be fulfilling their own personal desire .... (1964, 1994)

Coleman's view also reflects these observations:

> ... society consists of a set of independent individuals, each of whom acts to achieve goals that are independently arrived at ... This fiction derives in part from the fact that the only tangible actors in society are individuals and in part from the extraordinary impact that Adam Smith and other classical economic theorists, have had on the way we think about economic life. (1990, pp. 300–301)

According to Carr (1964, 1994) this fiction can be traced to the 'cult of the individual', which pre-dates Scottish classical economics. Carr contends the provenance of this cult was identified by Burckhardt's, in his *The Civilization of the Renaissance Italy*. Buckhardt argued that the cult of the individual began when man, who had hitherto been 'conscious of himself only as a member of a race, people, party, family, or corporation ... became a spiritual individual and recognised himself as such'. Moreover, this cult became the '... most pervasive of modern historical myths'. For example, the cult was connected with the 'rise of capitalism and Protestantism ... and with the doctrine of *laissez faire*' (*ibid.*, p. 33). Literature provides a number of examples of the individual cult, most famously from Daniel Defoe (1660–1731), who created an individual apart from society: an individual with no associational life, though the castaway, 'Robinson Crusoe' (1719) was soon given Man Friday as a companion. Another example is Dostoyevsky's (1821–1881) 'Devils' (1871) in which Kirilov demonstrates his complete individualism through suicide, 'the only perfectly free act open to individual man' (Carr, 1964, 1994). Incidentally, another precursor noted by Portes (1998) is Durkenheim's classic study of female suicide, which noted the importance of isolation as a casual factor for suicide: atomised individuals lacked a supportive network and were therefore more susceptible to extreme actions.

In sum, economics (both classical and neo-classical) posits the model of an atomised, rational, self-interested 'economic man'. In contrast, the 'embedded' socio-economic approach argues that in pre-capitalist society, capital and individualism did not predominate; rather economic activity was integrated into prevailing social relations and power structures that were collective. For example, in medieval pre-capitalist Europe markets were explicitly trammelled, guilds controlled craft industries and the aristocratic elites' defined merchants' trading terms (Postan, 1972, pp. 205–232). Thus the power of the market was transparently circumvented. The argument runs that these market boundaries were only breached in the modern era, under the sway of classical economics, as developed by Scottish philosophers of the Enlightenment (Patterson, 2000, pp. 39–55; Polanyi, 1944/2001). Therefore it can be argued that mainstream economics forged and established the model of the economically rational autonomous individual.

However, though the 'cult of the individual' and the Scottish origins of modern social theory, and specifically of social capital itself are significant in explicating the meaning of the economic form of social capital, Portes is nevertheless correct to state that an exercise tracing the intellectual background, '... would not reveal, however, why this idea has caught on in recent years or why an unusual baggage of policy implications has been heaped on it' (1998, p. 2). Therefore it is necessary to explore the more recent trajectory of theoretical refinement to understand its contemporary ubiquity and meaning.

2.8. CONTENDING PERSPECTIVES: CULTURE WARS, TAKING THE CLASS OUT OF SOCIETY AND NETWORKS

A deeper understanding of the meaning of the economic form of social capital can be achieved by examining the contemporary socio-economic and political context, as this broader context helped shape the social capital debates and predictably these debates reflect a familiar left/right divide. For example, Fukuyama's partisan social capital interpretation can be understood as a conservative and neo-liberal input into a wider debate, concerning competing notions of the direction of civil society. These competing notions of society have been termed 'The Cultural Wars' in America, and this section will contend that social capital resonated with other influential paradigms, integral to the 'Cultural War' disputes over the direction of American society. In short, social capital captured the political Zeitgeist, and consequently experienced 'take-off'.

Social capital also can be classified as belonging to a sequence of theories bolstering the prevailing socio-economic status quo (Paxton, 1999, pp. 88–127). For illustration, in 1993 President Clinton wrote an effusive letter to Amitai Etzioni, praising his book, *The Spirit of Community* (Wheen, 2004, p. 221), and Etzioni's moral communitarianism can be identified as an immediate precursor to Putnam's social capital, in terms of theorising and diagnosing society's ills, suggesting broad sweep remedies and also in the political attention the concept garnered. The concept therefore has utility in debates over the benefits that derive from integrated communities with shared normative values. Robert Putnam, for instance, '... the single most influential theorist of social capital' (Baron, 2004, p. 5), has advocated the desirability of replenishing American society's stock of social capital to reach the levels attained in the 1950s: the emblematic book-cover image, of bowling alone, needs to be replaced with an image reflecting Putnam's own experience in the 1950s of bowling in a team (2000). He asserts that the benefits of high levels of social capital are multitudinous: to mention a few, increased economic prosperity (*ibid.*, pp. 319–325); better mental health (*ibid.*, p. 331); higher educational achievements (*ibid.*, pp. 307–318); and lower levels of crime (*ibid.*, pp. 307–318).

In the United Kingdom the then Prime Minister's Strategy Unit produced an 80-page paper, which states in Putnam inspired language that social capital is important because it:

> ... may contribute to a range of beneficial economic and social outcomes including: high levels of growth in GDP; more efficiently functioning labour markets; higher educational attainment; lower levels of crime; and more effective institutions of government. (2000)

Conversely, social capital sceptics contend that the concept is in essence driven by reactionary politics. From this perspective social capital is interpreted as a component of a conservative viewpoint on social change and the collective action problem, which emphasises that exclusion and poverty can be explained with reference to social factors, to the exclusion of economic disadvantages. Once these social factors have been addressed, and the excluded have become the included, then the market can function that much more efficiently. For instance social capital provides solutions in terms of how to render labour more mobile and flexible in the face of competitive pressures wrought by globalisation: to paraphrase a best seller, the successful employee calls on their social capital to adapt and doesn't waste time complaining that their cheese has been moved (Johnson, 1999). In consequence, critics claim that the concept should be identified (and dismissed) as a conservative notion that accentuates consensus and social cohesion, which also means preserving and not challenging the economic and social status quo. This critical interpretation further argues that the concept embodies a reactionary view of social change and which also offers a normative perspective on how society could be organised for greater productivity and social cohesiveness. This line of reasoning also posits that social capital provides a conduit to by-pass adversarial politics. Thus social capital is taken as promoting a paradigm of social harmony and shared values and interests, which are underpinned by a dynamic of co-operation: contrasting adversarial paradigms stress ideological discord and conflict to gain access to scarce resources. Rather revealingly one of Putnam's earlier books, *The Beliefs of Politicians: Ideology, Conflict, and Democracy in Britain and Italy* (1973) concludes a chapter entitled, 'Conflict in Society' with the following observation:

> ... there is a link between ideological principles and orientation towards conflict. The Left, attacking an established social order, finds the origin of injustice in conflicting interests. The Right, defending the existing social order, argues that no one is 'really' disadvantaged by that order and that issues must be resolved, not by conflict, but 'on their merits'. It is obviously no accident that Burke, the great conservative, extolled social harmony, while Marx, the great revolutionary, stressed social cleavage. (p. 107)

In summary, the argument is that the unskilled, marginalised and poor need to become better social capitalists in order to pull themselves out of their disadvantaged state. In this understanding social capital functions as a deficit concept: the poor are poor because they don't have enough social capital. Moreover, the argument is also that state activity is inimical to social capital because it crowds out voluntary associations. Fukuyama, for instance takes this conclusion to the extreme, claiming the failure of market reforms in the former Soviet block is attributable to the low levels of social capital, a legacy of the communist system that conspired to destroy all forms of community, other than those of the state. According to Fukuyama this example stands as a, '... cautionary tale against over-centralised political authority' (1995, pp. 360–361).

In contrast, critics (usually from the Left) contend that social capital provides a convenient and over-simplified normative concept to explain, the widely perceived, decline in society's social and moral fabric. In social capital literature this decline is attributed to individual preferences, such as watching too much TV, the drift towards suburban living and changes in family structure (Putnam, 2000). Critics argue that following this line of reasoning social capital can be viewed as an explanatory concept that gives impetus and bogus intellectual sustenance for policies that purport to generate social cohesion. Further, from this optic, these policies are bound to disappoint, as they do not address the central role of class in society and therefore fail to address prevailing power relations. For example, Fine and Green have developed this position to argue that conceptual debates have attempted to reduce the social to the individual, given: '... neo-classical economics, besides being excessively formalistic at its core, is fundamentally asocial. Because it is constructed on the foundations of methodological individualism' (2000, p. 78). Thus, in this critical interpretation, social capital provides theoretical underpinning for free market policies, to be garbed in progressive language and cool sounding jargon (Champlin, 1999, pp. 1302–1314; Levitas, 2004, pp. 41–56).

To conclude, from a sceptical point of view the concept falls within the parameters of Burkean conservatism, promoting social harmony and dismissing other (leftwing) analyses. The concept can also be placed in a tradition that identifies a decline in community and relates the analysis to political outcomes (Paxton, 1999, p. 88). It is also no coincidence that the organisations and structures commonly lauded in social capital literature, including voluntary groups such as church organisations and charities, also provide convenient alternatives to deliver social services in the aftermath of gaps in social provision left by 'reforms', instigated by (neo-liberal) ideological policies, bent on cutting public spending and shrinking the state. Thus, the concept contributes to an attempt to address the negative developments of a market-orientated economy by launching an analysis that refutes the importance of class and asymmetrical wealth distribution. Social capital therefore offers a society-wide concept that takes the class out of society.

2.9. THE EXPONENTIAL RISE OF SOCIAL CAPITAL: WHY NOW?

It is egregious to find consensus in social capital. However, both sceptics and enthusiasts concur that in recent years there has been an extraordinary burgeoning of scholarly research into the concept.[8] Aldridge, Halpern and Fitzpatrick, for instance have charted the, '... exponential growth in references to social capital in the academic literature, 1985–2000' (2002, p. 9). Further the process has continued, perhaps even accelerated, and this then leads to the puzzle of why the concept has recently gained such wider currency. One answer, proposed by Lin avers that there was a theoretical convergence and, '... only in the 1980s, when several sociologists, including

Coleman, independently explored the concept in some detail, did it capture the interest of the research community' (2000). Thus theoretical development, according to Lin was achieved by the uncoordinated convergence, from different disciplines of scholars who happened upon the same theoretical approach. However, this emphasis on serendipity is not entirely convincing: it is more plausible that there were additional causal factors for the meteoric rise in social capital research and application.

Hirsch and Levin's conclusions on umbrella constructs are also apposite as explanatory factors explaining how a concept becomes 'en vogue': they cite two reasons that drive the process. First, they consider that umbrella perspectives, '... are necessary to keep the field relevant and in touch with the larger, albeit messier world' (1999, p. 2). An umbrella concept can have cognitive value for organising related concepts in field of inquiry that lack a, '... unified paradigm that can be efficiently developed'. And second that: 'The more a field lacks theoretical consensus, the more it will rely on umbrella constructs to tie together different research elements' (*ibid.*, p. 7). In social capital's case, Portes and Sesenbrenner contend that the 'umbrella' field in question, is 'economic sociology' (1993, p. 1320), and that interest in the concept, '... has sparked renewed interest in what sociology has to say about economic life' (*ibid.*, p. 1321). From this perspective social capital can be understood as an attempt to analyse economic action from a 'sociological perspective', which stands in contrast to neo-liberal market interpretations of economic action. However, though Portes and Sensenbrenner's evaluation of the social capital's utility is theoretically possible, in praxis the sociological perspective has been most influentially deployed to offer an analysis, which complements and nourishes the 'Colonization of the Social Sciences' by Economics' (Fine & Green, 2000, pp. 78–93). Fine and Green contend that social capital allows the perspective of the utility maximising individual to be introduced into the social sciences, and thus the concept is an intellectual: 'Trojan horse ... in which more and more areas of social science are claimed for economics' (2000, p. 91). Wallis, Killerby and Dollery concur: 'The recent interest in governmental effectiveness reflects an effective "capture" of social capital by mainstream economists' (2004, p. 243).

Moreover, Hirsch and Levin, second explanation for concept development, which they term 'political', is perhaps more persuasive in explaining the recent ubiquity of the social capital concept:

> A researcher can make others take interest in and accept his or her work by paying homage to the current, institutionalised umbrella construct. Doing so makes the individual's research more legitimate, both among fellow scholars and in the eyes of funding

agencies ... umbrellas are often necessary for establishing intellectual linkages among otherwise isolated researchers. (1999, p. 7)

Paldam reaches the same conclusion, stating the social capital has the potential to amplify communication in the social science: 'One of the main virtues of social capital is that it is close to becoming a joint concept for all social sciences' (2000, p. 631).

Further Baron et al. (2000, pp. 12–14), in a chapter introducing social capital, consider the timing of social capital's inter-disciplinary ubiquity when they pose the question: 'Why Now?' They offer a number of answers pointing to the 'narcissism of the elites' who find that the concept, '... chimes with their personal circumstances. (It)... resonates with their own inability to find enough time for family and non-professional activity'. Second they cite a concern for the, '... excess of individualism' that has been brought to the fore by contemporary critics of globalisation, such as Gray (1998). Moreover, they consider the less than sterling results of market reform and concomitant failure to establish civil society in the post-Soviet block has also acted as a compelling impetus to the conceptual debate: Fukuyama's, 'second generation' reform in economic development (1992). A third explanation, which is also reached by Portes (1998), is that, 'ideas live in cycles' and, '... this is simply a re-branding of ideas that have never really gone away: what fluctuates is the attention paid to them'. Thus they highlight the cyclical nature of social science concepts.

A fourth answer proffered is the most telling: that is the concept's utility, '... though not consciously planned by any set of individuals − (aimed) to reintroduce the social element into capitalism'. In methodological terms to open, '... up the way for different approaches to modelling social relations, which address some of the moral and technical complexities of their protean character' (Baron et al., 2000, pp. 13–14). Thus they consider that the concept had instrumental value in capturing qualitative phenomena, which contrasted with the exclusively quantitative and asocial perspective, which had hitherto dominated. For example, criticism has been levelled at development agencies, such as the WTO and IMF, for a reliance on overly quantitative models for analysis and policy recommendations. The argument is that these quantitative models failed to give adequate weight to the impact of social relations on economic activity. Thus they abstracted or disembedded economic activity from its social context developing this argument they also state that the concept has heuristic value for policy analysis; therefore for improving policy co-ordination by allowing 'purchase' on the 'dynamic fluidity of social and economic life' (*ibid.*, pp. 33–38).

Fukuyama also reaches the same conclusions, claiming that social capital analysis is important because: 'It constitutes the cultural component of modern societies' (1999, p. 1).

Therefore, it is possible to accept Lin's serendipitous, interpretation of concept 'take-off', in the sense that there was no co-ordinated attempt to promote the concept as part of a wider programme. However, it is also plausible to suggest that there were factors driving interest in the concept as there was something about the latter part of the twentieth century that made social capital particularly appositive to the times. Further, drawing on Baron, Field and Schuller's causal factors, it is also plausible to argue that social capital appealed to elites and played to intellectual fashions that were grasping at a means to couple the social sciences to rational economics. For illustration, Dasgupta, summarises the concept as producing a 'warm glow': 'Offering an alternative to impersonal markets and coercive states, the communitarian institutions built around social capital have looked attractive to scholars in the humanities and social sciences' (2005, p. 2).

Paldam's (2000, pp. 363–367) analysis over the operationalising of the concept is also significant. He credits the influence of Putnam's proxy measure or 'Instrument' as it came to be termed, as causal factor in the explosion of interest in the concept. This was the quantification approach that measured social capital by researching associational life. In Paldam's words: 'It appears to be precisely because Putnam proposed such a simple and operational proxy that social capital moved from being a speciality of network sociologists into a major research topic for many professions'. Thus, the concept achieved greater ubiquity, propelled by the influence of Putnam among the political elites and the masses, and through the ease that his 'instrument' suggested the concept could be quantified – see Chapter 3 for a detailed discussion of Putnam's quantification methods.

Social capital's 'linguistic ambiguities' are also valuable in allowing disparate research to shelter under the same conceptual covering. Lin's assertion is therefore apposite; '... the premise behind the notion of social capital is simple and straightforward: investment in social relations with expected returns in the marketplace. This general definition is consistent with various renditions by all scholars who have contributed to the discussion' (2001, p. 19). Therefore Lin argues that there is a central conceptual core, or 'idea' of social capital, into which scholars can ground their work into, while permitting multi-interpretations beyond the core. Thus social capital's all encompassing big tent quality can serve as a theoretical meeting place for scholars with disparate research interests and in this sense, the concept's definitional ambiguity, while raising challenges for validity, can be interpreted as a causal factor for its popularity.

In sum it is possible to assert that interest in social capital as a theoretical tool was attuned to the times, given that new right, free market solutions informed policy making, especially in the Anglo-Saxon economies. Further the concept had utility for debates over the cultural contradictions of neo-liberalism; for instance did capitalism, in particular the more unfettered capitalism of the 1980s onwards, deplete values necessary to the sustenance of social capital? For illustration, Fukuyama considered this question and concluded that capitalism does not deplete social capital's 'moral relationships', but rather the culprit could be found in, 'technology and technological change' (1999, p. 262). Again this is an example of how the concept has been merged with earlier insights on the economy; in this case there is a lineage to Schumpeterian entrepreneurial 'gales of creative destruction' (1947). Thus social capital served to address any unwelcome developments evident in the neo-liberal, free-market model. For instance, in terms of addressing rising crime and increasing inequality with the argument that they were both caused by a lack of social capital among the poor. For illustration, according to Fukuyama the explanatory factors for the failure of economic progress and record levels of imprisonment among black Americans, are due less to the failings of the economic system, which had casualised many hitherto highly paid jobs – traditionally taken by urban communities – but rather, are a result of their community's deficit of social capital: 'The contemporary black underclass in America represents what is perhaps one of the most thoroughly atomised societies that has existed in human history. It is a culture in which individuals find it extremely difficult to work together for any purpose from raising children to petitioning city hall' (Fukuyama, 1995b).

2.10. CONCLUDING COMMENT

This review has also identified a number of themes that are significant in social capital's provenance. Fine and Green (2000, pp. 78–93), for example, have concluded that the concept: '... appears to constitute a new weapon to deploy at the perennial skirmishes between economics and other social sciences' (2000, p. 78). This literature review (and the previous chapter) has also argued that certain conceptual precedents possess more weight than others. For illustration, the influence of the Scottish philosophers of the

Enlightenment (Patterson, 2000, pp. 39–55), who developed the duality between the social motivations of the 'passions' and the purely economic motivations of the 'interests' remain at the heart of the debate (Granovetter, 1985, p. 506). Further, communitarian approaches, dating from the Tocquevillian analyses on associational democracy, are also an influential antecedent: Putnam refers to him as the 'patron saint of American communitarians' (2000, p. 24) and Fukuyama references him extensively.

CHAPTER 3

THE LEADING SOCIAL CAPITAL SCHOLARS

3.1. INTRODUCTION

This chapter will review the leading theoretical scholars, who are significant in any appraisal of social capital concept, but have also been selected because of their direct relevance to the focus into the economic significance of social capital. For illustration, Coleman attempted to integrate rational choice economics and sociological structure; Putnam's 'Big Idea' promoted the sociological importance of the concept supported with detailed statistics gathered from proxy indicators; and Fukuyama's socio-political treatment emphasised the importance of culture, trust and the morality in communities for economic efficiency. Therefore, as these scholars are explicitly interested in the economic importance of social capital this literature review will consider their theoretical treatments in detail.

In addition the chapter will review social capital scholars who work in the social network analysis (SNA) field of research. The exclusivist claims of network theory will be rejected as hyperbole: social capital is understood as being multi-dimensional, rather than being uni-dimensional. However, the importance of networks for theoretical understanding will nevertheless be stressed, and in consequence this chapter will examine Granovetter's socio-economic and social network insights; as well as Burt's research into social capital reputation processes; and Lin's resource-based view of social capital.

3.2. THE SEMINAL SOCIAL CAPITAL SCHOLARS

In most literature reviews the key theoretical scholars are identified as, Bourdieu, Coleman and Putnam who represent the, 'three relatively distinct tributaries of social capital theorising (that) are evident in recent literature' (Foley & Edwards, 1997). Adam and Roncevic concur, evaluating these scholars as the, 'three fathers of the concept' (2003, p. 157). However, this review will consider these founding theoretical authors, as well as number of further leading social capital scholars exclusively as their research applies to economic activity. Further this review is not exhaustive, but aims to be illustrative of the most important social capital observations on the economy.

The review will first consider Pierre Bourdieu, whose understanding of social capital stands in contrast to the other seminal authors. Second, the review will discuss the arch rationalist Coleman (1990) who interpreted social capital from a sociological perspective interested in, '... a large variety of benefits that social capital provides for the individual or selected groups of individuals' (Hooghe & Stolle, 2003, p. 5). Third, Putnam, who drew on a political tradition that conceptualises social capital, '... to a relatively normative view as social capital is often linked to largely societal benefits, mostly defined in terms of democratic goals' (*ibid.*). The review will also investigate Fukuyama's cultural consideration of social capital. In synopsis, this review will identify Coleman, Putnam and Fukuyama as the most significant scholars for the economic form of social capital. Moreover, although these scholars share common assumptions, including social capital's role in developing collective action, they also have diverse theoretical understandings.

Moreover, Coleman defined social capital in relation to social network concept, and the literature review will also examine the leading social capital structuralists or social network theorists, including, Granovetter (1973, 1985, 2005), Burt (1990, 2004, 2005) and Lin (1999, 2001). These social network theorists constitute another literature stream that understands social capital in terms of network characteristics, such as network morphology and embeddedness.

3.3. PIERRE BOURDIEU: A GALAXY OF CAPITALS

Bourdieu was an intellectual polymath who wrote extensively across academic disciplines, though he was most eminent as a sociologist of culture and it was in this field that Bourdieu introduced his understanding of the social capital in *Reproduction* (1985), '... initially as a metaphor linked with a galaxy of other forms of capital' (Baron, Field, & Schuller, 2000, p. 5).

Thus Bourdieu extended the scope of capital as a unit analysis contending that social space is not only defined by class but by individuals' amounts of social capital. Moreover, although he remained convinced of the 'primacy of the economic' (*ibid.*, p. 5), social capital increasingly featured in his work both as metaphor for power relations and for playing a crucial role in identity formation.

According to Bourdieu, social capital concept explained why the reproduction of elites, such as the ruling and intellectual classes, were self-perpetuating. This was linked to his earlier theory of habitus, which, '... can be understood as the values and dispositions gained from our cultural history that generally stay with us across contexts (they are durable and transposable)' (Webb, Schirato, & Danaher, 2002, p. 36). Moreover, Bourdieu's initial notion of social capital was '... part of a wider analysis of the diverse foundations of social order' (Field, 2003, p. 14). Bourdieu eventually defined the concept as, '... the aggregate of the actual or potential resources which are linked to possession of a durable network of more or less institutionalised relationships of mutual acquaintance or recognition' (1985, p. 243).

To illustrate his notions of social hierarchy Bourdieu and Coleman considered the instrumental role of social capital in the education system's reproduction of social inequality and underachievement. In Bourdieu's analysis, social capital was a form of capital that enabled the powerful to remain powerful from generation to generation. In this treatment social capital was conceptualised as an agent for the efficient means of hereditary transmission of capital: effective because it was subtle and therefore hard to regulate, whereas economic wealth could be readily limited by targeted taxed such as death duties. To give a contemporary example, the social capital of powerful connections, based on shared cultural capital, is more enduring than capital based on qualifications, as the latter is more vulnerable to 'credential inflation' than the former (Field, 2003, p. 16).

Bourdieu's, seminal role in theoretical development has been acknowledged by Portes who asserts that: 'The first systematic contemporary analysis of social capital was produced by Bourdieu' (1998, p. 3). Moreover, Portes, regards Bourdieu as having produced the, '... most theoretically refined of those who introduced the term into sociological discourse' (*ibid.*, p. 3). Bourdieu anchored social capital in neo-capital theories, emphasising the fungibility of all forms of capital, which he defined as 'accumulated human labour' (*ibid.*, p. 3). Portes further considers that Bourdieu's 'treatment of the concept is instrumental, focussing on the benefits accruing to individuals by virtue of participation in groups and on the deliberate creation of sociability for the purpose of creating this resource' (*ibid.*, p. 3). Portes also laments Bourdieu's lack of visibility in the current social capital discourse.

In contrast, Baron et al.'s evaluation of Bourdieu is more critical. They acknowledge Bourdieu's achievement for establishing the framework for theoretical development. However, they are critical of Bourdieu's 'marginal use' of the concept, and for the 'contrast between sophisticated theoretical claims and weak empirical data' (2000, pp. 3–4). From the network perspective, Lin concludes that Bourdieu's concept of social reproduction, which results in 'symbolic violence': that is, the pedagogic process by which the dominant culture and values are accepted without conscious awareness or resistance is consistent with 'a lineage of capital to Marx' (2001, p. 15). However, Lin also acknowledges that Bourdieu falls outside the orthodox Marxist tradition, for instance in the significance he places on 'acquired capital and the market' (2001, p. 16). Moreover, Lin is critical of Bourdieu in not delineating between different levels of analysis; that is, at the group as opposed to the individual levels (*ibid.*, p. 25).

Field (2003) also criticises Bourdieu for being too Marxist, as well as more perceptively criticising Bourdieu's view that social capital was the 'exclusive property of elites' (*ibid.*, p. 17). Further Field identifies the limitations of Bourdieu's over 'static model of social hierarchy' unsuited to the 'loose social relations of late modernity' (*ibid.*, p. 18). Consequently, in Field's view Bourdieu does not consider that the less privileged, such as Portes' immigrant groups (2003) would have access to social capital. According to Field, another criticism that can be levelled at Bourdieu – and incidentally Coleman and Putnam – is that he represents, '… social capital as largely benign, at least for those who possess high volumes of it' (*ibid.*, p. 19). Thus the dark side or dis-utilities of social capital are under-explored in Bourdieu's theoretical treatment.

In summary, Bourdieu's use of the concept is seminal. However, Bourdieu is not responsible for the current interest in social capital in the world of work and his interpretation of the concept, as means whereby the dominant class maintains its group solidarity and its dominance is in stark relief to the more popular interpretations detailed below. Moreover, Baron et al. note: 'In 1989 Bourdieu and James Coleman co-organised a conference on "Social Concept for a Changing Society" (Bourdieu & Coleman, 1991) which despite their both having published seminal work on social capital scarcely addressed the issue' (2000, p. 5). This suggests that Bourdieu didn't attach as much importance to the social capital as the scholars who followed him.

3.4. JAMES COLEMAN: THE FICTION OF ADAM SMITH

Coleman (1926–1995) was a leading social theorist, who achieved eminence in the field of education sociology and public policy. Coleman's theoretical method was based on rational choice theory, which he espoused as a sociology professor at Chicago University. His most influential and also controversial research was entitled: 'Equality of Educational Opportunity', known widely as the 'Coleman Report' (1966),[1] which led directly to policy makers instigating measures to promote racial integration, for instance by bussing pupils to distant schools. Moreover, Coleman's subsequent educational research was highly controversial, as he performed a 'volte face' and was critical of these policies for creating 'White Flight'. This educational controversy is one reason why he remains perennially out of favour with Leftist social scholars. In addition, Coleman also became associated with the controversial hypothesis that the effectiveness of spending on schools is limited by their social context: a view that Coleman himself found unsettling and an over-simplification. However, leaving aside these controversies there is no gainsaying that Coleman actively engaged with societal problems by constructing theories on the patterns of social behaviour.

In terms of social capital Coleman fully developed his theoretical treatment in Chapter 12 of the voluminous tome, *Foundations of Social Concept* (1990). In his view: 'Social capital is defined by its function. It is not a single entity, but a variety of different entities having two characteristics in common: They all consist of some aspect of social structure, and they facilitate certain actions of individuals who are within the structure' (1990, p. 302). Moreover, Coleman's avowed objective was to introduce into social concept, the concept of social capital paralleling other capitals, '... but embodying relations among persons' (2000, p. 38).

Further, Coleman aimed to introduce social structure into the 'rational action paradigm' (see Chapter 1). He argued that sociology and economics has 'serious defects' (*ibid.*, pp. 18–19). In Coleman's view sociology had denuded the actor of an 'engine of action'; that is, the actor is assumed to be shaped entirely by their environment. Whereas, economics suffered from the fiction that society consisted of independent individuals expressed, 'most graphically in Adam Smith's imagery of an "invisible hand"' (Coleman, 1990, p. 300). Thus according to Coleman, economics was still directed by the 'extraordinary impact' (*ibid.*, p. 301) of Adam Smith and classical economists whose theories were founded on methodological individualism. In contrast, Coleman's aim was to, '... import the economist's principle of rational action for use in the analysis of social systems proper .... and to do so without discarding social organizations in the process' (2000, p. 19). Therefore Coleman was concerned with the fusion of sociology and economics within his own rational choice paradigm (as already detailed in Chapter 1).

In this task Coleman was influenced by the human capital, rational choice concept of fellow university of Chicago professor (and 1992 Nobel Prize winner) Garry Becker. To restate, Coleman's variant of rational choice concept posited that all action results from actors pursuing their own interests of maximising utility and minimising loss of their preferences.[2] According to Coleman, social interaction and cooperation should be interpreted as forms of exchange motivated by self-interest. This means individual actors cooperate because they evaluate that it is in their interests to do so, which also explains why actors may avoid acting opportunistically in the short term, on the instrumental assumption that the longer term pay-off is in all probability going to be more rewarding.

Furthermore, Coleman identified a number of economists that had already attempted to address the asocial nature of their discipline, including Oliver Williamson, who had published extensively on transaction costs (1985, 1993). Williamson (1985) theorised that costs involved in transaction included: obtaining relevant information; bargaining and decision-making costs as well as the costs associated with the policing and enforcing of contracts. Opportunistic behaviour occurred when, guided by self-interest, agents sought to promote their interests on the assumption that their misleading or false information would incur no penalties of punishments. Moreover, the costs for business could be onerous, given that it could be difficult to gauge who is likely to behave in this disreputable manner. This perspective then considered the costs of economic exchange and falls within a general approach termed, 'new institutional economics'. This school drew its antecedents to Ronald Coarse, and, in particular, his influential article of 1937, rhetorically entitled: 'Why do Firms Exist?' The answer given was to improve the flow of information and reduce exchange costs, a function analogous to that ascribed to social capital in Coleman's theoretical treatment.

Coleman also mentioned network theorists and his theoretical treatment is consistent with network concept. For example, Coleman approvingly introduced Granovetter's concept of embeddedness and the latter's criticism of the 'under-socialised concept of man' (1985). Coleman, concludes that Granovetter's approach is, '... an attempt to introduce into the analysis of economic systems social and organizational relations' (1990, p. 302). Lin's work on actor's instrumentality for, 'purposeful action' is also briefly mentioned.

Coleman further asserts that social capital along with other forms of capital, '... is not entirely fungible, but may be specific to certain actions'. However: 'Unlike other forms of capital, social capital inheres in the structures between actors and among actors' (Coleman, 2000, p. 20). Coleman illustrates these views with an examination of three forms of social capital: the first, 'Obligations, Expectations, and Trustworthiness of structures'. This is a network approach that notes the importance of the 'level of trustworthiness in the environment ... and the actual extent of obligations held' (Coleman, 1990, p. 306). To illustrate this observation, Coleman references the high levels of trust in the New York diamond trade, which is controlled by a Jewish 'closed community' (2000, p. 20), though he weakens his case by not considering the role played by the De Beers cartel in this arrangement. Coleman concludes: 'Reputation cannot arise in an open structure and collective sanctions that would ensure trustworthiness cannot be applied' (2000, p. 28). This conclusion also corresponds with network concept, concerning network closure assisting the development of reputation (Lin, 2001, p. 244).

The second form of the concept is to provide 'information channels' to facilitate purposeful action. This is an important form of social capital as it provides contemporary and contextualised information, which is often essential in achieving economic success: in the vernacular this form of social capital can be thought of as facilitating the process of 'learning the ropes', which is consistent with M. Polanyi's concept of 'tacit knowledge' (1958).

The third channel is for providing 'norms and effective channels', which are '... important in overcoming the public goods problem that exists in collectives' (Coleman, 2000, p. 26). This is an age-old problem of balancing self-interest against those of the collectivity; termed the collective action problem. This has been variously referred to as the tragedy of the commons' in relation of how to prevent over-grazing if the land is open to all; or the public good problem in terms of who should pay for the lighthouse when every vessel will use its guiding light? The problem therefore is how to enforce behaviour and counter the 'free-loaders'. One solution, suggested by Coleman, is that prescriptive 'norms' enforce behaviour: that is, the actor forgoes self-interest and acts in the interest of the collectivity as they have internalised these collective norms. An extreme form of a prescriptive norm, to facilitate action, is referred to as zeal, which carries negative implications. Moreover, Coleman is transparent in detailing the asymmetrical nature of norms in facilitating some actions yet constraining others. Moreover, 'zeal' also has religious connotations and Coleman, warming to this theme considered that: 'an ideology of self-sufficiency ... which is a basis of much Protestant doctrine, can inhibit the creation of social capital' (1990, p. 321). For illustration, SME owner-managers may pride themselves on their rugged independence, based on their efforts as 'self-made men'. Thus owner-managers may develop an exaggerated sense of individualism, while at the same time these very qualities may inhibit the development of social capital.

Coleman also considers social capital's creation. In his view: 'Social capital, however, comes about through changes in the relationships between persons that facilitate action' (2000, p. 22). And '... organization, once brought into existence for one set of purposes, can also aid others, thus constituting social capital available for use' (*ibid.*, p. 29). Thus according to Coleman social capital is created by the acquisition of skills and new processes by individuals; there is therefore, a relationship between social capital and the creation of human capital. Moreover, he considers social capital's creation to be mainly a by-product of other activities, given its 'public goods quality':

> Yet, because benefits of actions that bring social capital into being are largely experienced by people other than the actor, it is often not in his interest to bring it into being. The result is that most forms of social capital are created or destroyed as by-products of other activities. This social capital arises or disappears without anyone willing it into or out of being. (*ibid.*, p. 38)

It follows that in Coleman's understanding of social capital it would be difficult, if not impossible, to design effective policy measures for creating social capital. It is also worth noting that Coleman also observed that social capital is more likely to be created as an oppositional response, '... where one type of actor is weaker in a relationship ... the actors of this type will be likely to develop social networks that have closure, in order to strengthen their position relative to the more powerful type of actor' (1990, p. 319). This observation suggests therefore that contingencies are crucial in the success or otherwise of fostering social capital.

Coleman (1990, 2000) also analysed community norms and sanctions and highlighted the importance of continuity in social relations. For instance he noted that social capital is eroded as individuals became less mutually dependent: 'When, because of affluence, government aid or some other factor, persons need each other less, less social capital is generated'

(1990, p. 321). Moreover, social capital also diminishes as 'strong families and strong communities' decline (2000, p. 38): an observation that has raised the ire of more liberal social scientists,[3] though this observation is also open to the criticism that it offers an undifferentiated view of relations and affluence. An example of contrary conclusion is, Cairns, Van Til and Williamson's social capital research, which suggests that affluence increases social capital formation: 'Higher socio-economic status was found to be associated with higher levels of social capital' (2003, p. 4). Moreover, one could use Coleman's own observation, over social capital being formed in opposition, to suggest that single household families may band together to form increased levels of social capital more readily than traditional households because they are in opposition to prevailing, though changing social mores.

3.4.1. Perspectives on Coleman

Coleman has attracted considerable criticism for his 'rather vague definition' (Portes, 1998, p. 5). Reflecting this conclusion, Lin criticises Coleman's theoretical treatment a: 'social capital is defined by its function' (2001, p. 26). And that this, '... functional view may implicate a tautology ... the potential causal explanation of social capital can be captured only by its effects ... Thus the causal factor is defined by the effectual factor' (*ibid.*, p. 28). Portes agrees, disparaging Coleman's functional use of the concept: 'Equating social capital with the resources acquired through it can easily lead to tautological statements' (1998, p. 5). According to Portes this has led to, '... setting the stage for confusion in the uses and scope of the term' (Portes, 1998, p. 6). From this critical optic therefore Coleman can be held culpable for the proliferation of interpretations, for producing such an ambiguous and amorphous theoretical understanding that interpreted norms, trust, sanctions and networks as forms of social capital. Thus, if the concept does have a 'circus tent quality' (Lappe & Du Bois, 1997, p. 111), Coleman in this critical optic is the original circus master.

Conversely, Baron et al. have argued that because the concept is relational it: '... requires us to look at social phenomena from different angles to capture the changing nature of analysis' (2000, p. 29). Thus Coleman's functional and sketchy definition allows for a complexity in theoretical engagement, as do other non-linear conceptions, such as race and class. Moreover, Baron et al. (2000) consider that: 'Coleman's work has strongly shaped the contemporary debate' (p. 7). Inkpen and Tsang concur, observing that the concept evolved through Coleman and Burt (2004, 2005, p. 150). For example, Coleman's enduring influence over social capital can be identified in Nahapiet and Ghoshal's operationalisation of social capital (1998), which they readily admit was developed from Coleman's theoretical understanding (see Chapter 3). In synopsis Baron et al. characterise Coleman's understanding of social capital as being focussed on, 'a concern for social capital as a source of educational advantage' (2000, p. 7). Further, they acknowledge Coleman's insights on the importance of, '... primordial relationships', for facilitating strong levels of trust and promoting information sharing, within the confines of network closure and bounded ties. However, Baron et al. also noted Coleman's failure to recognise the advantages of structural holes, weak and loose ties as well as the opportunities they presented for brokerage in social systems. They conclude that Coleman interpreted social capital as: '... the key generic tool in his wider project of integrating rational choice concept with an understanding of the social' (2000, p. 244). They also note that Coleman drew attention to the contribution of social capital to equity and justice (2000, p. 45).

From a more critical perspective, Portes agrees on the significance of Coleman and credits him with: '... introducing and giving visibility to the concept in American sociology' (1998, p. 6). However, Portes also considers that Coleman was being disingenuous, when he described social capital as an 'unanalysed concept' (Coleman, 1990), given the earlier work of Bourdieu. Portes, incidentally, also emphasises Coleman's failure to acknowledge Bourdieu as curious, given that both scholars understood social capital as pivotal in the acquisition of educational credentials.

Field's (2003, p. 28) comparison between Coleman's and Bourdieu's notion of social capital is also illuminating. According to Field, Bourdieu's interpretation of social capital boils down to, '... privileged individuals (who) maintain their position by using their connections with other privileged people'. Whereas: 'Coleman's view is more nuanced, in that he discerns the value of connections for all actors, individual and collective, privileged and disadvantaged'. However, Coleman is also criticised for being 'naively optimistic' in acknowledging only the benign functions of social capital and for not allowing for the dark side or dis-utilities of the concept. Field further points to inconsistencies and weaknesses in Coleman's analysis. However, he is generous enough to highlight three strengths in Coleman's account:

> The strength must include his ambitious attempt to integrate social capital into a wider theory of the origins of social structures: his recognition that social capital could be an

asset for disadvantaged groups and not solely an instrument of privilege; and his interests in the mechanics of social networks. (*ibid.*, p. 29)

Fukuyama also concurs on the significance of Coleman's contribution to conceptual development (1999, p. 2). In sum, Coleman's peers acknowledge his pioneering scholarship, though his definition and interpretation are nonetheless mired in controversy due to his rational choice framing methodology, as discussed in Chapter 1. However, though Coleman's influence remains fundamental, in educational disciplines and for research into the economic significance of social capital, it has been claimed that he is, '... now overshadowed by Putnam in the wider public debate' (Baron et al., 2000, p. 8), and it is to this scholar that the literature review turns to next.

3.5. PUTNAM'S BIG IDEA: BOWLING WITH INFLUENCE

Putnam established his reputation with his ambitiously titled: *The Beliefs of Politicians: Ideology, Conflict, and Democracy in Britain and Italy* (1973), which drew directly on Edward Banfield's deeply flawed: *The Moral Basis of a Backward Society* (1958/1967). Putnam's hallmarks of detailed empirical research and a plethora of statistical data are already evident, as are a number of themes that were to inform his later work. He noted, for instance that there is a 'conflict-consensus syndrome', which is analogous to the 'left-right spectrum' (1973, p. 107). In terms of social capital's lineage Putnam's next significant publication, *Making Democracy Work* (1993) was based on research into Italian regional government, and was written in collaboration with Italian scholars, Robert Lonardi and Y. Nanetti. This research introduced incipient themes that were later to form the basis of Putnam's ever-evolving social capital understanding. For example, Putnam attempted to address the power of the past with reference to 'path dependency': thus '... where you can get depends on where you're coming from, and some destinations you simple cannot get to from here' (*ibid.*, p. 179). Moreover, according to Putnam this could lead to a 'path-dependent social equilibria' (*ibid.*, p. 180). For example: 'North America inherited civic traditions, whereas the Latin Americans were bequeathed traditions of vertical dependence and exploitation' (*ibid.*, p. 179). In Italy, Putnam considered regional government as a starting point to reach conclusions about the nature of society, culture and the collective action problem. According to Putnam, Banfield's 'amoral familism' in the Mezzogiorni had been self-reinforcing in Southern Italy from the Middle Ages (*ibid.*, p. 180). Thus Putnam contends that the Southern Italy was caught in a self-perpetuating 'vicious circle', which, '... reproduced perennial exploitation and dependence' whereas, the North had greater stocks of social capital due to its 'virtuous circle' (*ibid.*, p. 162).

This book also offers an early description of social capital as '... features of social organisations, such as trust, norms and networks that can improve the efficiency of society by facilitating coordinated actions' (*ibid.*, p. 167). According to Putnam social capital is a resource that, '... increases rather than decreases with use and which becomes depleted if not used' (*ibid.*, p. 169). Further: 'One special feature of social capital, like trust, norms and networks, is that it is ordinarily a public good ... (which) must often be produced as a by-product of other social activities' (*ibid.*, p. 170). Thus Putnam's original understanding of social capital is in its substantive points indistinguishable from Coleman's interpretation of the concept.

3.5.1. Putnam and American Social Capital: A Tocquevillian Analysis

Following his investigation of the civic traditions of Italy, Putnam turned his analytical gaze to his native country, America, specifically to its perceived declining levels of civic engagement (1995a, 2000). In synopsis his argument was that: 'The quality of public life and the performance of social institutions are powerfully influenced by norms and networks of civil engagement' (Putnam, 1995, p. 66). Moreover, Putnam drew inspiration from de Tocqueville's, *Democracy in America* (1835/1956), which characterised the fledgling American republic by its citizens' proclivity to form voluntary associations and willingness to maintain healthy levels of civic vigilance. Putnam's analysis concluded that the recent past had witnessed declining levels of social capital, which had followed a period of social capital formation associated with a long 'civic generation'. However the post-war baby boom generation had neglected social capital and the subsequent, so-called 'generation X', had further denuded the nations stocks. Thus, there had been intergenerational collapse of social capital and Putnam in response argues that 'lessons from history' can be used to replenish the nation's social capital, which he discussed in detail in the final part of his *Bowling Alone* (2000), in terms of: 'What is to be done?' In response Putnam's argues that there needs to be a 'Great Re-awakening' to be driven by educational and religious forces.

Putnam also developed his definition so that social capital was considered in terms of social interaction, such as networks, norms and trust that enable participants to act together more effectively to pursue shared objectives. Thus:

> Whereas physical capital refers to physical objects and human capital refers to properties of individuals, social capital refers to connections among individuals – social networks and the norms of reciprocity and trustworthiness that arise from them. In that sense social capital is closely related to what some have called 'civic virtue'. The difference is that 'social capital' calls attention to the fact that civic virtue is most powerful when embedded in a dense network of reciprocal social relations. A society of many virtuous but isolated individuals is not rich in social capital. (2000, p. 19)

It is also notable that Putnam's observations on the concept's long-term antecedents are linked to a reference to Alexis de Tocqueville analysis on American individualism. This is revealing, as de Tocqueville is Putnam's most cited historical source: 15 references in the index of *Bowling Alone* (2000). Fukuyama, perhaps the second most influential and well-known writer on social capital, also quotes liberally from de Tocqueville; 12 times in his *Trust: The Social Virtues and the Creation of Prosperity* (1995b). The question then needs to be posed as to why this liberal French aristocrat is so attractive to the two leading writers on contemporary social capital? Certainly, de Tocqueville was a writer of genius whose work echoes down the ages. However, his methodology would not pass muster: by contemporary standards of scholarship. For example, many of his conclusions are based on intuition and are deficient in evidential and/or statistical supporting material. R. D. Hefner (the editor of a recent edition of *Democracy in America*) is accurate therefore to criticise de Tocqueville's: '... too easy assumptions and his desire not to report, but rather to summarize, interpret and generalize' (1835/1956). However Hefner also notes that: 'For all his obvious inadequacies and the rather distressing subjectivity of his approach, still many of his generalizations concerning politics, religion government, art and even literature in democratic America are amazingly perceptive in their way' (1835/1956, p. 16), which is a balanced evaluation of de Tocqueville. Of course, as an historical figure it would be anachronistic to accuse him of failing to apply modern standards of scholarship, given he was writing from his own historical perspective as a Regency French liberal in the 1820s. However, the question remains as to why this writer, as is given such a prominent place by both Putnam and Fukuyama. The answer, which is perhaps more transparent in a close reading of Fukuyama, is that de Tocqueville's liberal 'Weltanschauung', for instance, of criticising authoritarianism, centralisation, while praising the US citizenry's proclivity to group membership and 'self-interest rightly understood', sits very comfortably with the conservative view of society espoused by Fukuyama and to a lesser extent by Putnam – the admiration and frequent references to de Tocqueville will also be discussed in reference to Fukuyama, another neo-Tocquevillian, below.

Thus, Putnam's central themes, with regard to civic community (2000, pp. 87–93) have their antecedents in de Tocqueville's *Democracy in America* (1835/1956). Further, Putnam's themes of civic engagement; political equality; solidarity, trust and tolerance and finally associations as social structures of cooperation, are also all identifiable Tocquevillian themes. It also can be contended that the reliance on de Tocqueville can connect Putnam's social capital to 'communitarianism', which has been similarly influenced by de Tocqueville's observations. Therefore there is an unbroken intellectual chain, originating in de Tocqueville that subsequently runs through numerous social commentators, including communitarians[4] leading to Putnam's Italian-inspired interpretation of social capital.

Putnam, also cautions over the 'Dark Side of Social Capital' (2000, pp. 350–363) and concedes that there is a, '... classic liberal objection to community ties: community restricts freedom and encourages intolerance' (*ibid.*, p. 351). For example in the 1950s a, '... surfeit of social capital seemed to impose conformity and social division' (*ibid.*, p. 352). Thus it is possible to consider that there is a continuum from liberty to community: '... the individualist society with much liberty but little community, and the sectarian society with much community but little liberty' (*ibid.*, p. 355). Furthermore, social capital, '... often reinforces social stratification', and: 'Social inequalities may be embedded in social capital' (*ibid.*, p. 358). However, Putnam, who is solidly in favour of the concept's normative value, for the collective and individual good, inevitably interrupts his consideration of the negatives of the concept, to suggest that social capital, '... may help produce equality' and, '... has been the main weapon of the have nots' (*ibid.*, p. 359).

In response to the theoretical dilemma of differentiating between beneficial and harmful social capital, Putnam introduces two types of social capital: bonding or exclusive capital, and bridging or inclusive capital. This is an ingenious solution to a core difficulty with the existence and promotion of social capital in that it has positive and negative outcomes. For instance the positives include social capital facility to 'mobilise solidarity' and negatives include its tendency 'to bolster our narrower selves'. However, he admits the categories are not mutually exclusive but rather, '... more or less dimensions along which we can compare different forms of social capital'.

Putnam summarises, mixing metaphors: '... Bonding social capital constitutes a kind of sociological superglue, whereas bridging social capital provides a sociological WD-40' (*ibid.*, p. 23). One can sympathise with Putnam for recognising the problem of inward looking social capital, which tends towards sectarianism and ethnocentrism. Further, the view that groups bond to the disadvantage of outsiders has long been noted (Smith, 1776/ 1999, pp. 232–233).

Putnam also considers 'Connections in the Workplace' (Chapter 5) and notes the comments of labour economist, Peter Pestillo made 20 years earlier, as being prescient: 'The young worker thinks primarily of himself. We are experiencing the cult of the individual, and labour is taking a beating preaching the comfort of coalition' (*ibid.*, p. 82). Putnam continues, and refutes the suggestion that workplace social capital, formed for instance in the queue for the photocopier, has replaced other declining sources. Putnam is therefore under-whelmed by recent management movements aimed at increasing human and social capital, including: TQM, quality circles, team building initiatives and creative spaces, labelled 'watering-holes', 'conversation pits' and 'campfires', where workers warm their hands. In conclusion Putnam still asserts: '... I know of no evidence whatever that socializing in the workplace, however common, has actually increased over the last several decades' (*ibid.*, p. 87).

Recent organisational changes also fall within Putnam's analytical gaze, including 'right-sizing', 're-engineering' and economic restructuring. Putnam's conclusion is measured: these developments have led to some gains, in terms of improved productivity and less paternalism. However, in terms of social capital Putnam's evaluation is unequivocal: '... their impact on trust and social connectedness in workplace. On that score, the balance sheet is negative' (*ibid.*, p. 88). For example, 'outplacement' can be linked to 'survivor shock' and this 'job churning' and has also been linked to a fall in 'the returns to tenure', in terms of wages and other benefits from seniority (*ibid.*, p. 89). Overall, Putnam offers a balanced consideration of the effects of organisation change, noting that more time at work and teamwork may improve informal workplace social capital. However, he still concludes:

> ... all these structural changes in the workplace – shorter job-tenure, more part-time and temporary jobs, and even independent consultancy – inhibit workplace social ties ... social capital takes time and concerted effort. Birds of passage, whether by choice or by necessity, generally don't nest. (*ibid.*, p. 90)

Putnam, further considers trust and trustworthiness and refers to the work of Gambetta (1998) on the Mafia, who maintains that societies that rely on force are likely to be costly, inefficient and unpleasant (*ibid.*, p. 136). For example, discussing transaction costs, Putnam concludes, '... trusting communities, other things being equal, have a measurable economic advantage' (2000, p. 135). He continues that, 'dense social networks' encourage 'trust', and: 'An effective norm of generalised reciprocity is bolstered by dense networks of social exchange'. Moreover, collaborators, 'have reputations at stake that are almost surely worth more than gains from momentary treachery. In that sense honesty is encouraged by dense social networks' (*ibid.*, p. 136). Thus 'thick' trust, where relations are embedded in personal relations that are strong, frequent and nested in wider networks, encourages the development of reputation. Moreover: 'Thin trust is even more useful than thick trust, because it extends the radius of trust beyond the roster of people whom we know personally'.

Furthermore, in a chapter entitled, 'Economic Prosperity' (Chapter 19) Putnam puts the case that social capital leads to economic prosperity and links the concept with Alfred Marshall's 'industrial districts', '... which allow for information flows, mutual learning, and economies of scale' (*ibid.*, p. 325). Examples offered of industrial districts, with concomitant high levels of social capital, include: north-central Italy with crafts and consumer goods; western Michigan with furniture; and Rochester, New York with optics. Perhaps the most interesting example is taken from Silicon Valley, whose success is contrasted with the relative failure and traditional business practices of its main regional competitor, 'Route 128', by Boston. Putnam attributes Silicon Valley's success to 'horizontal networks of information and formal cooperation that developed among fledgling companies in the area'. Moreover, the industry was in a state of flux and this encouraged and reinforced, '... the value of personal relationships and networks' (*ibid.*, p. 324). Thus according to Putnam, social capital development and utility played a key role in perhaps one of the most successful business cluster in the world. However, it could be argued that this is perhaps another example of Putnam's tendency to reduce complicated phenomena to a prime determinant; in this case the instrumental value of social capital in creating a cluster of cutting edge IT firms that created a 'virtuous circle' of technical and economic advantages.[5]

3.5.2. Putnam Conclusions

Putnam offers a theoretical treatment replete with detailed empirical data, analysing a widely perceived though hitherto barely articulated perception over the decline of social activity. Further, Putnam's success in promoting the concept to a mass readership, as well as to political elites, can be attributed to both his persuasive literary gifts, and to his ability to simplify social capital so that it could be readily understood.

Of course success focuses attention, not always complimentary, and Putnam has been subject to a number of interconnected criticisms, the most significant of which be classified into two themes. First and most tellingly are criticisms of Putnam's theoretical approach and research methods. For example, Putnam's draws on data collected by other researchers for different purposes and his measurement instrument, which uses proxy indicators, has provoked scepticism over the validity of measuring a relational asset by its supposed effects. Second, Putnam's formative theoretical research based on his, '... reading of Italian society (which) has caused a vast scholarly debate animated by Italian scholars and Italinists abroad' (Huysseune, 2003, p. 212). It is instructive to take each criticism in turn, as they illustrate Putnam's strengths and limitations, before reaching a conclusion over his contribution to theoretical debates.

First, Putman's use of the concept has also attracted criticism for lacking clarity.[6] For example, Portes levels the charge of 'logical circularity' (1998, p. 6). Thus because Putnam defines social capital as the property of nations and communities and not individuals, '... social capital is simultaneously a cause and an effect' (*ibid.*, p. 19).[7] Putnam therefore stands accused of tautology, inferring social capital's existence from its outcomes. According to Portes, this flawed approach to analytical deduction was popular in American sociology in the 1940s and 1950s. Thus, to reiterate if a community is economically successful, such as North Italy then this is because it has high levels of social capital: if a region is less successful, such as South Italy then it is because it has low levels of social capital (Fukuyama, 1995a; Putnam, 2000, pp. 344–345). It also can be argued that Putnam's historical analysis is over-determinist, which can be characterised as 'the arrogance of the present', which attempts to explain the present by projecting trends from the past as their causal factors (see below for a discussion of the Whig view of history).

It is also worth detailing Portes' evaluation of Putnam's work as it provides a good example of the general tenor of the criticisms of Putnam's sociological methods. For instance, Portes accuses Putnam of logical circularity (1998, p. 19), definitional tautology (*ibid.*, p. 20) and erroneous analytical induction (*ibid.*, p. 20). Portes also highlights other authors who have noted, '... the unacknowledged class bias in Putnam's book'. And, '... the elitist stance of the argument, where responsibility for the alleged decline of social capital is put squarely on the leisure behaviour, rather than on the economic and political changes wrought by the corporate and governmental establishment' (*ibid.*, p. 19). Skocpol's review of Putnam's analysis is also described as trenchant when she asserts:

> How ironic it be if, after pulling out of locally rooted associations, the very businesses and professional elites who blazed the path toward local civic disengagement were now to turn around and successfully argue that the less privileged Americans they left behind are the ones who must repair the nation's social connections. (1996, p. 25)

Thus, there is a collection of criticisms that interpret Putnam's social capital as class based, and elitist for providing a bulwark in favour of the prevailing economic policies. For example, according to Halpern: '... to a European eye at least, the limited discussion of economic inequality and the potential positive casual role that might be played by the state is especially striking' (2005, p. 230). However, Putnam's concern to improve the well being of the disadvantaged, for instance with his campaigning Saguaro Seminars – named after a hardy plant that flowers in the desert and his http://www.Bettertogether.org, suggest that these criticisms are less than trenchant. Further, it could be argued that these 'Leftist' critics conflate Putnam's interpretation with more reactionary interpretations; these criticisms levelled at Fukuyama would possess more credence. For example, Fukuyama, consistently argues from a neo-liberal vantage of the unintended consequences of social engineering: in other words, his vantage is one of scepticism towards the hubris of grand schemes of social engineering which leads to the conclusion that markets know best – see below.

However, it is true that Putnam does not place emphasis on politics in his social capital treatment[8] and in this omission of class he reflects general analytical lacunae: outside of the hard Left, class analysis is arguably the great taboo in contemporary American social science. Further although he fails to consider class in any detail, the evidence for being elitist and having an unacknowledged class bias, meaning anti-working class, is unconvincing. For instance, a consideration of Putnam's scholarship from his early work on social capital 1973 to the present, suggests that he conceives of society in a consensual and inclusive framework. This means Putnam's politics are ambiguous and hence his popularity among politicians of various hue. Moreover, Putnam's analytical focus is broad, in contrast to Bourdieu who interpreted social capital as an asset exclusively of the privileged. Further, Putnam does not focus on one class to the exclusion of the rest of society, and his stinging criticisms of 'gated communities' (2000, p. 210) would seem to contradict the putative class bias: gated communities are expensive and therefore these criticisms are aimed at the affluent, middle and upper classes. In addition, Putnam has criticised the effects of 'the privatisation of leisure time', due to the proliferation of electronic entertainment, as a casual factor in the decline of America's stocks of social capital (2000, p. 284).

Leftist critics of Putnam have been discussed above, and their criticisms derive from a conviction that Putnam's consensual optic is essentially conservative. Thus they argue the concept is attractive to policies intent on undermining socialist principles and legislation. For example, in the United Kingdom critics have concluded that social capital rhetoric has been deployed to assist in the dismantling of the welfare state and replacing it with charity, the latest version of which is 'The Big Society' (Baron, 2004, pp. 5–16; Baron et al., 2000, p. 2; Levitas, 2004, pp. 41–56). In overview, critics consider that Putnam's social capital is little more an anti-statist, authoritarian neo-communitarianism, which argues for more personal responsibilities and fewer rights. Consequently, Putnam's social capital is read as advocating a new form of communitarianism, which stresses the need for the 'civic deficit' to be cut not by state intervention, for example by introducing a more progressive taxation regime; but rather by encouraging individuals to join 'legitimate' voluntary NGOs. Therefore, the responsibility for social exclusion is shifted onto the poor: it becomes their individual responsibility to join-in and improve their stock of social capital. In this analysis to further exacerbate the negatives, the recognised legitimate community organisations, which tend to be those groups that are long established, are then drawn into partnership with right-wing or 'reformist' policies. Moreover, the consequence of these relationships is a tendency, to subvert the NGOs original purposes, as unwittingly they end acting as organisational fig leafs for welfare cutting policies.

However this body of criticism is overstated. For example, according to Baron et al., Putnam is '… not advocating a compassionate conservatism, with hierarchical classes peacefully bound to each other by mutual obligation'. Instead he sees social capital as '… incompatible with high levels of inequality; it is a complement, not an alternative to egalitarian policies' (2000, p. 10). Further, they suggest that Putnam has further refined his definition of social capital: 'Most recently, in the Alfred Marshall lectures delivered in Cambridge in 1999 Putnam has applied Occam's razor with even greater rigour, identifying social capital directly with networks alone' (*ibid.*, pp. 10–11). They also assert that: 'Putnam's latest work shifts the emphasis from trust to reciprocity' (*ibid.*, p. 11). Thus Putnam's developing, or shifting notion of social capital fails to focus on politics, and in the sense that he interprets society through a consensual optic the criticism that Putnam is conservative has validity.

The second body of criticism relates to Putnam's historical and contemporary interpretation of Italian society, which is contentious, as it draws on the equally flawed work of Banfield (1958/1967). Thus, Putnam's conclusions and policy recommendations, which are drawn from an analysis based on a spatial North/South division of Italy, and from a consideration of Italy's social fabric, are open to alternative interpretations. For example, Putnam argues that there is a fissure in Italian society, dividing the prosperous North from the more Catholic, familistic South. In the Italian vernacular: 'Garibali, didn't unite Italy, he divided Africa'. However, there are a number of facts that contradict Putnam's conclusions. For example, one can argue that the idea of Italy was imposed on long established city states in 1861 and any spatial analysis needs to consider the boundaries of city states in more detail. In consequence, the fissure dividing Italy between North/South is too simplistic to capture the city-state boundaries that played a more influential role in Italy's civic and social development. Moreover, Putnam's also implies that Northern Italians, are more likely to 'play by the rules' given their levels of 'civicness'; but one can point to examples when the 'civicness' rules being followed are not ones suggested by abundant stocks of social capital.[9]

Putnam is aware of these charges and has sought to answer his critics. For example, he has argued forcefully that social capital's temporal dimensions; that is, its deep historical roots do not mean it cannot be reconstructed for the present. According to Putnam social capital has both a heritage and contemporary dimension. For instance Putnam has campaigned vigorously in his 'Saguaro Seminars' for greater social connectedness in American society. Moreover, he claims that his 'path dependent social equilibria' (1993, p. 180) is far from 'an invitation to quietism' (ibid., p. 184). However, these arguments run counter to the single factor, mono-casual interpretation of social capital that typifies Putnam's scholarship (1993, 1995a, 1995b, 2000). Thus, according to Putnam the unending dialogue between the present and the past is reduced to a 'prime determinant': Putnam therefore has a Whig view of history.[10] In consequence, a criticism of Putnam is that his historical narrative is extremely reductive and runs counter to trends in historiography to stretch, not shrink the historical canvas. Further, Putnam's reading of Italian history is controversial, perhaps because Putnam is neither a medievalist nor an Italian historian.[11]

It is also worth noting that Putnam is still refining his theoretical interpretation and in his latest treatment, social capital is defined in a 'lean and mean way' as society's 'social networks and the associated norms of reciprocity' (2004, p. 143). This is an unexpected development, as Putnam has not previously emphasised researched or measured social capital in network terms. One can speculate that Putnam has been inspired to construct his new definition to assist in his avowed aim to produce 'actionable' policy-making to build and nourish social capital: networks and norms of reciprocity are arguably easier to focus on than the previous, more intangible definitions and supporting concepts, such as trust. Further, sceptics on the left have been especially scathing, perhaps because they evaluate Putnam's conceptual interpretation to be a competitive challenge to their beliefs and in praxis as a fig leaf to cloak welfare cuts. Thus, '... while his account of social capital is interdisciplinary, its roots lay in political science' (Field, 2003, p. 39). And the political science Putnam's notion is grounded in is not of the Left. Other critics point to Putnam's research flaws, arguing that he neglects or underestimates the importance of informal and developing forms of social capital and furthermore that he fails to consider the intensity of associational activity in sufficient detail. His conclusions are also controversial, and according to critics reflect a perennial sense of American exceptionalism, and perhaps Italian exceptionalism. Moreover, blaming declining levels of social capital on intergenerational change may be correct, but it is a limited answer that prompts further questions.

To conclude, criticisms of Putnam are substantial (Sobel, 2002, pp. 139–154). However Putnam's treatment of social capital is persuasively developed and *Bowling Alone* (2000) became a sensation because it articulately targeted and offered convincing (to a point) explanations and solutions to widely held perceptions of society's drift towards atomisation. Therefore Putnam's influence, among political elites, academics and with the general public will probably remain significant for as long as the social capital is considered important. Thus Putnam is a seminal, if flawed social capital author.

3.6. FUKUYAMA: SOCIAL CAPITAL AND THE END OF HISTORY

According to Fukuyama: 'The first known use of the term *social capital* was by Lydia Judson Hanifan in 1916, to describe rural community centres'. Jane Jacobs is also credited with using social capital in her classic, *The Death and Life of Great American Cities* (1961), though it is worth noting that her use of social capital is fleeting – she used social capital on only one instance. Fukuyama further identifies the origins of the concept in: 'The economist Glenn Loury, as well as the sociologist Ivan Light, (who) used the term social capital in the 1970s to analyse the problem of inner city development'. In addition, Coleman is referenced for bringing the term into wider use in the 1980s, and Putnam is credited with stimulating an, '... intense debate over the role of social capital and civil society in Italy and the United States' (Fukuyama, 2000, p. 19). However, demonstrating a characteristic willingness to speculate, Fukuyama asserts:

> Perhaps the most important theorist of social capital was someone who never used the term but who understood its importance with great clarity: the French aristocrat and traveller Alexis de Tocqueville. Tocqueville observed in 'Democracy in America' that in sharp contrast to his native France, America possessed a rich 'art of association', that is, a population habituated to come together in voluntary associations for purposes both trivial and serious ... This ability to, in effect self-organise not only meant that the government did not have to import order in a hierarchical, top-down manner, civil association was also a 'school of self-government' that taught people co-operative behaviour they would carry over with them to public life. (2000, pp. 19–20)

Thus Fukuyama acknowledges various scholars' contributions to theoretical development though in his interpretation social capital draws its primary inspiration from de Tocqueville; both in terms of tracing the concept's origins, and for its contemporary application. Fukuyama's approach is to employ the concept on a macro level to analyse countries and cultures from a prism shaped by Tocquevillian and to a lesser extent Weberian values. For example, it is significant that Tocqueville cautioned over democracy in America tending towards tutelary despotism. Thus, in Tocqueville's analysis the risk was that the heavy hand of the masses would nullify risk and excellence from society, and impose a stifling conformity emanating from an over-powerful centralised state. The link to Fukuyama anti-statist conservatism, stressing individual responsibility, is therefore direct and explicit. For instance, Fukuyama is forthright in rejecting 'big government', claiming, in a distinctly de Tocquevillian analysis that: 'There are, of course, good reasons why countries should restrict the size of their state sector for economic reasons. On top of this, one can add a cultural motive of preserving a sphere for individual action and initiative in building civil associations' (2001, p. 18).

de Tocqueville also cautioned against 'excessive individualism', which he predicted would destroy civil society and this vacuum would inevitably lead to the emergence of a centralised state; '... amongst democratic states the notion of government naturally presents itself to the mind under the form of a sole and central power, and that the notion of intermediate power is not familiar to them' (1840, p. 297). The importance of dense civil society is therefore paramount to prevent creeping state power and interference. For example, he claims that his, 'Trust: The Social Virtues and the creation of Prosperity' is '... a cautionary tale against over-centralized political authority' (1996, p. 361). Further according to Fukuyama, communism in Eastern Europe, '... envisioned the destruction of an independent civil society and the creation of a new socialist community centred exclusively around the state' (1996, pp. 360–361). It follows therefore that the states which had 'retained nascent civil societies', such as Poland, the Czech Republic and Hungary were able to generate capitalist economies more successfully than former communist countries where the 'artificial communities' of communism had obliterated any alternative forms of community and voluntary associations. In these benighted states, such as Russia, economic and civil society development was thwarted as the sense of community could only readily be formed around family, ethnic and delinquent groups, such as criminal gangs.

Moreover, Fukuyama is also a self-avowed intellectual cheerleader for conservatives: 'Dan Quayle was right' (2000, p. 274), and in particular American neo-conservatives. Therefore it is unsurprising that he employs the social capital concept as part of his broad sweep analysis of cultural change and as a right-wing evaluation of relative degrees of national democratic and economic success. For illustration of his standpoint: 'We can think of neoclassical economics as being, say eighty per cent correct' (2000, p. 13).

In overview, Fukuyama's definition of social capital is varied and draws on a number of interrelated concepts, such as trust, game theory and network theory. For example, he defines social capital as '... an instantiated informal norm that promotes cooperation between two or more individuals ... by this definition, trust networks, civil society, and the like which have been associated with social capital are epiphenomenal, arising as a result but not constituting social capital itself' (1999, p. 2). Further, social capital is generated spontaneously: '... as a product of iterated Prisoner Dilemma games' (Fukuyama, 2001, p. 160). It also has been suggested – contradicting the above definition – that Fukuyama '... more or less equates social capital with trust' (Preuss, 2004, p. 155). Fukuyama therefore stands accused of 'fuzziness' in definition and application. For example, on one occasion Fukuyama has asserted that:

> Social capital can be defined simply as a set of informal values or norms shared among members of a group that permits co-operation. If members of the group come to expect that others will behave reliably and honestly, then they will come to trust one another.

Trust is a lubricant that makes the running of any group or organization more efficient. (2000, p. 16)

Whereas on other occasion he has stated that: 'Social capital is a capability that arises from the prevalence of trust in a society or in certain parts of it' (Fukuyama, 1995a). Thus there is opaqueness in Fukuyama's use of social capital and trust. Another example of this ambiguity is in his assertion that: 'Trust is a key by-product of the co-operative social norms that constitute social capital' (2000, p. 29). Moreover, he further claims that:

If we understand a network not as a type of formal organisation, but as social capital, we will have a much better insight into what a network's economic function really is. By this view, a network is a moral relationship of trust. (2000, p. 199)

Therefore, in Fukuyama's theoretical treatment social capital and trust have a floating, ill-defined connecting relationship.

Fukuyama also contends that social capital '... constitutes the cultural component of modern societies' (Fukuyama, 1999, p. 2). Thus: 'Social capital, the crucible of trust and critical to the health of the economy, rests on cultural roots' (Fukuyama, 1999, p. 33). Further, according to Fukuyama '... the most effective organizations are based on communities of shared ethical values', and '... this kind of moral community ... requires habituation to the norms of a community and, in its context, the acquisition of virtues like loyalty, honesty, and dependability' (*ibid.*, pp. 26–27). Fukuyama further develops this assertion to contend that, '... familistic societies', such as Taiwan, Hong Kong and the People's Republic of China, lack: '... a generalised social trust and, consequently, a strong propensity for spontaneous sociability' (*ibid.*, p. 29). This is in contrast to '... high trust societies with plentiful social capital – Germany, Japan and the United States' (*ibid.*, p. 30). Thus Fukuyama shares a perspective with Coleman, who also recognised that classical economics failed to give sufficient weight to the importance of social life in economic activity. Fukuyama's view is that: 'As Adam Smith well understood, economic life is deeply embedded in social life, and it cannot be understood apart from customs, morals, and habits of the society in which it occurs. In short, it cannot be divorced from culture' (1996, p. 13).

Fukuyama also seeks to clarify his definition by coining another concept: 'the radius of trust', which he details by stating that: 'All groups embodying social capital have a certain radius of trust, that is, the circle of people among who cooperative norms are operative' (2001, p. 8). A wider circle of trust produces positive externalities. He continues that a narrow radius of trust creates internal cohesion and negative externalities. Therefore the radius of trust offers different language to describe phenomenon labelled bonding and bridging capital by Putnam (2000, pp. 22–24). For illustration, Fukuyama develops this observation by contending that traditional societies are characterised by narrow radii of trust (*ibid.*, p. 9). In contrast, modern societies possess Granovetter's 'weak ties' (1973, 1985) which, '... permit multiple membership and identities' (2001, pp. 9–10). Moreover, Fukuyama considers this insight to be significant as a key explanatory factor for relative levels of economic and civil success. For example, Southern Italy and the African-American urban poor are deficient in social capital possessing, '... neither strong families nor strong associations outside of kinship' (2001, p. 93); hence their desperate plight.

Further, according to Fukuyama: 'The economic function of social capital is to reduce transaction costs associated with formal coordination mechanisms like contracts, hierarchies, bureaucratic rules, and the like' (2001, p. 10). Thus as: 'No contract can possible specify every contingency that may arise between the parties; most presuppose a certain amount of goodwill that prevents the parties from taking advantage of unforeseen loopholes'. He continues, 'spontaneous sociability' constitutes a 'subset of social capital' and explains how; '... highly sociable Americans pioneered the development of the modern corporation in the late nineteenth and early twentieth centuries, just as the Japanese have explored the possibilities if network organizations in the twentieth' (Fukuyama, 1995a). Thus, according to Fukuyama: '... large modern, professionally managed corporations' hierarchical corporations' developed first in societies with high trust and social capital: Germany, Japan and the Unites States'.

What is more, these 'informal norms' and 'internalised professional standards' are becoming more crucial as business becomes increasingly, 'complex and technologically sophisticated' (Fukuyama, 1995b). Therefore: 'If people who have to work together in an enterprise trust one another because they are all operating according to a common set of ethical norms doing business costs less' (*ibid.*, p. 27). It follows therefore that: 'Low trust societies, in contrast, must fence in and isolate their workers with a set of bureaucratic rules' (*ibid.*, p. 31). Fukuyama thus notes the economic importance of social capital for the 'changing methods of coordination'. Moreover, he notes that notions of decentralising and empowerment are not new and have long practised at firms, such as General Motors and Du Pont Chemical (2000, p. 196), at the same time he also avers that centralised corporate hierarchies have become increasingly vulnerable because

'... they cannot deal with the informational requirements of the increasingly complex world they inhabit' (2000, p. 195).

Technologically driven process of increasing economic complexity has also created the problem of how to coordinate the decentralised organisation, where power resides throughout, including among the lower level employees. The response, according to Fukuyama, has been the 'Rise of the network', which rather ironically, he considers ill-defined. Moreover, he notes networks are, 'as old as human communities themselves' (2001, p. 202) and have been associated with negative phenomena: '... like nepotism, favoritism, intolerance, inbreeding and non-transparent, personalistic arrangements' (ibid., p. 202). For modern firms networks provide an organisational model that does not rely on authority relationships, but rather relies on shared informal norms, which facilitate information flow for workers in highly skilled processes involving, diffuse, tacit or difficult to communicate knowledge and processes. Thus networks permit individuals or small units within large organisations, which are intimately connected to market changes and particular local conditions to iteratively interact and innovate. However, Fukuyama, also cautions that network organisations face a potential '... huge liability when a company entrusts a single low-ranking individual with the authority to "bet the firm". This is in effect what happened to the venerable British investment house Bearings' (2000, p. 225). Fukuyama also warns that network-based decentralisation can lead to, '... tribalism, where one's division's chief interest lies in beating another division rather than an outside competitor' (ibid., p. 226).

Fukuyama further contends that economic activity is moving from 'low trust to high trust production'. Thus in the United States, low trust or perhaps more accurately no trust, Taylorism has been superseded by high trust, 'lean manufacturing'. Further, Fukuyama also contends that social capital is important for regions and networks. He argues that the regional advantage of Silicon Valley over Route 28 as residing in 'informal links and trust necessary to share technology with rivals' (2000, p. 209). And also that: 'The social capital produced by such informal social networks permits Silicon Valley to achieve scale economies in R&D not possible in large, vertically integrated firms'. The same observation on the advantages of social capital in economic networks is also identified in Japanese Keiretsu networks (ibid., p. 210). Further, Fukuyama notes that: 'The importance of social capital to technology development has some paradoxical results'. For example, he notes that 'proximity remains important', citing the 'mutual trust and respect evident in places like Silicon Valley'.

3.6.1. Fukuyama Criticisms

There are a number of criticisms that can be levelled at Fukuyama's interpretation and application of social capital. For instance a key argument espoused in *Trust: The Social Virtues and the Creation of Prosperity* (1995) is that trust creates spontaneous sociability and this in turn explains why firms in high trust countries are more likely to grow into modern corporations than their counterparts in low trust cultures, which tend to remain 'familistic' in structure and outlook. The biologist, Matt Ridley's evaluation of this argument is telling: 'You can take this too far. Francis Fukuyama argues unconvincingly that there is a broad difference between successful economies such as America and Japan and unsuccessful ones such as France and China because of the latter's addiction to hierarchical power structures' (Ridley, 1996, p. 251). Thus Fukuyama stands accused of overstatement.

Fukuyama's trait for generalising is also evident in his historical methodology. It is true, of course, that historical facts are never pure and rather, '... are always refracted through the mind of the recorder' (Carr, 1964). However, Fukuyama's refraction is too narrowly focussed on contemporary concerns, for instance with what he terms, 'The Great Disruption', which is explicitly revealed in the book's subtitle, *Human Nature and the Reconstitution of Social Order* (2000). Thus Fukuyama is unashamedly fighting the 'cultural wars' for conservatism and at times this agenda has led to a reading of the past which fails to appreciate the complicated nature of history. Fukuyama therefore employs a historical method that, 'studies the past with reference to the present', which is a 'Whig Interpretation' of history that marshals events from the past to support a particular, in Fukuyama's case ideologically conservative, view of the present. To take an obvious example, Fukuyama, draws on the work of Banfield (1958/1967) and Putnam (1973, 1993) to reach a number of sweeping conclusions on the effects of trust, social capital and the harmful effects of Catholicism, as explanatory factors for current levels of economic development and civic engagement in Italian regions. Thus, in his account Southern Italy is less developed than Northern Italy due to differing historical experiences; that is, '... the celebrated Norman feudal aristocracy of the South and the fertile communal republicanism of the North' (1996, p. 108).

However, Fukuyama's Whig approach can be criticised on a number of grounds. For instance, it privileges one epoch over another: why for instance was late medieval history more important in explaining contemporary Italy than any other epoch? Further Norman feudalism flourished across Western Europe and as a social system produced different outcomes throughout the continent. Thus the link Fukuyama's attempt to connect feudalism with Southern Italian 'amoral familism' is tenuous. It could also be argued that Fukuyama, in common with Putnam, has an exceedingly idiosyncratic reading of feudalism: it is significant that both omit to reference any of the leading authors on feudal society. Another example is Fukuyama's claim that '... the French capacity for spontaneous sociability was effectively destroyed beginning in the sixteenth and seventeenth century by a victorious central monarchy' (1996, p. 28). However, this was the age of European Absolutism and the process of centralisation occurred across most of Europe and therefore it is difficult to see why the process had more profound effect in France than in other parts of Europe. Moreover, if centralisation by an absolute monarchy destroys social capital, then Japan, a society Fukuyama quotes approvingly for its high levels of trust and social cohesion (1996, pp. 171–183), should have seen its stock of social capital plummet during the Meiji Restoration, which saw Japan centralise under a powerful monarch at a greater pace and to a greater extent than any processes that occurred in France. Thus Fukuyama's reading of history is tendentious in places and a key weakness. Further, Fukuyama also displays a typical neo-liberal Francophobia (1995, pp. 55–56, 113–125) arguing that France's social capital is limited and consequently its future bleak.[12]

Fukuyama also can be criticised for inconsistencies. For instance his unit of analysis varies. Italy (1996, pp. 97–111) and Korea (*ibid.*, pp. 140–144) are afforded a regional consideration, whereas Germany (*ibid.*, pp. 209–219), France (*ibid.*, pp. 113–121) and the United Kingdom (*ibid.*, pp. 249–51) are analysed as single entities. Fukuyama's history can also be factually incorrect or, by omission misleading. For instance, he claims that Germany '... has been extraordinarily successful for a very long time' (*ibid.*, p. 209). Conversely it is reasonable to argue that before unification in 1870 Germany was relatively poor in relation to its neighbours and carried less diplomatic weight than the 'Great Powers'. Moreover, unification was achieved after a war with France, and while Germany was unified from 1871 to 1945 it instigated two bloody world wars: these facts then would also leave one to question Fukuyama's evaluation of Germany as an 'extraordinary success'. Another example of Fukuyama's partial use of historical fact is in his telling of the history of Shell Oil. For illustration, according to Fukuyama, Marcus Samuel who founded Shell succumbed to the leisured values of the British aristocracy and in the process dissipated his original entrepreneurial zeal. Further, according to Fukuyama, this move into the aristocracy allowed Henry Deterding, head of Royal Dutch to oust Samuel as the former '... retained more of the classic middle-class virtues and was not seduced by the appeal of fox hunting or charitable social events' (*ibid.*, p. 250). However, what Fukuyama fails to mention is that although Deterding may not have been seduced by foxhunting, but he was seduced by Hitlerism, and to describe the ousting of the Jewish Samuel without reference to the influence of Nazism is a grave weakness in the narrative of events.

Fukuyama also describes himself as a neo-Weberian and he considers that '... the impact of culture on economic life ... revolves around a single work, Max Weber's 'The Protestant Ethic and the Spirit of Capitalism' (*ibid.*, p. 43). According to Fukuyama: 'Max Weber's famous Puritans did not seek wealth by capital accumulation; they sought to demonstrate their status as elect in the eyes of God. But as an accidental consequence of their frugality, self-discipline, and desire to prove election, they created businesses in the here and now that were ultimately the source of enormous wealth' (2000, pp. 256–257). Conversely, it can be argued that importance of the Weberian 'moral character' of economic activity is governed by contingencies. For example, Puritan values did not produce 'enormous wealth' in Cromwellian England,[13] and perhaps only did so in America given the continent's abundance of natural resources: the Puritan's would have been hard pressed not to produce 'enormous wealth' in the natural treasure trove of North America which lay untapped prior to the arrival of Europeans.

Fukuyama treatment of social capital is then problematical: his interpretation, methods of inquiry, conclusion and utility for the concept are all contentious. However, the weight Fukuyama affords to culture, defined as 'inherited ethical habit' (*ibid.*, p. 34) is significant for a thorough understanding of social capital. In Fukuyama's view, in the post-Cold War world '... the most important distinctions between nations are no longer institutional but cultural' (2001). He continues to opine that traditional arguments between left and right over the role of the state miss the point as: 'The character of civil society and its intermediate associations, rooted as it is in non-rational factors like culture, religion, tradition, and other pre-modern sources, will be the key to the success of modern societies in a global economy' (*ibid.*, p. 103). Thus Fukuyama places culture, with its features of trust and social capital as the wellspring of civil and economic success.

Fukuyama also emphasises that: 'Social capital is frequently a by-product of religion, tradition, shared historical experience and other factors that lie outside the control of any government' (2001, p. 18). It follow that Fukuyama considers that it is easier to destroy than to create social capital. However, he does acknowledge that the sources of social capital can be encouraged, for instance by '... efficiently providing necessary public goods, particularly property rights and public goods' (*ibid.*, p. 18). In developing countries he asserts that religion and globalisation (*ibid.*, p. 19) can increase stocks of social capital. Moreover, curiously echoing Bourdieu he also claims that '... the area where states have the greatest ability to generate social capital is education'. And: '... one of the greatest safeguards against corruption is to give senior bureaucrats high quality professional training and to create *esprit de corps* among this elite' (*ibid.*, p. 18). Fukuyama therefore identifies that social capital is partly a cultural phenomenon, and as such has low and non-rational components. However, he also notes that it can be encouraged by '... providing necessary public goods'; that is, social capital is fostered by good governance. It is also encouraged as a by-product of education (*ibid.*, p. 18).

In synopsis, Fukuyama offers a synthesis of disparate, but relevant interdisciplinary material. This material offers a number of provocative perspectives on social capital. Moreover, Fukuyama's influence on social capital extends beyond his natural constituency on the Right, with his emphasis on the importance of culture adding value to any understanding of social capital.

3.7. SOCIAL CAPITAL AND SOCIAL NETWORK ANALYSIS

This section will examine the meaning of social capital as a network concept, which according to social network theorists offers the optimum approach for understanding social capital. In overview, the social network approach to social capital can be characterised as sharing a common notion that '... all network structures have some effect on the action of the actors enmeshed in these networks' (Flap, 1994, p. 29), or in Granovetter's view that all social and economic phenomena is embedded in social networks (1985).

It is also worth noting that both Coleman and Putnam understood networks as integral to social capital. Coleman, for instance emphasised the necessity of network closure and stability for developing reputation (1990, p. 320) and also argued for the significance of context to be acknowledged (*ibid.*, p. 302). Putnam also associated dense social networks with effective norms of generalised reciprocity. For example: '... honesty is encouraged by dense social networks' (2000, p. 136).

3.7.1. Granovetter and Embedded Social Network Analysis

Granovetter's, 'The Strength of Weak Ties' (1973) is the seminal network paper, in part because the paper eschewed technical mathematical models, and was illustrated with examples that confirmed everyday experiences, such as successful job searches being prompted by, 'Not a friend, an acquaintance' (Granovetter, 1973, p. 1372). Thus, '... blue-collar workers find out about new jobs more through personal contacts than by any other method' (*ibid.*, p. 1371). And: 'From the individual's point of view, then, weak ties are an important resource in making possible mobility opportunity' (*ibid.*, p. 1373). In network terminology, they are more likely to transmit non-redundant information than dense close ties.

Granovetter also noted the importance of weak ties for establishing a 'sense of community' and he considered '... why some communities organize for common goals easily and effectively whereas others seem unable to mobilize resources, even against dire threat' (*ibid.*, p. 1373). Granovetter developed this insight by analysing the Italian community in Boston's West End, which failed to resist urban renewal. Granovetter suggests that the community was 'completely partitioned into cliques'. This is important as: '... people rarely act on mass-media unless it is transmitted through personal ties' (*ibid.*, p. 1374). In this instance the mass media can be taken as efforts to transmit information, resisting urban renewal. Thus it was difficult to organise resistance, as there was a dearth of leaders deemed trustworthy. Moreover, Granovetter noted that diffusion studies have demonstrated the importance of trusting a leader who then transmits information through personal ties. However, in this community: 'The local phenomenon is cohesion'. The structure then was of cohesive groups within, at the macroscopic level, a fragmented whole. Thus 'unique clusters' (*ibid.*, p. 1375) with strong ties were the defining network characteristic of this community. There was an absence of weak ties because the '... two common sources of weak ties, formal organizations and work settings, did not provide them in the West End; organizations membership was almost nil and few worked within the area itself, so that ties formed at work were not relevant to the community' (*ibid.*, p. 1375). This example is relevant for understanding the returns of social capital, as Granovetter's observation argues for the importance of weak ties for establishing trust in leaders, who then act as opinion formers and influence norms in the networks. For a community to establish leaders therefore there needs to be personal ties to transmit influence. Moreover: 'Trust in leaders is related to the capacity to predict and affect their behaviour' (*ibid.*, p. 1374). Thus, the link with reputation mechanisms is that if establishing trust in a leader requires loose ties, then establishing reputation, which is closely related to trust involves similar processes.

In 'Economic Action and Social Structure: The Problem of Embeddedness' Granovetter discusses the origins of the under and over socialised conceptions of action and concludes that '... purposive actions are embedded in concrete, on-going systems of social relations' (1985, p. 487). For example, he discusses how clever institutional arrangements, such as implicit and explicit contracts, including deferred payment, have evolved to discourage the problem of malfeasance. However, he also considers that these arrangements: '... do not produce trust but are a functional substitute for it' (*ibid.*, p. 489). Further, he notes that conceptions that have an exclusive focus on institutional arrangements are '... under-socialized in that they do not allow for the extent to which concrete personal relations and the obligations inherent in them discourage malfeasance' (*ibid.*, p. 489). He also cautions that if malfeasance was controlled entirely by clever institutional arrangement then a malign cycle could develop in which economic life would: '... be poisoned by ever more ingenious attempts at deceit' (*ibid.*, p. 489). Thus, he develops his embedded notion of economic action to stress that networks of social relations generate trust and discourage malfeasance. For example:

> The widespread preference for transacting with individuals known reputation implies that few are actually content to rely on either generalized morality or institutional arrangements to guard against trouble. Economists have pointed out that one incentive not to cheat is the damage to one's reputation; but this is an under-socialized conception of reputation as a generalized commodity, a ratio of cheating to opportunities for doing so. (*ibid.*, p. 490)

Moreover, according to Granovetter, we seek information about an actor from a trusted informant for four reasons. First, it is cheap. Second, one trusts one's own information to be more nuanced to one's needs. Third, continuing relations have an economic motivation to be trustworthy so as not to discourage future trade and fourth the social content of the ties discourages opportunism. Furthermore, he notes rational actors rely on knowledge of relations. 'They are less interested in general reputations than in whether a particular other may be expected to deal honestly with them – mainly a function of whether they or their own contacts have satisfactory past dealings with the other' (*ibid.*, p. 491). Thus: '... business relations are mixed up with social ones' (*ibid.*, p. 495). For example, he quotes a businessman describing a network norm: 'You can settle any dispute if you keep the lawyers and accountants out of it. They just do not understand the give and take needed in businesses' (*ibid.*, p. 496). These observations are relevant for social capital's reputation processes as they indicate the importance of embedded social relations. Granovetter also describes how sustained relationships enable reputation to develop, which incidentally reflects Coleman's observation on the importance of a stable network for reputation development. Further the veracity of Granovetter's views over imposing 'clever institutional arrangements' in isolation of 'getting the relations right', is demonstrated at the macro, state level by the struggles between 'casino capitalism' (Bohatá, 1997; Fuxman, 1997), and the efforts to impose western style market economies in post-Soviet states (Fukuyama, 1995, pp. 360–361).

Granovetter further contended in a subsequent article that: '(1) The pursuit of economic goals is typically accompanied by that of such non-economic ones as sociability, approval, status and power'. Further, according to Granovetter: '(2) Economic action (like all action) is socially situated and cannot be explained by reference to individual motives alone. It is embedded in on-going networks of personal relationships rather than being carried out by atomised actors. (3) Economic institutions ... are socially constructed' (1992, p. 25). Granovetter therefore understood economic action as being relationally embedded. Further, Granovetter adopted a 'weak embedded position' that emphases the continuity of relationships down the ages, implicit in this conclusion is that, although technologies and market structure are subject to historical change, the nature of relations remains significant, regardless of the economic conditions (1992, p. 28).

In addition, Granovetter considered, 'The Impact of Social Structures on Economic Outcomes'. His view was that social networks were important for three main reasons: they affected the quality and flow of information; they affected reward and punishment; and social networks also encouraged trust'; '... by which I mean the confidence that the others will do the right thing' (1995, p. 33). For social capital processes this paper raises a number of relevant points. First, according to Granovetter '... collective action that depends on overcoming free-rider problems is more likely in groups whose social network is dense and cohesive, since actors in such networks typically internalise norms that discourage free riding and emphasise trust'. And '... larger groups have lower network density because people have cognitive, emotional, spatial and temporal limits on how many social ties they can sustain ... the larger the group' (*ibid.*). This observation suggests that social network density is limited by innate human capabilities.

To conclude, Granovetter's scholarship is worthy of incorporation into the social capital understanding for two principal reasons: first, for his embedded view of the economy, which is complementary and enhances the social capital analysis. The second reason is that Granovetter's social network analysis is also complementary to social capital literature, in terms of detailing network processes, which are integral to social capital processes.

3.8. BURT AND THE NETWORK ADVANTAGE

Ron Burt's notion of the social capital focuses on advantages created in social structure. In his view social capital has become a core concept because of the '... coordination capability gap bedevilling our time' (2005, p. 4). According to Burt's analysis the new economy is characterised by networks of flexible adaptive networks, as opposed to the traditional economy's vertical bureaucratic authority structures, whose closure blocks the 'vision advantage'. Thus the modern economy is structured in clusters with the market coordinating cluster specialisation. Moreover, Burt considers that, '... there is a network residue to social history, a network in which individuals are variably connected as a function of prior contact, exchange and attendant emotions' (*ibid.*, p. 101). Thus social activities have a network history. Burt also agrees with Granovetter's observation of preferring to trade with known others, discussing the '... homophily bias in networks'; that is, 'birds of a feather will flock together' (*ibid.*, p. 12). Therefore: 'Whether communities in a geographic region, divisions in a corporation, groups in a profession, to people in a team, people specialise within clusters and integrate via bridges across clusters' (*ibid.*, p. 13).

Burt also argues that networks can be understood using the conceptual tools of brokerage: the activities of those whose networks bridge the structural holes between dense clusters; and closure: the level of coordination within the networks. Thus: 'Brokerage is about coordinating people between whom it would be valuable, but risky to trust. Closure is about making it safe to trust' (*ibid.*, p. 97). In Burt's structuralist syntax, brokers have 'vision advantage' and are 'rewarded for their integrative work' by being, 'at greater risk of having creative ideas and (are) more likely to see a way to implement ideas' (*ibid.*, p. 7). However, the difficulty of moving ideas across groups is exacerbated by the extent of group closure. For example: 'Opinions and behaviours within a group are often expressed in a local language, a dialogue fraught with taken for granted assumptions shared within a group. The local language within a group makes it possible for people in the group to exchange often-repeated data more quickly' (*ibid.*, p. 17). Thus Burt's argument is that, '... people connected across groups are more familiar with alternative ways of thinking and behaving, which is an advantage in detecting and developing rewarding opportunities. Specifically there is a vision advantage' (*ibid.*, p. 59). This insight is important '... because so much of business leadership is about bringing together ill-connected functions, organizations or market segments – in other words building bridges across structural holes' (*ibid.*, p. 87). It is therefore reasonable to suggest that brokers would develop strong reputations based on their business leadership.

Burt further detailed an understanding of social capital with reference to reputation mechanisms. In his view, 'bandwidth' is essential for the transmission of news: 'A closed network provides wide bandwidth for the flows of stories as packets of people data ... The more closed the network the more penetrating the data'. Thus a closed network can efficiently transmit gossip, which controls behaviour. For example, news of opportunistic behaviour will be disseminated rapidly through the network. Further: 'Social obligation and identity are defined with reputation' (*ibid.*, p. 107). Thus:

> The more groups with which you are affiliated, the more alternative reputations you have ... A person affiliated to only one group – for example, their family, their team, or a neighborhood – has only one reputation, which must necessarily be their social identity. Lose the group and you lose your identity ... To the extent that reputation-protection is a motivation, people in closed network have a single source of reputation and can be expected to protect it. (*ibid.*, p. 108)

It follows then that control can be eroded by connections to multiple groups. Thus in a closed system reputations are transparently defined in the network by people monitoring and discussing behaviour, therefore network closure facilitates reputation and trust. In addition, the identity formation hypothesis creates a perception that people within a social network are more trustworthy than strangers: the social and emotional costs of opportunism within than without the network and these ties create a tendency for 'comfort in interaction'; that is, experience creates relational embedding that in turn 'lower coordination risk and cost' (*ibid.*, p. 138).

Burt also proposes a reputation generating theory based on two hypotheses, first in term of the 'bandwidth hypothesis', in which the actor own their reputation, in the sense that they define their behaviour, which in turn, defines their reputation. Second, under the 'echo hypothesis', reputation is not owned by the individual but rather is owned by '... the people in whose conversations it is built, and the goal of those conversations is not accuracy so much as bonding between the speakers' (*ibid.*, p. 196). For instance, if a firm breaks a contract in one project, because they consider the terms of employment to be inequitable then they will have influenced their reputation, and under the bandwidth hypothesis they can argue their actions were justified and therefore there should not be any detrimental effect to their reputation. However, under the echo hypothesis it is how the contract dispute is interpreted and gossiped about across the network that is most significant. In this hypothesis the reputation is not owned by any individual, but rather by their relational network through which its 'reputational-sculpting stories pass' (*ibid.*, p. 219). Thus: 'The key to establishing a good reputation is to get people in closed networks talking to one another'. Moreover, under the echo hypothesis first impression is crucial for setting in chain favourable impressions. And: 'Reputations do not emerge from good work directly so much as from colleagues stories about the work' (*ibid.*, p. 218). In consequence:

> Bandwidth and echo are processes by which closure can carry reputation across projects, bandwidth ensures that people in the new project group are informed about you, so you construct an identity as you work that will be with you across projects, which is expected to make you careful about your behaviour. Echo ensures that people in the project group hear stories about you, positive if the new group is predisposed towards you, negative otherwise. Reputation is beginning anew in the sense that the new group affects what they hear, but more specifically there will a social construction of you that begins with an uninformed audience reacting from their predispositions to the stories that most often circulate about you. You enter a project saying hello to strangers who feel they know you. (*ibid.*, p. 196)

Burt's echo hypothesis means inconsistent reputations can develop in different networks. Moreover: 'You do not have one reputation; you have as many as the groups in which you are discussed'. And network closure's relation with trust is amplification towards extremes: 'It is associated with more certain, intense feelings' (*ibid.*, p. 222). Thus under Burt's echo hypothesis it is possible to have multiple actors engaged in assassinating character and furthermore, this negative perception will not be easily influenced by changes in behaviour because '... the source of the reputation is stories third parties are telling one another' (*ibid.*, p. 219).

Burt also stresses that the effects of social capital are more significant in 'extreme network condition' (*ibid.*, p. 225). This conclusion reflects Coleman's notion that social capital is destroyed in unstable structures (1990, p. 320) and is most easily formed in opposition to an external threat (*ibid.*, p. 319).

In sum, Burt has been included in this review for analysing networks in terms of their advantages, which Burt argues are the advantages of social capital. These advantages that Burt elucidates (from a network perspective) are in terms of networks' coordinating, knowledge and identity or reputation returns. To conclude this book agrees with Burt that these advantages are the advantages of social capital and consequently his masterful exposition of these processes justifies his inclusion in this literature review.

3.9. LIN: THE FUNCTIONALIST VIEW OF SOCIAL CAPITAL

Lin places social capital in 'A Theory of Social Structure and Action' (1999) asserting that it belongs to a family of capital theories. He defines capital as: '... investment in resources with expected returns in the marketplace. Capital is resources when these resources are invested and mobilized in pursuit of profit − as a goal in action' (*ibid.*, p. 3). He elaborates that: 'The notion behind the premise of social capital is rather simple and straightforward: investment in social relations with expected returns in the marketplace ... capital captured through social relations'. Moreover, according to Lin resources are '... material or symbolic goods' (*ibid.*, p. 19). He also defines '... social resources or social capital, as those resources accessible through social connections. Social capital contains resources (e.g., wealth, power, and reputation, as well as social networks) of other individual actors to whom an individual actor can gain access through direct or indirect social ties' (*ibid.*, p. 43). Further, for Lin resources are valued good in society: they correspond to wealth, reputation and power. Thus: 'Social capital consists of resources embedded in one's network or associations' (*ibid.*, p. 56).

Lin also argues that: 'The theory focuses on those actions that are taken for the purpose of either maintaining or gaining valued resources' (*ibid.*, p. 55). These resources are: '... (1) wealth: economic assets, (2) power: political assets and (3) reputation: social assets' (*ibid.*, pp. 61−62). Lin's theoretical analysis further distinguishes between two classes of actions. First for expressive purposes; that is, actions for their own sake with actors who have similar resources: in Lin's network terminology, homophilious interactions. And second, for instrumental purposes; that is, actions with a purpose of achieving certain goals with actors with different resources: heterogeneous interactions (*ibid.*, p. 58). Lin also considers that strong ties are positively associated with expressive action and weak ties with instrumental action (*ibid.*, p. 76). Moreover, this observation on homophilious action – the more pervasive – and heterogeneous action, is similar to Burt's notions of closure and brokerage. The research implication is that network stability is determined by the dynamic tension between these two types of action. In Lin's conceptual interpretation: 'Instrumental action is taken to obtain resources not possessed by the actor, whereas expressive action is taken to maintain resources already possessed by the actor' (*ibid.*, p. 244). It follows that '... a stable social system requires a balance between homophilious and heterophilious exchanges' (*ibid.*, p. 180). Thus, if a stable system promotes reputation, the two types of action need to be evident. Too many heterophilious exchanges will result in structural instability and a lack of network solidarity, identity and cohesion: too few opportunities for heterophilious exchanges will result in fragmented immobile actors with over-developed intra-level solidarity and conflict. Therefore the sources and extent of tensions within a social system are significant to its social stability and consequentially to the formation of social capital.

In addition, Lin draws attention to the significance of relations in exchange and notes that neo-classical economist, such as Willliamson (1985) acknowledge the role of relations in exchange, though in Lin's view they underplay relational significance, as just another 'transaction cost' (*ibid.*, p. 147). In contrast, Lin reaches a converse position arguing that exchange is often motivated by '... social approval, esteem, liking ... Notably, in exchanges where the transactions are imbalanced' (*ibid.*, p. 147). Thus these exchanges create a 'symbolic reward' that 'represents value' and therefore the argument is that exchanges can be motivated to create social standing; that is to develop reputation. Lin develops this insight to propose a network analysis of social standing, status and prestige, which he considers is: '... based on the accumulation and distribution of reputation (as indicated by the extent of recognition in social networks and collectives)' (*ibid.*, p. 150). Therefore relational rationality can be motivated exchange to generated resources: the resources are social status and reputation.

Lin further develops this idea of relational rationality, by referencing Coleman's notion of social credits; that is, 'credit slips' on which an actor in a network can draw if necessary (Coleman, 1990, p. 306). In Coleman's conception '... creating obligations by doing favours can constitute a kind of insurance policy'. Moreover, according to Coleman it can be rational to avoid favours in order to avoid obligations (*ibid.*, p. 310). Lin's observations reflect Coleman's analysis, for instance: 'The critical element in maintaining relationships between partners is social credits (and social debts)' (Lin, 2001, p. 151). And: 'Transactions are means to maintain and promote social relations, create social credits and social debts, and accumulate social recognition' (*ibid.*, p. 152).

The research implication of this observation is that reputation depends on the willingness of network actors to create persistent relations based on unequal transactions, which have obligations of social credits and debts. If they are not prepared to conduct these socially motivated transactions, then it follows that reputation will not develop. For illustration, J. Hutchinson's (Hutchinson & Vidal, 2004) paper 'Social Capital and Community Building in the Inner City' observes that while: 'Creating and later paying of obligations is a cornerstone of social capital ... The aversion of Pico Union residents to engagement in neighbourly actions reveals a general rejection of reciprocal indebtedness of any kind ... Respondents expressed a generalized resistance to relationships that would create obligations' (2004, p. 172). She concludes that: 'The community-based analysis described the almost universal aversion to interpersonal reciprocal relationships identified by this study as vital survival strategy' (*ibid.*, p. 174).

Lin also considers how reputation is promoted by '... recruiting actors with a reputation established elsewhere in society' (1999, p. 154). Further, in Lin's interpretation reputation is both an asset for groups and individuals and can be built/acquired, maintained/attained or lost with different levels of reputation and ill repute (*ibid.*, p. 158). Thus reputation has an individual and social or collective nature, and is open to change.

In summary, Lin offers an explicitly rational understanding of social capital from a network perspective. His conclusions reflect and complement Granovetter and Burt's appreciation of network processes. To conclude, Lin has been included in this review for his detailed explication of network processes to do with rational and instrumental economic exchanges; for his views of relational rationality; and for his insights into social capital's network processes of identity and reputation development.

3.10. CONCLUSION: A FAD WITH SUBSTANCE

Putnam has recently argued that social capital researchers: '... have gradually but unmistakably converged on a lean-and-mean definition that focuses on social networks and the associated norms of reciprocity' (2004, p. 145). However, the reverse is true, as the ineluctable expansion of social capital literature has led to an increase in theoretical diversity. In response this chapter and the preceding chapter have defined the terms of the research, established the economic returns of social capital, reviewed the contemporary intellectual context, background and benefits of social capital and then proceeded to critique the leading social capital scholars. This chapter's aim, and Chapter 2's aim, has been to gain a synoptic understanding of the concept as it applies to this research agenda into the economic form of social capital. Moreover, the lack of theoretical consensus, which has been identified in these chapters, '... matches the spirit of an uncertain, questioning age' (Baron, Field, & Schuller, 2000)), which in part explains the attractiveness of social capital to contemporary scholars.

This chapter has also identified a number of complementary, but distinct literature streams established by leading social capital scholars. Moreover, from this literature review it is plausible to reach the conclusion that the economic form of social capital is most influenced by American authors. Social capital also can be characterised as a conservative concept that is largely uncritical of contemporary capitalism, other than in the sense of trying to render it more rational and efficient. Thus the social capital discourse does not, '... question the economic concept that dominates the World Bank or, indeed, much contemporary economics' (Bebbington et al., 2004, p. 36). This reflects the literature on trust, which can be thought of as an ontological component of social capital, '... the significance of trust has been over-emphasised and that this serves ideological purposes, contributing to a "soft" view of capitalism' (Harris, 2002, p. 3).

To be sure, Bourdieu's neo-Marxist treatment stands in contrast to the predominant rational and 'neo-Tocquevillian' interpretations of the concept. Moreover, there have been attempts to introduce Bourdieu's treatment of social capital into economic analysis (Svendsen & Svendsen, 2004), though Bourdieu's academic sympathisers have tended to criticise the economic form of social capital rather than interpret it for their purposes. For example, Levitas has concluded that social capital, '... simultaneously obscures and legitimates wider social inequalities, and provides a lens through which the rich become virtually invisible' (2004, p. 49). In this perspective if neo-liberal markets are about 'getting the incentives right' then social capital is a complementary concept about 'getting the social relations right'. Thus, there has been a tendency from the left to dismiss the economic form of social capital rather than attempting to reclaim it from a Bourdieusian perspective – as evidenced by the literature reviewed in this chapter.

This literature review has also argued that the recent interest in social capital has been driven by key authors who have gained theoretical influence among academics, elites and the masses by producing hypotheses that go with the grain of the times: more than anything this has been a process driven by contemporary politics and economics. For example, Coleman's broad sociological approach to social capital is contentious, '... setting the stage for confusion in the uses and scope of the term' (Portes, 1998, p. 6). However, in attempting to introduce into social theory, 'capital embodied in relations among people' (*ibid.*, 1998, p. 38) Coleman succeeded in stimulating interest in the concept. Moreover, by combining intellectual streams from sociology and economics to introduce, '... social structure into the rational action paradigm' (*ibid.*, p. 17) Coleman was transparent in promoting Chicago University's robustly market-driven agenda. In contrast, Putnam's political interpretation of the concept builds on Tocquevillian assumptions of associational behaviour to analyse communities in terms of 'social networks and norms of reciprocity' (Putnam, 2004, p. 143). Further, this literature review has contended that Putnam's treatment of social capital is conservative in nature, and is deployed to support the status quo, which also reflects his views on consensus being the default setting of right-wing analysis, as expressed in one of his early publications (1973, p. 107).

Fukuyama's analysis of national and regional communities, which interprets social capital in terms of cultural values, is also a political analysis that in this instance extols neo-liberalism. Thus the three key authors' notion of the economic form of social capital are broadly conservative, in the sense that the concept is understood as being charged with rendering the dominant economic and social systems more efficient, as opposed to mounting a theoretical challenge to this system and its predominant values. Economic social capital is therefore a consensus form of social capital with instrumental value for conservative notions of society and economic activity. For example, Putnam who focuses on associational activity by considering reciprocal norms and social networks has been accused of 'having an unacknowledged class bias' (Skocpol, 1996). And Fukuyama further retains the core neo-liberal belief that any social engineering should be limited, as it inevitably leads to punitive unintended consequences (1995, pp. 349–354). It can be argued therefore that social capital achieved take-off because it offered a way of addressing cultural, political and economic concerns that complemented, rather than challenged the prevailing economic and political nostrums; for instance poverty could be alleviated if the poor became better social capitalists or social entrepreneurs, conversely the importance of context, that is with the poor having limited resources and power was ignored in this social capital debate. Thus the social capital discussion is deemed consistent with the 'post-Washington Consensus' notion that there is a role for non-market interventions to resolve market imperfections' (Bebbington et al., 2004, p. 36). From this perspective social capital is in vogue: '... as a collective good or resource possessed by a social system that helps the system as a whole solve problems' (Briggs, 2004, p. 151).

Further, social capital is resistant to a holistic definition. For instance, while Portes concludes that there is a growing consensual definition that '... social capital stands for the ability of actors to secure benefits by virtue of membership in social networks or other social structures' (1998, p. 6). He also acknowledges − as do other authors − that the concept suffers from overstretch (Lin, 2001, p. 26; Preuss, 2004, p. 155): it is logical to conclude that if the social capital was precisely defined then it could not easily be overstretched. Therefore, any consensus is incomplete and there remain a number of competing interpretations (Adler & Kwon, 2002, p. 7). Moreover, this lack of theoretical agreement contributes to a core theoretical controversy over the trajectory of social capital. For illustration, Putnam refers 'in postmodernist jargon' to 'declensionist narratives' (Putnam, 2000, p. 24); conversely Lin argues that it is in the ascendant, due to 'virtual communities' and new forms of association (2001, pp. 210−243); or is social capital in equilibrium, changing its countenance to match societal developments, but neither increasing nor decreasing its aggregate levels (Paxton, 1999, pp. 88−127)? The interpretive nature of this debate is also illustrated by Fukuyama's evaluation that increased litigation might be sign of increased social capital as: '... rather than appeal to a hierarchical sources of authority to resolve disputes private parties seek to work out equitable arrangements among themselves, albeit with the help a legion of highly paid lawyers' (2000, p. 24). In contrast Putnam notes this rise in litigation and reaches an opposite conclusion: 'For better or worse − we rely increasingly − we are forced to rely increasingly − on formal institutions, above all on the law, to accomplish what we used to accomplish through informal networks reinforced by generalised reciprocity − that is through social capital' (2000, p. 147).

Further, this 'honeyed' term which is overwhelmingly understood as a positive attribute has yet to adequately consider the drawbacks of social interaction and social structures, which include bonding capital's nepotism, and other forms of discriminatory structures, disputes over the legitimacy of knowledge ownership, as well as rights to privacy in the workplace. For instance, Portes' comments that social capital literature is over-optimistic and needs balancing with an acceptance of the dark side of the concept: 'Indeed it is our sociological bias to see good things emerging out of sociability, bad things are more commonly associated with the behaviour of *homo economicus*' (1998, p. 15). Portes summarises the negativities as four-fold: 'exclusion of outsiders, excess claims on group members, restrictions on individual freedoms and downward levelling of norms' (1998, p. 15). Fukuyama, also notes the dark side of social capital and quotes Partha Dasgupta that: 'Social capital is a private good that nonetheless is pervaded by externalities, both positive and negative'. For instance: 'Many groups achieve internal cohesion at the expense of outsiders, who can be treated with suspicion, hostility or outright hostility'. For example, social capital can result in '... hate groups and inbred bureaucracies'. And, '... group solidarity is often purchased at the price of hostility towards out-group members' (Fukuyama, 2001, p. 8). In Fukuyama's view groups with 'narrow radius of trust', what Putnam refers to as 'bonding capital', are most likely to create these negative externalities.

It is also worth noting that both Putnam (1973, 1993) and Fukuyama (2000, pp. 97–111) draw inspiration for their conceptual treatment from Italy. For example, Fukuyama refers to 'Italian Confucianism', which acknowledges Putnam's arguments crediting the importance of the past; that is in 'path dependency' in shaping the present. However, as empha-sised there are significant weaknesses with Putnam's (and Fukuyama's) historical method, which are a 'Whig view of history', with all the attendant weaknesses.

Finally, for this research it is also worth emphasising that the social capital scholars reviewed in this chapter, with the exception of Bourdieu, all adopt a rationalist understanding of social capital that assumes individuals pursue their economic self-interest. Granovetter who works within literature streams associated with both socio-economics and social network theory, also claims to be influenced by rational notions of motiva-tion and behaviour, as detailed in Chapter 1 (1985, pp. 505–506) and Appendix B.

CHAPTER 4

METHODOLOGY: A HOLISTIC EXAMINATION OF THE MANAGEMENT OF SOCIAL CAPITAL PROCESSES

4.1. INTRODUCTION

The research follows an ethnography in the tradition of Herbert Blumer's Chicago School. The research aim is to develop understanding of the owner-managers' interpretations, experiences and shaping of the management of social capital processes. Accordingly, this research takes an interpretivist approach that acknowledges the inter-subjective nature of social reality. In the words of Robert Prus:

> The interpretivists envision human group life as actively constituted by people in interaction with others. Human behaviour is seen as denoting an interpretative, interactive process. The primary methodological procedures are ethnographic (participant observation, observation, and open-ended interviews) in nature. Human life is studied as it is experienced and accomplished by the very people involved in its production. The interpretivists are centrally concerned with the meaning people attach to their situations and the ways in which they go about constructing their activities in conjunction with others. (1996, p. 9)

Thus, the research understands social capital processes as an interpretive process of interaction and consequently investigates how its management is accomplished (interpreted, experienced and shaped) by the actors involved in its production. Moreover, the research is, '... centrally concerned with the meaning people (owner-managers) attach to their situations and the ways in which they go about constructing their activities in conjunction with others' (*ibid.*, p. 9).

The research also aims to allow for sensitivity to context and to the participants' frames of reference with an emphasis on the significance of the quotidian, that is the taken for granted assumption that owner-managers share in the day-to-day social interactions. Further as social capital is 'situational' (see Chapter 1) the research will be conducted with reference to contingency factors to offer, 'contextual understanding of social behaviour' (Bryman & Bell, 2003, p. 295). Moreover, researching the management of social capital in its economic context entails investigating in an open system beyond the control of the researcher, and this is a further reason for following a qualitative research strategy (*ibid.*, pp. 279–311). Thus to achieve familiarity and insight into the world of the owner-managers, the primary methodological procedures will be ethnographic in nature: to include in order of importance semi-structured, open-ended interviews, observation and observation participation data collection methods. This research will also be inductive to produce a grounded model for generating hypothesis/ recommendations for further research.

In sum, this qualitative research will be based on an interpretivist epistemology, with an emphasis on the intersubjective and 'minded accomplishment of human activity' (Prus, 1996, p. xix).

4.2. DESCRIPTION OF METHODOLOGY

The research will research the lived experience in the management of social capital. Ontologically this research understands social capital as being characterised by 'Macro-to-Micro and Micro-to-Macro Transitions' (Coleman, 1990, pp. 19–29), and also as an asset for individuals (external) and structures (internal), as detailed by Adler and Kwon (2000). However, the emphasis will be on social capital as an individual level endowment, while also acknowledging the integrated ontology of the theory. Thus the research will examine the management of social capital at the individual level, in this instance at the level of owner-managers.

Chapter 1 detailed the research aim as:

- To develop understanding of the management of social capital processes as they are interpreted, experienced and shaped by owner-managers. Thus, to research owner-managers' perspectives and experiences on how they make sense and go about their management of social capital processes.

The aim can be decomposed into the following objectives (expressed as questions in Chapter 1):

1. To research the owner-managers' management of social capital process in terms of rational, self-interested, opportunistic utility optimisation method of analysis.
   o to research the management of social capital in terms of a narrow economic self-interest; that is in terms of notions of pecuniary maximisation of utility
   o to research the management of social capital in terms of a broader understanding of rationality. This understanding of rationality is taken from Coleman's 'methodological individualism', which contends that actors are 'purposive and responsible'. And '... much of what is ordinarily described as non-rational or irrational is merely so because the observers have not discovered the point of view of the actor, from which the action is rational' (1990, pp. 16–19).
2. To research the owner-managers' management of social capital process in terms of a low and non-rationality method of analysis.
   o Thus to research phenomena that are not readily reduced to notions of rationality (economic or otherwise) which are characterised by low or non-rationality, including instincts, emotions, ethics, habits, risk taking, the will to create, the adaptive unconscious and the role of intuition.
3. To research the owner-managers' management of social capital processes in terms of the interdependence between rational and low and non-rationality method of analysis.

4.3. ONTOLOGICAL FOCAL POINTS

The book's introduction argued that social capital lacked agreement and this theoretical diversity is reflected in the ontological status of social capital. For example, in Adam and Roncevic's view social capital's ontological status has yet, '... to be resolved coherently within a particular approach or research programme' (2003, p. 157). This research will therefore in keeping with the sociological, embedded understanding of social capital already discussed, stipulate the following ontological focal points to facilitate the research process.

First, social capital will be understood as an integrative, multi-dimensional theory of social interaction. Thus social capital is more than the sum of its parts, and although it can be de-composed into its component dimensions to assist research, nevertheless its essential qualities have to be considered in a synoptic or holistic purview. Therefore the reductivist approach of interpreting social capital by its constituent parts, labelled as bonding and bridging (Putnam, 2000, pp. 22–23) and/or linking capital (Woolcock, 2001) is rejected on the grounds that these sub-components considered in isolation are not social capital, as its sub-components interact and self-reinforce in a multi-dimensional process to form social capital. Further, for this research the owner-managers' inter- and intra-firm social relations are understood to aggregate to form social capital, as these dimensions are complementary, interconnected and also mutually self-reinforcing. Accordingly, to research these connections in isolation will result in an overly narrow view of social capital processes, as Adam and Roncevic put it: 'Claiming that social capital can be studied as a dependent or independent variable ignores the possibility of complex causal mechanisms, which are not the exception but the rule' (2003, p. 167). Moreover, the extent social capital can be decomposed, while maintaining its integrity as a unifying theory has also been raised by Maak (2007) and Anderson et al. (2007).

In consequence, for this research the understanding is that any sub-dimensions are complementary, interrelated and fluid (Liao & Welsch, 2005, p. 347), as opposed to being separate entities, as suggested by a number of authors including Patulny and Svendsen (2007) and Lee (2008). Thus, social capital's ontology is understood as integrative. Accordingly, the research sub-dimensions, which have been constructed to facilitate the research, are not understood to constitute social capital.

The second ontological focal point relates to the level of analysis in social, which acknowledges the interconnectedness and multi-level nature of the concept. Therefore the research will be cognizant of the synoptic and integrative nature of the concept. For illustration in Lin's view: 'Most scholars agree that it [social capital] is both collective and individual goods' (2001, p. 26). Moreover:

> To a large extent, the distinction between the individual resource, external view and the collective characteristic, internal view is a matter of perspective and unit of analysis. Some definitions are therefore neutral on this dimension. Moreover, these two views are not mutually exclusive. A collective actor such as a firm is influenced by both its external linkages to other firms and institutions and the fabric of its internal linkages: its capacity for effective action is typically a function of both. (Adler & Kwon, 2000, p. 93)

This ontological understanding also reflects Coleman's micro-to-macro, and vice versa, macro-to-micro perspective (1990, pp. 19–20); that is each level of social capital analysis is interdependent and aggregates from one level to another. Thus to fully understand macro or societal economic social capital requires an understanding of micro or individual firm levels of social capital. In social capital research therefore, one level of analysis can offer findings relevant at other levels, though care is needed in terms of 'ecology reference factors'.[1]

Further, it can be argued that it is only by examining how social capital is managed at the micro level, in this instance at the level of the individual owner-manager (by researching into social capital's interactive and individual nature) that understanding of social capital at any level can be established. To reiterate, in *Foundations of Social Theory* Coleman adopted an individual-level theory of action for '... examining processes internal to the system, involving its component parts, or units at a level below that of the system' (1990, p. 2). In Coleman's words: 'The interaction among individuals is seen to result in emergent phenomena at the systems level, that is, phenomena that were neither intended nor predicted by the individuals' (*ibid.*, p. 5). Thus Coleman's social theory made a micro-to-macro transition and took individuals as its starting point. This insight can be illustrated by recent research that suggests sector reputation (which is one return of social capital) frequently 'overspills', affecting individual firms (Yu & Lester, 2008, pp. 94–108). In synopsis, Coleman adopted an individual level approach, while at the same time arguing for social capital as an external or collective asset, which he stated were aspects of social structure that enhance opportunities of actors within that structure (1990, p. 302). Accordingly, this research will focus at the micro level as a private good (for the individual entrepreneur) but will also generate findings that aggregate to the group level (for the firm or sector).

The third ontological focal point is that the economic form of social capital is 'embedded' (as is all economic activity) in sociological phenomena and broader society. This insight is taken from socio-economics, and according to Portes and Sensenbrenner has its origins in classical sociology, including Weber who argued for the moral character of economic transactions (1993, pp. 1322–1327). Thus economic social capital is understood from a socio-economic perspective that takes the market as being embedded in the broader economy, which in turn is embedded in broader society.

The fourth ontological focal point is that social capital is situational and contingency factors are crucial therefore for any analysis. In Coleman's treatment: 'A given form of social capital that is valuable in facilitating certain actions may be useless or even harmful in others' (1990, p. 302).

Thus the research will appreciate that owner-managers' perspectives, experiences and shaping of social capital are subject to contextual variables (see Chapter 2).

4.4. EPISTEMOLOGICAL DIRECTION

The research will be driven by the ambition to investigate, 'the details of the situation to understand the reality or perhaps a reality working behind them' (Remenyi et al., 1998, p. 35). Moreover this epistemic direction is based on the understanding that being an owner-manager can be understood within an interpretivist and social constructivist perspective. This understanding is also consistent with Granovetter's conclusion that, '... economic institutions (like all institutions) are socially constructed' (1992, p. 25).

Further, the interpretivist perspective contends that, '... to understand a particular social action (e.g. friendship, voting, marrying, teaching), the inquirer must grasp the meaning that constitute that action' (Schwandt, 2000, p. 191). Social reality is also appreciated as being a product of sentient individuals, and consequently the research will focus on how owner-managers make sense, experience and shape their management of social capital, through their day-to-day social interactions. Thus the research is driven by the ambition to understand the deeper meanings of behaviour: in more prosaic terms to get inside the owner-manager's heads to find out what they are thinking, to understand their actions from their perspective. Moreover: 'These meanings emerge from the shared interaction of individuals in human society ... any complete understanding of human behaviour must include an awareness of this covert dimension of activity, not simply the observation of overt behaviour' (Meltzer et al., 1978).

The methodological and epistemological orientation of this research is also directed by 'symbolic interactionism' perspective, which has been characterised as research with an interest in, '... understanding how individuals take and make meaning in interaction with others. The emphasis is on the pressures of meaning-making in social organisation' (Marshall & Rossman, 1995, p. 2). Symbolic interaction can be thought of as, '... a general orientation, which is concerned to understand social phenomena through the micro-analysis of human affairs' (Burrell & Morgan, 1979, p. 79). Further, symbolic interaction's core proposition is that human behaviour and interaction relies on symbols and their meaning. Therefore, in the symbolic interaction perspective researching behaviour requires a focus on interaction, and this interaction relies on symbols, the most fundamental of which is language. Further, the influence that stimuli have upon human behaviour is shaped by the context of symbolic meaning within which human behaviour occurs. Thus, symbolic interaction '… may be envisioned as the study of the ways people make sense of their life-situations and the ways in which they go about their activities, in conjunction with others, on a day-to-day basis' (Prus, 1996, p. 10).

The symbolic interaction theoretical perspective contends that individuals interpret the world through an ongoing social process of interaction, in which they shape and are shaped by their social reality. In Mead's view, '… persons both control and are controlled simultaneously by their environments' (Meltzer et al., 1978). Further, most symbolic interactionists agree that there is an objective reality, 'the situation as it exists' referred to as 'situated reality', while simultaneously there is also a social reality: 'Humans therefore exist in a physical objective reality and in a social reality'. In addition: 'The important point is that we do not respond to this reality directly. Instead we define the situation "as it exists" out there and that definition is highly influenced by our own social life' (Charon, 2009).

There is also a consensus that symbolic interaction developed from American pragmatism (Charon, 2009; Meltzer, 1978), and that it was first expounded by John Dewey's tendency, 'that personal considerations affect all knowing' and that the mind or will is always active in perception and analysis (Joad, 1924, pp. 66–86). Pragmatists claim an affinity with Greek sophist Protagoras and his maxim: 'Man is the measure of all things', and with Aristotle's politics that people are social and are only fully human in a community, which is transparently a precursor for the symbolic interactionist perspective. However, symbolic interactionism as a discrete perspective is usually traced to the social psychologist, George, H. Mead (1863–1931), and paralleling Coleman's social capital, is also the product of Chicago University scholarship. Further just as social capital in its economic form has been characterised as a conservative theory, symbolic interaction has also been understood as 'geared to providing an explanation of the status quo', and Mead identified as a 'theorist of regulation' (Burrell & Morgan, 1979, p. 76). Moreover, besides pragmatism, Mead's symbolic interactionism was influenced by Darwinism (Mead understood humans as social animals) and behaviourism, in the sense that he thought that humans should be thought of in terms of what they do, by researching their actions, as opposed to examining the impact of social structural theories such as culture or class.

Mead's symbolic interaction was subsequently interpreted and developed through one of his students, Herbert Blumer and evolved into two schools of thought. In the Chicago school purview humans are active and thinking in creating the social environment, which interact to influence behaviour. Further: 'These meanings emerge from the shared interaction of individuals in human society ... any complete understanding of human behaviour must include an awareness of this covert dimension of activity, not simply the observation of overt behaviour' (Meltzer et al., 1978). In this view individuals are taken, '... as active agents in creating the social environment which, in turn, influences their behaviour' (Meltzer, 1978). In contrast, the alternative Iowa school argues for a positivist methodology and a structural conception of the self and society.

Thus, there are two schools that encompass a number of interpretations of symbolic interaction (Crotty, 1998, pp. 71–78), and the approach taken for this research is drawn from the Chicago school, which emphasises the origin and development of meaning. For illustration:

> Methodologically, the implication of symbolic interactionist perspective is the actor's views of actions, objects, and society has to be studied seriously. The situation must be seen as the actor see it, the meaning of objects and acts must be determined in terms of the actors meanings, and the organisation of a course of action must be understood as the actor organizes it. The role of the actor in the situation would have to be taken by the observer to see the social world from their perspective. (Psathas, 1973, pp. 6–7 quoted in Crotty, 1998, p. 75)

Blumer, the most significant interpreter of Mead, also understood the latter's symbolic interactionism, '... as being essentially concerned with the meanings which underlie the processes of interaction and as an attempt to understand society in these terms' (Burrell & Morgan, 1979, p. 81). Blumer argued that interaction, '... consists in the fact that humans beings interpret or "define" each other's actions instead of merely reacting to each other's actions ... (and) interaction is mediated by the use of symbols, by interpretation, or by ascertaining the meaning of one another's actions'. He also highlighted the significance of the process of interpretation in which: 'Instead of individuals being surrounded by an environment of pre-existing objects which play upon him and call forth his behaviour, the proper picture is that he constructs his objects on the basis of on-going activity' (Blumer, 1962, p. 197). Further, a central notion of symbolic interaction is to take the standpoint of those being studied (owner-managers) and hence the only way this can be achieved is through interaction and more specifically symbolic interaction:

> ... for it is possible only because of the 'significant symbols' – that is language and other symbolic tools – that we humans share and through which we communicate. Only through dialogue can one become aware of the perceptions, feelings and attitudes of others and interpret their meanings and intent. (Burrell & Morgan, 1979, pp. 75–76)

In sum, this research is influenced by Blumer's understanding of symbolic interaction in terms of being sensitive to the owner-managers' perspectives. Further social capital is researched as phenomenon constructed on the basis of ongoing activity at the micro-analytical level of day-to-day interactions. This research will therefore be guided by the view that: 'To understand how others define reality is to interpret their acts not from our perspective but from theirs' (Charon, 2009). Thus the research aims to understand action from the perspective of those who act, as Blumer argues there is a need, insightfully, 'to feeling one's way inside the experience of the actor' (Meltzer et al., 1978).

Moreover, reflecting social capital's stated ontological focal point, in symbolic interaction, '... the individual and society are inseparable units. While it may be possible to separate the two units analytically, the underlying assumption is that a complete understanding of either one demands a complete understanding of the other' (Meltzer et al., 1978). In consequence, from this perspective there is a mutually interdependent relationship between the individual and society, a view also reflected in Coleman's micro-to-macro view of levels of analysis (1990, pp. 19–20).

In synopsis, a symbolic interaction perspective contends that society is dynamic and continually being created and recreated by sentient individuals who are active participants in shaping and being shaped by their social interactions: this a processional as opposed to static or mechanical view of social reality. In this perspective, individuals interpret and shape, and are shaped by their environment. In consequence, social reality can only be understood in terms of what the actors (owner-managers) themselves believe about their reality. Moreover, objective reality, the 'situation as it exists' is defined within a perspective developed from social interaction. Individuals therefore exist in a physical objective reality, which is understood from a social reality developed in dynamic and emergent symbolic interaction processes. The core of these symbols is language and words.

Finally, it is worth noting that symbolic interaction has been criticised on the grounds that it underplays the importance of emotions and the unconscious, which is a valid criticism as interaction is often based on emotional motivations. Further, according to Meltzer symbolic interaction has also been criticised for an a-structural or microscopic bias, with too much focus on the transient, episodic and fleeting.[2] The symbolic interaction perspective can also be criticised for offering an over-optimistic 'liberal' (American) view of social reality. However, Blumer's response, in 'Society as Symbolic Interaction' (1962) argues that society is comprised of individuals constructing and sharing their social worlds through processes of interaction. Hence, Blumer rejects collective (and biological) determinism, arguing against the idea that individuals are entirely malleable by societal level and historical phenomenon, in part because society is dynamic and these macro-level structures are constantly being refined. Moreover, Blumer makes a case against the distinction between macroscopic and microscopic levels of reality. Further, it can be argued that Blumer's optimistic perspective on society and individuals, as active agents in a process of creating their own environment, which in turn influences their behaviour, is appropriate for research into owner-managers who typically display an optimistic and 'can do' view of their environment (Chell, 2008, pp. 134−137 on self-efficacy theory).

4.5. RESEARCH IMPLICATIONS

The research lens will be at the microscopic individual level as suggested by symbolic interaction theory. Moreover, the management of social capital by owner-managers will be researched in action, reflecting a core proposition of symbolic interaction that social reality is dynamic and emergent through processes of interaction. Further the research aims 'to take the role of the acting other', and this will be achieved in part by face-to-face interviews which are sensitive to individual and social symbols, in this case analysis their owner-managers' words.[3]

It is also relevant that Mead contended that, '... all group life is essentially a matter of cooperation' (Manis & Meltzer, 1978, p. 16). And, taking the role of others into account is essential to this cooperation and can be thought of as 'social intelligence' (Charon, 2009). Thus taking the role of the other is essential for social cooperation to examine this aspect of social capital the research will aim to achieve 'sympathetic introspection' with the individual owner-manager. Thus the research will aim to view the owner-managers' social world from their own perspective. The research will accord therefore with Blumer's aspiration for, 'feeling one's way inside the experience of the actor' (Meltzer, 1978). Meltzer also recommended case studies and interviews, of the free and non-directive type, as being relevant for this research aspiration (both of these research approaches are discussed below).

4.6. METHODOLOGICAL PROCEDURES

The methodological procedures of this research are ethnographic[4] and will therefore follow in previous small firm ethnographic investigations, including Ruth Holliday's influential study of small firms (1995). According to Holliday (with reference to Bryman, 1988) ethnographic research can be characterised as:

> seeing through the eyes of the researched; a reliance on description; the contextualisation of events within the social system under study; an emphasis on process, both in terms of studying process and the study as process; flexibility in research – there are no proscribed frames of reference; and the emergence of theory and concepts through description. (1995, p. 21)

Further, the methodological procedures aim to achieve familiarity and insight into the world of the owner-manager to investigate how these actors interpret, experience and shape their management of social capital. There are three primary ethnographic methodological procedures in this research.

In order of importance, the first of these procedures were semi-structured, open ended, face-to-face, rapport interviews (based on an interaction of mutual understanding and agreed trust). These interviews were approached as interactions in which the interviewer actively probed and developed the dialogue to gain greater detail and understanding of social capital processes. Further, in keeping with the symbolic interaction methodological perspective, the interview interactions aimed for 'sympathetic introspection' or ethnography, purposefully striving to take, 'the role of the other' (owner-managers), to '… achieve intimate familiarity with human group life as it is actually accomplished' (Prus, 1996, p. 130). For example, in each interview the owner-managers were asked to describe and reflect on the management of social capital for research interactions lasting over one hour. Collectively these interviews offer a multi-voiced narrative (in the owner-managers' own words) on their perspectives and experiences of the management of social capital. The final length and direction of the interviews was dependent on the nature and extent of emerging data, with most of the owner-managers being interviewed on two occasions. However, all of the owner-managers were interviewed for over one hour on each occasion, with the longest interview interaction (which took place over three sessions) lasting for six and a half hours. These interviews were all recorded, subsequent to being transcribed, verbatim for analytical purposes. Further in subsequent chapters quotes from the owner-managers are used to categorise the data by presenting their words to support the thematic analysis.

Second, the research relied on data from observation. These sources of data have been defined by Silverman as, '... text as a heuristic device to identify data consisting of words and images that have been recorded without the intervention of the researcher (e.g. through an interview)' (1985). Further this understanding is also consistent with the view that observation, '... encompasses not only things that one witnesses through one's visual and audio senses, but also includes any documents, diaries, records, frequency counts, maps, and the like that one may be able to obtain in particular settings' (Prus, 1996). For this research 'observation' material included owner-managers' power point presentations, as well as induction and training documents, websites and various internal and external texts. For example, most of the owner-manager's had firm-specific websites, and the research also had access to a range of internal and external texts. For illustration, 'IT Solutions' research data included extensive face-to-face interviews, as well as an analysis of the company website and internal textual sources, including an award winning staff induction programme, and 'PowerPoint' presentations.

The third source of data was participant-observation with the researcher in a number of instances directly advising the owner-manager on operational and training matters. The researcher also participated in a number of networking events with owner-managers.

Moreover, words, 'symbols that are spoken or written' (Charon, 2009) are the most important, and the base for all other symbols: for this research the symbols to be analysed were words deriving from the owner-manager's interviews; or from observation in terms of words in textual sources; or from their words about participant-observation.

4.7. ANALYTICAL STRATEGY: SENSITISING SUB-DIMENSIONS

The research will use the symbolic interaction method of 'sensitising concepts', to suggest directions along which to investigate. Further, sensitising concepts are in harmony with the symbolic interaction perspective of social reality as being fluid, and also for offering a humanistic interpretation of the actor's ability to shape their own social reality. Conversely, Blumer characterises 'defining concepts' as providing restrictive prescriptions on the nature of social reality (Meltzer, 1978).

The analytical strategy is also open ended enough for a symbolic inter-actionist perspective to produce a 'focused interaction' in face-to-face inter-views. For example, the research aims to develop their knowledge of the vernacular of the subject group (owner-managers). It is also worth stressing that the open-endedness of the interviews offered the following advantages:

1. It allows respondents to use their 'unique ways of defining the world'
2. It assumes that no fixed sequence of questions is suitable to all respondents
3. It allows respondents to 'raise important issues not contained in the schedule' (Denizen, 1970).

Denizen & Lincoln has also described this 'in-depth' approach as a 'rea-list approach to interview data' (1970).

To facilitate the investigation a sensitising two-dimensional/themed research framework has been developed from theoretical literature (reviewed in Chapter 2). The purpose of this framework is to offer initial themes for 'fixing attention upon one or a few attributes' (Stake, 2000, p. 44). In symbolic interaction terms the framework can be understood as providing 'sensitising dimensions to guide the research of where to look as opposed to definitive analytical categories' (Meltzer, 1978).

This approach is also consistent with Anderson et al.'s methodology to review social capital to provide:

> ... a preliminary theoretical framework about the nature and categories of social capital ... so that emergent themes that we 'recognized' were those associated with the qualities of social capital that we had described earlier. (2007, p. 255)

In consequence, the research rejected the view that ethnography should be entirely without pre-coding, which is based on the assumption that find-ings will somehow emerge by 'going native'. Further for this research among 'hard-headed' owner-managers, the necessity to explain the aims and general research approach meant that the researcher had to present the research as being semi-structured. Thus, a characteristic of the owner-managers was that they wanted to know what the research was about, as well as requiring an explanation of the logic for the research design before they would commit any of their time to the research. Thus, in the researcher's view an unstructured approach would have created significant, perhaps insurmountable problems in gaining access and cooperation from the owner-managers. This research understanding is also consistent with Silverman's criticisms on 'simplistic induction' (1985) in favour of acknowledging that without a theoretical focus 'one would not recognise the field one was studying' (Silverman, 2005, pp. 78–80). This research further acknowledges Silverman's concern that qualitative research needs to, '... reflect the subtle interplay between theory, concepts and data' (2005, pp. 78–80).

The analytical strategy is also consistent with a 'descriptive framework', as recommended by Yin for analysing case studies (1994, pp. 104–106). This research design combined a semi-structured thematic pre-coding together, in terms of flexible sensitising sub-components, together with a flexible and emergent inductive approach to data analysis. Therefore the pre-coded dimensions were constructed on the understanding that they would be elastic enough to permit inductive findings to be recognised. In summary, the research design combines a semi-structured and thematic pre-coding, together with a flexible, open-ended and emergent inductive approach to data collection and analysis.

Textual sources that have been defined as, '... data consisting of words and images that have been recorded without the intervention of a researcher (e.g. through an interview)' (*ibid.*, p. 825) are also analysed within the same analytical strategy as the interview interactions.

4.8. CODING APPROACH

The understanding that social capital can be decomposed into various dimensions is commonplace among theoretical scholars. For example, Adler and Kwon consider that social capital can be de-composed into three dimensions, which they label as networks, shared norms and beliefs (2000, p. 97). Further, reflecting this three-dimensional approach, Halpern proposes a three-tier typography, which considers social capital's main components, levels of analysis and its function (2005, pp. 26–27). In contrast, Putnam's most recent understanding of social capital is more parsimonious, limiting the theory to two dimensions: 'Researchers working with the concept of social capital have gradually but unmistakably converged on a lean and mean definition that focuses on social networks and the associated norms of reciprocity' (2004, p. 143).

However, Nahapiet and Ghoshal's (1998) typography is the most influential in recent social capital research: for example Edelman, Bresnen, Newell, Scarbrough, and Swan (2004) and Liao and Welsch (2005) have both adopted this typography when conducting recent research into the economic significance of social capital. In more detail, Nahapiet and Ghoshal categorise social capital into three interrelated clusters or dimensions to capture the various facets of the theory and explicitly stated that they were influenced in constructing this typography by Granovetter's discussion on structural and relational embeddedness published in 1992 in his 'Problems of Explanation in Economic Sociology' (1998, p. 244). It is also notable that Nahapiet and Ghoshal were also transparently influenced by Coleman and Bourdieu theoretical treatments (1998, pp. 243–245).

A note of caution is necessary however, as Nahapiet and Ghoshal constructed their dimensions with reference to their research into intellectual capital, stating their third 'cognitive dimension', '... is of particular importance in our consideration of intellectual capital, including shared languages and codes' (*ibid.*, p. 244). Therefore, though the model has been transposed unadulterated (Edelman et al., 2004; Liao & Welsch, 2005), there is a danger in this approach in that the model was designed for a specific purpose which is not necessarily appropriate in different contexts.

In summary, the research was operationalised by decomposing social capital into a flexible and integrated sensitising framework, taking Nahapiet and Ghoshal's model as its inspiration. These 'a priori' dimensions moreover were constructed from the theoretical literature discussed in earlier chapters. Furthermore, this 'top down' pre-coding was modified and complemented by emergent 'bottom-up' thematic coding, which was inductively developed as the research data was analysed.

4.9. DIMENSION ONE: STRUCTURAL EMBEDDEDNESS

The first research dimension researched the networks of the owner-managers. There are a number of different networks associated with SME.[5] However, the initial focus for this research was on the owner-managers' external network relations with stakeholders, with a lesser reference to internal stakeholders. The logic for this inter-firm, as opposed to intra-firm emphasis, was that the research was concerned with the management of social capital in economic life, and the assumption was that the market was more external than internal to the firm. However, it also worth noting that influential research into intangible processes, including reputation mechanisms has concluded that external reputation reflects internal capabilities (Dowling, 2001). Further the ontology of social capital is that it is an integrative theory and thus internal and external social capital processes are interconnected (see Chapter 3). Moreover, as the research developed the distinction between external and internal networks became difficult to maintain as discrete sets of connections, given that they were often overlapping (see below for a discussion of the emergent research design).

In synopsis this dimension, '... refers to the overall pattern of connections between actors, that is, who you reach and how you reach them' (Nahapiet & Ghoshal, 1998, p. 244). This dimension comprises network ties, network configuration and appropriable organisation, meaning how easily social capital can be transferred from one context to another, that is the extent of its fungibility (*ibid.*, p. 251). In addition, network roles, rules and precedents were also researched (Grootaert & Bastelaer, 2002, p. 19). Overall, this dimension focused on externally observable network structures and their characteristics, including their formal and informal rules and procedures.

4.10. DIMENSION TWO: RELATIONAL EMBEDDEDNESS

This dimension, '... describes the kind of personal relationships people have developed with each other through a history of interaction ... It is through these on-going personal relationships that people fulfil such social motives as sociability, approval and prestige' (Nahapiet & Ghoshal, p. 244). This dimension comprises 'trust, norms, obligations and identification' (*ibid.*, p. 251). Further, this sensitising dimension is concerned with beliefs, attitudes, values and norms of behaviour. In consequence this dimension will examine the significance of business ethics or morality in the marketplace.

4.11. DIMENSION THREE: COGNITIVE/ COMMUNICATION EMBEDDEDNESS

This dimension '... refers to those resources providing shared representations, interpretations, and systems of meaning among parties' (Nahapiet &

Ghoshal, 1998, p. 244). This dimension comprises shared codes and language and shared narratives and was developed from the 'strategy domain' with 'particular importance' for researching into the authors' focus into intellectual capital. However, Nahapiet and Ghoshal also admit that this cluster '… represents an important set of assets not yet discussed in the mainstream literature on social capital' (*ibid.*, p. 244). And this research was unable to generate sufficient distinct data within this dimension, rather the data generated from this dimension replicated data from the structural and relational dimensions. Therefore the research design was modified to omit this dimension.

In summary, the research was operationalised with pre-coded, sensitising dimensions constructed with reference to the books' literature review. Nahapiet and Ghoshal's tri-dimensional approach was adapted to construct three 'a priori' dimensions, which were subsequently modified into two guiding dimensions. Further, this dissertation's ontological understanding is that social capital is more than the sum of its parts, and thus these dimensions were viewed as overlapping and complementary.

4.12. SAMPLING APPROACH

For this qualitative, ethnographic inquiry, concerned with achieving sympathetic introspection, a snowballing approach was adopted as the most appropriate sampling strategy. This sampling strategy was chosen as there is a close fit between the snowballing approach and a qualitative research framework (Bryman & Bell, 2003, pp. 106–107). This non-probability sampling involved the researcher making contact with a number of owner-managers and then subsequently using these research connections to network with additional owner-managers, a fraction of whom were willing to participate in the research. Further, snowballing sampling can be further justified with reference to Coleman's view that it is appropriate when the researcher needs to consider the nature and substance of social relations. In his view tracing these social connections would be preferable to probability sampling (1958).

The sample is drawn from small business owners mainly from the service sector, with a limited number in the retail sector. This sampling strategy is followed because of the critical importance of intangible assets for firms in these sectors, arguably more so than firms producing tangible outputs.

4.13. THE AUTHORIAL VOICE

Anderson & Jack have commented that all analyses are subjective interpretations (2008, p. 256), and therefore it is worth reflecting on the researcher's perspective, though as Rabbie Burns noted self-perception is inevitably a difficult process: 'O wad some Power the giftie gie us/To see oursels as others see us'. However, within the reflection that any self-understanding will inevitably be fragmented and paradoxical, the following observations are germane.

First the researcher has over 10 years' experience of owner-management in a medium size family retail business. The legacy of this experience is that he was immersed in SME mores and values to the point that he was able to strike a rapport with a majority of the owner-managers during the research process.

Second, the research confirmed the author's prior view that owner-managers are heterogeneous, and consequently the search for a personality profile of a shared set of characteristics, as suggested by various trait theorists[6] is at best restricted to general and porous categorisations. For example, the research sample included owner-managers who could be characterised as opportunists, pioneers, innovators, brokers, organisers as well individuals who defied any classification. Thus, the research confirmed that owner-managers as a reference group exhibited limited stylistic consistencies of behaviour. Therefore the research confirmed the view that owner-managers lack consistent trait characteristics.

Third, it is also worth noting that the owner-managers were unaware of debates concerning the meaning of entrepreneurship, with most of them understanding the term in terms of working for themselves. However, this didn't mean they saw themselves as independent, as a common complaint related to work pressures resulting in limited freedom of actions. For instance, a number of the owner-managers acknowledged that they were reliant on larger clients in their roles as sub-contractors. Thus independence for these owner-managers was more theoretical than real.

Overall, the researcher's view is that entrepreneurs are a diverse set of individuals and thus they can be thought of as a reference group[7] with limited commonalities or shared stylistic behaviours. In consequence the researcher rejected the 'essentialist' approach, which has been defined as identifying:

> ... the essence of something is to distil that which is a necessary component without which the 'thing' would cease to be that particular class of thing. Applying this concept

to personality suggests that each person's personality comprises such essential components; one problem is that this is a very static view that does not permit change or development. (Chell, 2008, pp. 4–5)

Conversely, the researcher's view is that owner-managers are engaged in a social process and that experiential knowledge and learning is essential for firm survival and success. This view follows the epistemology of the research in understanding owner-management from a symbolic interaction perspective that places a premium on the individual's interpretation of social experiences. Moreover, the researcher's view is that owner-management is not just about responding to interaction, but also about influencing and reflecting on those interactions. This ability or flexibility to absorb and learn or adapt from day-to-day interaction was exhibited by all of the interviewees: though it was also obvious that a number of owner-managers had learnt the wrong lesson from their experiences. In sum, and in keeping with this theses' epistemological direction, the author views owner-managers as being engaged in dynamic socially constructed process that simultaneously they control and are controlled by. Moreover, this understanding follows the theses' epistemological direction as elucidated by Mead's perspective on pragmatism (1978, pp. 409–418).

4.14. RESEARCH LIMITATIONS

The research was limited by a number of factors.

First, the role of the researcher is fully acknowledged as being active in this research (see above for authorial voice). This viewpoint is consistent with Prus' understanding that:

Like those they study, researchers also work from pre-existing frames of reference and although they may explicitly attempt to put these pre-existing notions in suspension in order to maximise openness in their queries and assessment, the material is apt to be guided to some extent by certain aspects of their pre-conceptualisation. (1996, p. 251)

In consequence a limitation relates to the inevitable subjective nature of the qualitative research process.

Second, the research was limited by its focus on the firms' owner-managers. This means that other stakeholders connected to the firms are not researched directly. However, while this is a limitation in terms of stakeholder scope, this focus has advantages in terms of the depth of data that the owner-managers can reveal about social capital process. This approach is also consistent with Jack and Anderson's view that while the entrepreneurs selected, '... are not representative of the entrepreneurial universe they do provide useful data ...' (2000, p. 13).

Third, the research is limited by a gender imbalance, with 23 male and only 7 female owner-managers being researched. The research sampling criteria did not consider gender as a selection criterion, and consequently a limitation is in terms of considering if there are any gender-based differences to managing social capital processes.

Fourth, the owner-managers were selected from the service and retail sectors. In consequence the findings from this research are not generisable to other sectors.

Fifth, the importance of family businesses and the management of social capital processes were not considered as a selection criteria. Only four of the owner-managers described themselves as working in a family SME. However, 'shadow' owner-managers (mentioned below) resulted in a significant number of the firms being managed in conjunction with their partners. Further a majority of the owner-managers researched had established their firms less than five years earlier. The implication is that the majority of the owner-managers researched had the potential to develop into dynastic family firms.

Sixth, over the two year course of the data collection the economy deteriorated. In consequence the findings are limited by a constantly changing economic context, which means that the results could not be replicated.

Seventh, an emergent and unexpected limitation was that in a number of cases identifying the lead owner-manager was less than obvious, with the firm's entrepreneurial drive residing with the putative owner-managers' spouse. Thus, in a number of instances the owner-manager being researched had less influence over their business than their spouse or 'shadow' owner-manager.

CHAPTER 5

MANAGING SOCIAL CAPITAL – THE NETWORK DIMENSION

5.1. INTRODUCTION

The purpose of the chapter is to examine the owner-managers' perspectives, experiences and shaping of their network interactions and structures, with reference to the three research questions.

In this research networks can be understood as the quantitative component of social capital. Furthermore, as already discussed (Chapter 2) there is extensive theoretical convergence between network and social capital theory, with a number of scholars interpreting them as synonymous. For example, according to Anderson et al. '... social capital is a network phenomenon' (2007, p. 264), and that '... it is difficult, if not impossible to study social capital without looking at social networks. The two are so entwined that neither would survive without the other' (*ibid.*, p. 265). This viewpoint is further elaborated in detail by Lin (2001) and Burt (2005). It has also been contended that '... scholars familiar with the social network literature might well regard some of what is written on social capital as a reinvention of the wheel' (Casson & Della Giusta, 2007).

Moreover, as social capital and network literature are voluminous[1] there is a need to set boundaries to the chapter's theoretical analysis. Accordingly, this chapter's references consequently will be limited to scholars (already discussed in the literature review) who identify themselves as working in social capital literature from a network vantage, most significantly Lin (1999, 2001) and Burt (1990, 2000a, 2000b, 2004, 2005, 2006). This chapter's interpretation of networks is also framed by assumptions taken from socio-economic literature (Smelser & Swedberg, 2005), in terms of owner-management and entrepreneurship being embedded in both economic and social phenomena (Granovetter, 1973, 1985, 1992, 2005;

Polanyi, 1944/2001). Further, the chapter will reference a limited number of scholars who have researched and theorised networking in the SME sector (Blundel & Smith, 2001; Chell, 2008; Shaw & Conway, 2000, pp. 367–383).

The chapter's network understanding is also consistent with Blundel and Smith's egocentric network structures, which they define as being:

> ... created out of the personal contacts of entrepreneurs. New and existing links are 'enacted' in a variety of ways, to create new ventures (i.e. start-ups) and to redirect current business activities into other areas (i.e. diversifications, 'serial' and 'portfolio' entrepreneurship). (2000)

It is also germane that the research initially focussed on the owner-managers' inter-firm networks. However, the distinction between inter-firm and intra-firm networks became increasingly difficult to maintain as the research emphasised their integrated nature, and consequently this chapter will report on both network types. Moreover, this network interpretation reflects the conclusion that, '... the "network perspective" on industrial organisation is "blurring" firm boundaries, recognising that similar processes guide network linkages both within and between organisations' (Blundel & Smith, 2001).

The network themes that emerged during the research are organised into three sections, the first of which examines the owner-managers' perception on the primacy of their rational motivations, an understanding that they were most enthusiastic to volunteer as the driving force for their network interactions. Next, in order to analyse the interwoven nature of the owner-manager's rational and non-rational network motivations the second theme examines the temporal variables in networks. This theme will also examine rationality with reference to the path dimension of the owner-managers' networks, an approach which is predicated on the notion that networks continually evolve. This theme considers how, '... processes and outcomes in turn influence network development over time (networks as dependent variables)' (Hoang & Antoncic, 2003). In contrast the third theme investigates levels of rationality in shaping the morphological variables of networks.

In overview, the originality of this chapter will be to add to and complement orthodox network interpretations predicated on rational exchange theory (Coleman, 1990, 2000), and the homophily perspectives (Burt, 1990, p. 60; Lin, 2001, pp. 65–66; Putnam, 2000, pp. 22–24). In contrast this chapter will examine the role of rationality, low and non-rationality, and also the significance and inter-dependence of these factors for understanding actors' (owner-managers') perceptions, experiences and shaping of networks.

5.2. RATIONALITY AND NETWORKS

People and groups who do well are somehow better connected. (Burt, 2005, p. 5)

The research confirmed that the owner-managers were fully cognizant that it was in their financial self-interest to cultivate and maintain networks. As Karl of 'K.T' put it:

You cannot do business all by yourself. The more people and relations you are able to affect with your products, the more success you would have. It's as easy as that. Somebody once said that; 'the more people who are happy with you having been on this planet, the more success you have had'. I find that to be true.

This view corroborates an extensive theoretical and empirical literature over the benefits of networks in the SME sector (Anderson et al., 2007, pp. 245–272; Burt, 2005, pp. 58–162; Casson & Della Giusta, 2007, pp. 222–224; Hoang & Antoncic, 2003; Jenssen & Greve, 2002, pp. 254–267; Liao & Welsch, 2005, pp. 345–262; Shaw & Conway, 2000, pp. 367–383). In broad terms this perspective has been summarised as follows:

... people who live in the intersection of social worlds are at higher risk of having good ideas ... : Ways of thinking and behaving are more homogeneous within than between groups, so people connected to otherwise segregated groups are more likely to be familiar with alternative ways of thinking and behaviour which gives teem the option of selecting and synthesising alternatives. (Burt, 2005, p. 90)

An atypical example of the importance attached to networks was offered by Karl of 'K.T' who reflected that:

I am not dependent on other people to get things done. I work well on my own. But I acknowledge the fact that 'we as a group' can do much more than you can do by yourself. You gain knowledge as time goes by and you learn that some things are important, such as gaining knowledge from those around you, although when you're young you often tend to believe that you can do everything by your self.

Another typical understanding of networks was volunteered by Nils of 'POGO' who readily acknowledged his reliance on network resources:

With a lot of the things that I do, I am dependant on having such networks and working with others. Having a small business, I know some things and other people know other things. If I am to initiate a project, I cannot do that on my own. I must rely on others. Such as with the Bioenergy project in the developing countries. I am dependant on my technical partner. They know their things about the project, and I know mine, and without them I cannot make that specific project work. My business is built in a way which makes it necessary to network with other people.

An additional representative and succinct view of networks was offered by Nick of 'S.L.' who elucidated:

> There are no obligations but obviously without our local network we would be dead ... Skye is very much a traditional community in that somebody knows somebody who knows somebody so you can get virtually anything done by tapping into their network.

Nick gave details on the information value of his networks:

> I tell you one thing, this is an interesting one because I have 3 properties in Skye and 1 property in Fort William which is about 70 miles away and the joiner who works on my house in Fort William is also what's called a Crofter. Now I also own in Skye a croft, and he has informed me that he has managed to get 3 log cabins put onto his croft and as a Crofter you have the right to do that so you can become a cottage industry, which has opened a potential for me to exploit this small croft that I have got. His core competence to me is his network and the fact that he is sharing knowledge with me; I have found this network particularly useful.

Nick's rationality was also blunt in his approach to formal networks, as the following interview extract illustrates:

> Nick: There are two issues to do with formal networks. One is route to market, our referential value for Visit Scotland, the star rating gives us added value, and also when people look at the thing and they see the stars they know that the house is kosher. ASSC, we are a member of their group because they have a lot of insight, whereas the 'Visit Scotland' is very bureaucratic and civil service, if you want to put it that way, whereas the ASSC is very aware of the market and gives you a lot of intelligence. Then finally with regard to a shed load of other websites that we make sure we register with, it drives search engines towards us so we tend to get a good hit rate.
>
> Researcher: So it's all commercial then? There are no formal groups that you joined for any other reason than commercial reasons?
>
> Nick: No.

Charles of 'J.R.' also detailed the recurring economic rational understanding of the benefits of networks:

> Networks are extremely useful for gathering information in the form of: interviews, surveys and questionnaires. They also give me access to important business and political figures on the Jewish scene.
>
> • I was invited by Philip Green to his Arcadia offices for a talk by him and a tour around the Oxford Street 'Topshop'.
> • I have also been able to network with the British Board of Deputies, which is the representative organisation of British Jewry and advices parliament.

- Through these groups I have also had access to specific Washington senators and Israeli diplomats.

A further instance of the benefits of networks was offered by Sarah of 'S.W.' who stated that networks provided: 'Active referral generation, an increased breadth of knowledge and base of contacts, as well as the growth of a database of suppliers, imperative to my company'. This conclusion is therefore consistent with Burt's summary of the information benefits available in networks as relating to, 'Access, Timing and Referrals' (1990, pp. 62–65).

In overview, the owner-managers understood and approached networks from the rational perspective that they were business intangibles to be nurtured as commercially valuable resources. The returns of networks were also understood in terms of facilitating knowledge management and for generating positive 'word of mouth' (reputation). Networks were also valued for developing internal intangibles relating to the benefits of 'communities of practice' (Cohen & Levinthal, 1990; Lesser, 2000, pp. 13–14; Wenger et al., 2002). The owner-managers' views were consistent therefore with the literature that argues for entrepreneurship and owner-management being a social and network activity (Baron & Markman, 2003; Chell, 2008, pp. 137–140; Korsgaard & Anderson, 2011; Quince, 2001).

5.2.1. Network Rationality in Action

In the majority of the owner-managers' accounts there was a conviction that the rational, utility maximising approach, which instrumentalised network ties for self-interested utility, was the most realistic perspective for understanding, experiencing and shaping network interactions. For example, there was a recurring view that networks had to be judged with reference to opportunity costs incurred, as expressed by the following owner-manager.

I would say that generally we are all very busy in business and you have got to look at your time and think, does this add value and is this a good use of my time? (Darren: P.X.)

Phil of the eponymous 'P.B.' was also typical of the owner-managers in his rational cost/benefit analysis of the value of networks:

Networks can be helpful but I also find some to be a pain. There are so many types of networks now that it's hard to keep up. I use the networks and groups that I know and am happy with and tend not to join new ones just for the sake of it.

Stephen at 'A.G.' also argued:

> Networks must have some ultimate business benefit, short, medium or long-term. The contact in the network must also be a decision maker. In IT many people influence a decision, but very few take the decision.

In synopsis, the owner-managers emphasised that they evaluated each network on its respective benefits. Thus they rejected the notion that networks were always worth cultivating as resource, rather the particular network had to have an obvious returns to convince them to devote resources to cultivate their development. For illustration Charlotte of 'H.P.' described her approach to networks by asserting:

> I choose the people I get in touch with, I don't involve myself unless I can see a benefit for my business.

Aftab was also typical of the owner-managers in his cost/benefit calculations:

> They must have got the company name off Practice House and register and I don't think there is a week that doesn't go by that somebody isn't emailing me saying would you like to be a part of this or that. Some of them are quite interesting, to be honest and I wouldn't mind joining them, but it's always a delicate balance of time and resources ... Its not that I don't want to join, it's just a question of convenience.

The rational approach to networks was also apparent in the owner-managers' avoidance of networks on the basis of a negative cost/benefit analysis. For example, Darren of 'P.X.' stressed his reason for not joining Leeds Chambers of Commerce as it offered, 'poor value for money'. Further, a number of the owner-managers avoided formal networking events as they saw them as no more than cleverly disguised sales pitches. For instance, according to Neal of 'A.G.' his firm avoided network events to miss: 'Alumini stuff, places where I will be overtly sold services and products'. He was however willing to join: 'A broad groups of professional networks, including the British Computer Society', as he valued the knowledge and business benefits of these network connections. Another example was offered by Phil of 'P.B.', who stated that he declined: 'General membership of different wholesalers who annoyingly contact me with offers'. He also avoided connections with sectoral networks such as the 'Balloon Association' and the 'Play Providers Association'. In sum, if there was a rational, self-interested business case for joining a network then the owner-managers stressed that they would be enthusiastic to join for these commercial benefits. For example, Rob of 'F.B.' stressed that joining professional organisations could be an insurance requirement, and also that tangentially membership of professional organisations offered knowledge management benefits in terms of acting as a conduit for communicating regulatory and legal developments.

Moreover, the recurring owner-manager understanding of internal networks relates to the aforementioned theoretical literature concerning 'communities of practice'. Further the owner-managers understanding was nuanced with a tendency to rationally construct internal networks, while at the same time acknowledging that there was a limit to the extent that they could foster these inherently uncertain, organic structures. Thus the owner-managers took a dual approach, endeavouring to rationally plan internal networks, while accepting that internal networks grew out of unmanageable shared endeavours and reiterated interactions. In overview, the owner-managers view was that their most effective rational strategy was to set a favourable background context to cultivate the nurturing of these networks (Cohen & Prusak, 2001, pp. 13–14; Thorpe, Holt, Macpherson, & Pittaway, 2006).

The owner-managers also tended to stress that cultivating internal firm networks was essential for business success. For example, Neil of 'IT Solutions', expounded that he developed his internal firm networks by initiating rigorous recruitment and selection procedures, as well as developing detailed induction programmes, appraisal schemes and award winning training programmes.[2]

> I also have this document here which is an internal document for employee induction, and something I am very passionate about is the way need people to represent IT solutions, so we focus a lot on cultivating peoples' approach to work, customers, and each other's networks. We have this series of customer principles, people principles and how we interact with each other, we don't just pay lip service to these we drum them into people. We have a boot camp where we take people away on an away day.

Reflecting this view on the importance of developing internal networks David of 'R-Ices Ice-Creams' in addition stressed that:

> If you are going to be more than a sole trader, you have got to build a team, networks, management and quality and all that takes people.

It is also worth noting that a number of scholars have argued that entrepreneurs and owner-managers value their independence and consequently dislike joining groups (Curran & Blackburn, 2001; Jenssen & Greve, 2002, p. 255; Shaw & Conway, 2000, pp. 367–383). Chell also comments on the 'fortress enterprise' typifying, 'the small business owner's stalwartly independent nature – a tendency as it were to batten down the hatches against external interference, influence and intervention' (2008, pp. 133–137).

However, in this research the owner-managers did not describe themselves, or act in accordance with this isolationist/autonomy focussed approach to interaction and networks, which is also consistent with research that challenges the idea of the solitary entrepreneur (Dodd & Anderson, 2007). For example, Robert of 'T.W.' reflected:

> I don't like joining groups but I appreciate the massive value in doing it in a business context though I'd say entrepreneurs value their independence very much so.

Paradoxically, the owner-managers were of the view that the only rational way to preserve their autonomy was by joining groups and networking: to do otherwise would place their firms at a considerable disadvantage that would increase the likelihood of business failure and the ultimate cessation of their independence and autonomy. For example, Darren of 'P.X.' offered an atypical illustration of how the owner-managers rationalised the need to network:

> Some companies we are working alongside with people much higher up. I'm dreadful at going in and doing a CEO level presentation and don't feel comfortable with that high level, flashing a smile, corporate b*****, networking type of stuff but appreciate it's important for me, and not to go in and say yes sir, no sir, three bags full, but to go in and find out what their business problems are so that again we have a generic or a specific response to either that person or someone in a similar situation.

To conclude, the owner-managers offered a range of examples elucidating the rational business benefits of networks. This business case understanding of networks is therefore consistent with the rational cost/benefit approach to networks recently identified by Cooke et al., who concluded from research with SME entrepreneurs and owner-managers that:

> Respondents typically find it hard to hard to think of occasions on which network interactions do not involve financial transactions. (2005, p. 1068)

5.3. THE TEMPORAL VARIABLE OF NETWORKS

> Networks are constantly being socially constructed, reproduced, and altered as the result of the actions of actors ... Therefore networks are as much process as structure, being continually shaped and reshaped by the actions of the actors who are in turn constrained by the structural positions in which they find themselves. (Nitin & Eccles, 1990)

This section will detail that although social capital is best thought of as a self-reinforcing, evolutionary process, nevertheless there are phases when this evolution intensifies or atrophies. Further, the originality of this section will be to explicitly identify the phases when social capital tends towards either rapid accumulations or swift dissolution, framed by a consideration of the owner-managers' rational and non-rational motivations. In terms of theory the section is also consistent with scholarship confirming the importance of temporal variables for networks and social capital. For instance, Putnam considers that social capital has a historical or path dimension (1993, p. 179); and Cohen and Prusak also contend that social capital requires space and time to develop (2001, p. 4). This temporal variable also accords with the process perspective understanding of networks, interpreting them as dependent on a series of reiterated interactions (to establish connections) that facilitate norms and levels of reciprocity. Further this understanding was first elucidated by Harrison White, the founding scholar of social network analysis, who argued that actors are active, purposeful agents engaged in an on-going dynamic process towards taking control and achieving advantage in their networking (White, 1963).

Burt has also identified the importance of time in that: 'Experience seems to be the answer to questions about how people learn to be network entrepreneurs' (2005, p. 76). The significance of a residue of social interactions is also consistent with Anderson et al.'s view that social capital, '… is a misused metaphor for a relational artefact' (2007, p. 264). Thus the research agrees with a significant body of literature on the importance of time variables for networks and social capital. However, the research is novel in two ways. First, it will identify the most significant network phases for the management of social capital, and second it will examine these phases with reference to the research questions into rationality.

5.3.1. Prior Start-Up Networks

> … entrepreneurs rely primarily on informal sources in their personal contact network (PCN) to mobilise resources before the formation of a venture. (Blundel & Smith, 2001, p. 49)

The majority of the owner-managers were fulsome in acknowledging the business benefits derived from prior start-up networks. For instance, Neil recounted on the importance of his prior networks in gaining leads for 'IT Solutions':

> My first piece of business was from my ex boss in fact. He knew that me and the other guys were good programmers and we made the connection through a friend of a friend

down the boozer. Next thing we get call saying I believe you have set up in business Neil, I might be interested in working with you. So I was the one and only person from that company working in there and I got a good personal reputation.

Nils of 'POGO' was also atypical in emphasising the importance of pre start-up networks for facilitating the survival and prosperity of his firm:

I have a huge network behind me acquired through my years in Statoil ... You have my former colleagues from Statoil, where I have access to many resources when I should need them. People with experience on running projects, experience relating to climate, energy, etc. Though this is informal, they come when I ask them to.

Furthermore, the owner-managers also tended to emphasise that their prior networks were most critical in the start-up phase of their firms. For instance, Aftab of 'Easy Tech' recalled:

We were set up here in 2003. This company is a little bit of a development of a previous company from 1993−2000. So with this company in 2003 we already had a little bit of reputation that we could turn on the tap straight away.

Another representative experience of prior networks was offered by Darren of 'P.X.':

We sent out a very chatty email saying we are back in business if anyone is interested, we'd love to lend a hand, and hope things are great. Immediately within 3 hours we got a call. He said 'Darren, I was just lamenting this lunchtime that an organisation with people like you no longer exists when can you come and see us' so that's a personal net-work reputation thing. He had done business with a company I'd worked for previously, he had been lamenting the fact that the company no longer existed and then he received this email in his inbox and he was delighted. So that was previous personal company network and reputation which we managed to latch onto.

In sum, there were numerous examples of the owner-managers recognising that they had derived advantages from prior start-up networks. It is also significant that the owner-managers claimed that these resource rich networks had not been rationally constructed, as they had not been cultivated in terms of maximising economic returns; rather these networks developed organically, usually as a by-product of activities relating to previous employment. For example, according to Neil of 'IT Solutions':

Where do you start? The thing with networks is that very often they have built up unbe-knownst to you over a long period of time, a business isn't suddenly there. It is very rare a business is born and they say right lets get into widget manufacturing. It is usually because of a past experience, exposure and you know people so do you count those years or don't you? I think from the day I left Leeds Met, without realising it I was going to come to rely upon that network later on in life. So, I don't know where it starts.

Neil's understanding of these prior network ties was typical, in that he interpreted them as comprising a fortunate coincidence of resources to be exploited as circumstances permitted. Thus, in the owner-managers' perspective they had not cultivated these prior networks for any potential business advantage. However, if commercial opportunities arose seren-dipitously, then they would feel no compunction about utilising these networks for maximum commercial benefit. The key point was that they perceived and stated they had approached these prior start-up networks oblivious to any conscious rational commercial considerations. Therefore in the case of the prior start-up networks the owner-managers were willing to concede that they had not been constructed with reference to rational motivation, rather they viewed these connections as random and that any benefits were entirely a matter of good fortune. Thus prior network cultivation was characterised by the owner-managers as being of low or non-rationality.

In contrast, the research indicated that the avowed speculative approach to networks, though non-linear was in reality less random than as detailed in the owner-managers' accounts. For instance, Darren of 'P.X.' described a typical approach to this cultivation of networks:

> There is certainly the social side and I still keep in touch with many of my old incubator colleagues and why I do that? I can't say any business benefit coming out of it but also it is a very low effort to maintain and I enjoy it, and who knows something might come in down the street.

Moreover, though these connections had a random character, they were also driven by an intuition that networking in certain contexts could create a bank of valuable ties. For illustration, according to Karl of 'K.T':

> You have many different sorts of networks you can connect yourself to, however, we have based much of our business on the informal networks formed from connections in previous employment, as that's where things happen. We know a lot of people, from working in business for many years, and being active in this city for many, many years. We have put our signature on a lot of the things.

In theoretical terms the owner-managers' speculative approach to net-works relates to literature on entrepreneurial opportunity recognition (De Carolis & Saparito, 2006, pp. 41–42). Thus, typically the owner-managers would cultivate prior start-up networks without any consistent rational objectives; however the research also suggests that this approach to net-works was at a certain (subconscious) level driven by alertness to opportu-nities. The owner-managers thus tended to construct these prior start-up network connections based on an under-unacknowledged mixture of commercial insights, and various other cognitive processes (Chell, 2008, pp. 131–133), which served to direct them towards network contexts brimming with resource rich ties. For example, many of the owner-managers had extensive prior start-up networks in specific areas that related to their firms activities. Of course, networks would have developed organically in the course of previous employment, but in this research the owner-managers tended to cultivate and maintain strategic networks in excess of ordinary workplace connections (see below for section on network tie numbers). Furthermore, these prior start-up ties were often characterised with reference to what M. Polanyi termed the 'difficult to codify' skills based, tacit, insider knowledge (1958). This research observation is also consistent with the conclusion that:

> ... research into entrepreneurial processes supports earlier findings regarding the shape of entrepreneurial networks, notably their more extensive range and 'loose-knit' structure. (Blundel, & Smith, 2001, p. 50)

In sum, the owner-managers approach can be characterised – in network jargon – as cultivating 'weak' ties for 'brokerage benefits' (see below). Thus, the owner-managers, at a subconscious and non-rational and instinctive level, would set the boundaries for these 'random' networks to contexts that were likely to result in the cultivation of potentially commercially valuable ties. For instance the IT sector owner-managers all agreed that they constructed extensive networks in this sector, well in advance of their conscious efforts towards owner-management (Kevin of 'Cogs'; Neil of 'IT Solutions'; Darren of 'P.X.'; and Stephen of 'A.G.').

Further as this aspect networking was driven by subconscious motivations, it followed that the owner-managers underreported and perhaps misunderstood how they had accomplished these prior networks. This conclusion is also consistent with M. Polanyi's dictum, relating to tacit knowledge: 'That we know more than we can tell'. Chell's interpretation of Polanyi is also relevant for this conclusion:

> Nascent entrepreneurs cannot tell all they know: they absorb socio-cultural knowledge routinely through social interaction; some knowledge within the cognitive-affective structure becomes 'taken for granted'; socio-cultural beliefs and attitudes in particular form part of the individual's tacit knowledge and are enacted implicitly. It then becomes difficult (indeed impossible) for the entrepreneur to articulate how they know a product concept is not simply an idea, but an opportunity worthy of development. (2008, p. 258)

On self-reflection, the majority of owner-managers were also prepared to admit to the significance of these non-rational drivers, for instance in terms of 'gut instincts' which led them to network in certain contexts evaluated to be resource rich. A number of owner-managers were also willing to recognise that this approach to networks was driven by their 'people skills', a view that is consistent with trait theory in terms of social competence as a recurring quality or characteristic of entrepreneurs (Baron & Markman, 2003; Chell, 2008, pp. 137–140). Thus by being social the owner-managers would establish networks without any specific outcome, but predicated on the intuition or other non-rational motivation that these connections had the potential to be commercially valuable at an unspecified point in the future.

5.3.2. Start-Up Networks

The research confirmed that the majority of the owner-managers placed a premium on cultivating networks in the start-up stage as a key objective for establishing their firms. Further the owner-managers' views were consistent with an extensive literature on the benefits of networks to start-ups.[3]

For example, a typical understanding of start-up networks, in terms of developing ties with customers, was offered by Steve of 'P.S.' who recalled:

> I had a lot of customer meetings! I spent a lot of time on building further on customer relations. I had a lot of conversations, which made us able to build trustworthy relationships with our customers, for us to be able to come in the positions where we could deliver … It takes a lot of time and a lot of customer meetings, and things need to be sorted out. You need to convince your customers. The customer buys you, before they buy your products. It might sound a bit silly, but that's the way it is. If you are not able to sell yourself, you won't be able to sell your products.

However, the theme that strongly emerged in tandem with the owner-managers' pursuit of these valued resources, related to the difficulty of constructing networks to provide commercial returns. For example, according to Rob of 'F.B.':

> I spent a tonne of time at the beginning of opening the hotel doing local networking and went along to all event, and it can be a full time thing; and I didn't get a single piece of business from any of them. I realised I was doing it because I was being told to do it, get out there and network it's the right thing to do, but realised I wasn't targeting the right place. You find out who your customer is and go and ask them what they actually need from you, don't be embarrassed about it, people are a bit too secretive in business as they think by revealing their USP someone will rip it off straight away, this is not true, businesses can coincide harmoniously.

Nils of 'POGO' was also typical in describing his approach to start-up networks:

> Well, you get to spread the message ... You build your business reputation from taking part in these start-up networks and forums by new meeting people ... But I haven't gotten that much in return, I must admit.

Neil of 'IT Solutions' also offered a typical view of networks in the start-up phase, describing network connections as:

> In the local area I have done a lot of networking and I can honestly say I haven't got a penny's worth of business out of those and you find that the local support organisations bombard you with that stuff.
>
> I have been on courses on how to do networking, shake hands, tell them who you are, empathise with them, explain what you and your services do, exchange business cards etc and nothing has come of it. I've made some great friends, referred business to those people, so it works for some of those, but my point is you have got to be selective in the type of networking event you go to be effective for you and your business.

Darren of 'P.X.' gave another example of how the start-ups, were in his words, 'besieged' to join formal networks:

> But I tell you everyone was knocking on my door from Business Link, West Yorkshire Ventures, Connect Yorkshire, Leeds Chamber of Commerce, Incubators, and Private Incubators etc. Everyone is trying to offer advice on this, that and the other and trying to get you to join their organisation or network. What they can offer advice on is the mechanics of running a business i.e. VAT, HMRC, advice on looking at some of the contracts and stuff, so absolutely take advantage of that; but what I found was that particularly through some of the networking events I was going to, I was getting contradictory advice left, right and centre and if I hadn't been through it on my own prior to that I might have been trying to put into practice everything everyone was telling me.

The research therefore revealed that formal network events were targeted by the owner-managers in the start-up stage. Further there was ample evidence that the owner-managers also exerted themselves to cultivate networks in the start-up stage. However, there was a consistent view among the owner-managers that the majority of this networking activity had been futile: as Paul of the 'S.I. Property' put it when describing the numerous letting agency events he had attended: 'They're usually talking shops and a waste of time'. In sum, there was rare unanimity among the owner-managers that organised network events were unproductive venues for cultivating resource-rich ties and networks.

Moreover, this viewpoint was confirmed by the researcher's observation and participation in three separate networking events (with Neil of 'IT

Solutions', Kevin of 'Cogs' and David of 'R-Ices Ice-Creams'). The researcher's conclusion was that these forums were characterised by extreme rationality, with participants furiously 'networking' for their own self-interested advantage. In consequence, the three events attended were emotionless, soulless affairs, with a plethora of card exchange interactions, but at the same time with participants being extremely wary of being instrumentalised in these network transactions. Thus there was an observable caution to avoid being outfoxed, with participants being on a heightened sense of awareness driven by 'zero-sum' game calculations. In theoretical terms this understanding is therefore consistent with the arguments of R. Frank on rationality being unable to address the 'commitment problem', for instance in terms of a self-interested persons being unable to, '... make themselves attractive for ventures that require trust' (1988, p. 255). Accordingly, the most rational network generating approach, which was predicated on a reductive focus on the mechanics of networks, was understood by the owner-managers as the least likely platform for developing connections. In sum, these networking events assumed a rational actor, 'homo economicus' view of participants, resulting in an absence of human dynamics and a perceptible absence of trust. Hence, the rational self-interest approach led, in the language of economics, to a market failure in terms of the avowed objective of generating networks.

In consequence it followed that the owner-managers tended to be dismissive of formal start-up networks, as Tom of 'S.V.' expressed it:

> Some of the network meetings appeared to be great opportunities to acquire a skill or meet likeminded individuals and I thought maybe I can learn from that. After attending a few of them though I find them too intense, everyone is trying to sell you something or to gain one – up over you.

5.3.3. Developing Start-Up Networks: 'An Awful Lot of Frogs to Kiss' (Darren of 'P.X.')

Despite discussing at length the limitations of start-up networks the owner-managers were unable to pinpoint any detailed criteria for identifying the minority of network approaches that were likely to offer commercial resources. Thus, the owner-managers were deficient in any coherent or consistent approach or any general blueprint for developing networks. In the owner-managers' view cultivating networks was an idiographic trial and error, or contextual learning process, which would lead in an 'ad hoc' way to the individual being able to select the most appropriate network and networking events to cultivate. Theoretically this observation is consistent with the view that entrepreneurs and owner-managers are action orientated, with a consequent reliance on experiential learning (Rae, 2005).

Moreover, though the owner-managers stressed that it was impossible to accurately assess the potential value of networks in advance – with even the disparaged formal network events presenting the chance, albeit small, that an interaction would result in a win–win network encounter – there were nonetheless three optimum approaches to developing networks that emerged in the research. In order of importance the research highlighted that the best method for building networks was to make the first move and be altruistic, on the assumption that this increased the likelihood of generating reciprocated altruism. For illustration: 'If you want to build networks, take the initiative and be nice and do someone a favour' (Terry of 'A.C.'). Further the research revealed that the network benefits of this approach outweighed the dangers of being viewed as 'unworldly' or as economically naïve. This approach facilitated networks, as the tie would then be inclined to reciprocate favours and in the process form structural connections. From a theoretically perspective this research observation on cultivating networks is therefore consistent with previous research which concluded that:

> The employment of reciprocity, particularly the trading of reciprocal favours, was the most prominent activity used across all social capital relationships. (Bowey & Easton, 2007, p. 294)

For example, Kevin of 'Cogs' stated his self-interested, yet altruistic approach:

> We cultivate networks through conferences because they see me or one of my guys showing technical tips, giving away free codes, solve particular design problems and making them shine within their organisation. They tend to see who is an ally and a friend so when they are then in the **** we say why don't we get Cogs in, so they don't see us as being a threat. So we explicitly and deliberately build strong ties with targeted customers … . It's very difficult to say well you're not worth much to me so I'm not going to spend much time with you because what goes around comes around. You have got to be consistent.

Steve of 'A.G.'IT Limited' gave a further illustration of how altruism could be based on economic rationalism: in this instance predicated on the assumption that sharing knowledge would lead to greater knowledge management returns, as well as to the establishment of robust commercial networks, which is consistent with literature that characterises knowledge as 'leaky' (Cohen & Prusak, 2001). Moreover, the implication of the 'leaky' understanding of knowledge is that if knowledge could not be corralled then the best approach was to trade it for additional resources, as Neal elaborated:

> In principle I absolutely agree that many organisations work on a basis of knowledge is power and indeed people think this the contractor or sub contractor, mentally and it is confusing. They think well I know how to use DB2 or TSQ or whatever, why should I share with someone else because that's my competitive advantage. We work on the exact reverse principle, on the basis that if you share a little known fact with 5 other people they share 5 things with you and you have learnt 5 things. Whereas, if you just hold that one thing close to your chest you have only known that one thing. You need to really reach the creativity and the people who are working with you, to not be frightened of sharing ideas and questioning authority.

Another example of this iterated altruisms was from David of 'R-Ices Ice-Creams' who described how the 'The Regional Food Group' had advised him not to pay for membership for their group, as it would not be good value for money till his business had become more established. In David's words 'they had done him a favour' which coloured his subsequent view of 'The Regional Food Group':

> Yes, going forward we've started to develop products that are not just dependent on our own retail, but our market and I think we use them more and more.

Second, the research identified that the owner-managers consistently developed commercial networks derived from their social networks. This conclusion is therefore in agreement with a broad range of literature, reviewed by Jenssen and Greve that contends that entrepreneurs use their social connections to launch start-ups (2002, pp. 254–55). Chapter 5 will also examine the relational aspects of managing social capital and social connections, however as far as networks are concerned the following observations are relevant.

One observation was that the exploitation of social networks was driven by self-interested, rational calculations. Thus, appropriating social networks for commercial gains was understood an efficient approach for maximising network advantages. This view was predicated on the assumption that networks could be constructed readily on already established ties, which was considered a much easier option than establishing new network ties. For example, George of 'C.W.' was unabashed in describing how he exploited his social networks to create commercial networks: in George's description he used his friends to publicise and staff his events. Therefore in George's case the owner-manager's commercial networks were inseparable from his social networks. George was also typical of a minority of owner-managers who did not make any distinction between social and commercial networks, which is consistent with the view that:

> The extensive personal ties used by entrepreneurs often lead a blurring of business and social life, with mixed consequences. (Blundel & Smith, 2001, p. 49)

However, George was in the minority in his lack of discrimination between social and commercial networks. In contrast, the prevailing owner-manager approach to exploiting social networks for commercial benefit blended George's rational self-interested approach to social networks, together with low or non-rational social motivations. For example, the owner-managers typically were driven by social instincts that moderated their economic rationality, including the drive to preserve socially based friendships. For illustration of this perception of networks, Terry of 'A.C.' reflected that:

> It can be difficult this 19th hole thing, it is a bit like selling a friend a car, you have got to be careful about doing that kind of things as it can easily sour relationships. This guy and I we were very up front about doing this and we said look if we are the wrong business for you just tell me, there will be no love lost because I value your friendship and would rather keep going around with you and out for dinner etc than mess it all up through work, so there is a big danger there.

Another example of this rational approach to exploiting social networks blended with low and non-rational motivations was offered by Robert of 'F.B.':

> However, my partner, who is a Christian, is part of a Christian Network, and through the network that he is a part of we have gotten several valuable contracts, in fact. We have used his network on various occasions but you have to be careful because he sees these networks as far more than business networks: they are about his beliefs.

There was also a theme that commercial networks could be encouraged by adopting a long-term perspective that combined rational economic exploitation of connections, together with contradictory low and non-rational motivations. The ability to combine and act with reference to these conflicting motivations was taken as the key to cultivating commercial networks. For example, Julia of 'H.T.S.' acknowledged that she approached networks motivated with this duality of (economic) rationality and low and non-rationality (to be part of a community), in her words:

> The most important aspect is to use your social networks to find business opportunities, and how I might use a network to gain an advantage, while also working to develop the

network itself, which is very important. These things go both ways ... You can't just grab the things you want, and to expect that you don't have to give anything back.

My motivation is that ... Firstly, I want to be a part of a community ... Second I want to see if you can get any contacts which you can do some business with. It can be social and personal related groups, who you can build business related relationships with.

5.3.4. Networks and Change of Ownership

A number of owner-managers also identified that during a change of ownership firms were subject to an intense phase of network accumulation, or conversely to the dissolution of existing network ties. This understanding was based on the owner-managers taking an 'egocentric' view of firm networks that interpreted networks as being embodied in the owner-manager, as opposed to residing in the firm as a separate entity. Thus, if the owner-manager sold up and left it was assumed that their networks would leave with them. The firm would still have connections but the human content would be removed, resulting in those connections being hollowed out and bereft of substance. Accordingly, the owner-managers emphasised that the best network approach when purchasing a firm was to think of it as a start-up, in which it was essential to establish new networks or to reestablish previous networks. Thus, the owner-managers' stressed it would be a grievous error to assume that previous networks would seamlessly transfer over during the change of ownership.

The research further revealed that one approach to networks in a takeover was to tie the previous owner to the business, to ensure a bridge for the transition of existing networks to the new owners. For instance, during the research Neil of 'IT Solutions' described this process in terms of 'earn out':

If its all about you and your tight knit team and you have great customer relationships and networks the buyers are not going to hand over £10 million to you and let you walk off into the sunset whilst they are left holding this empty shell. So the concept of an 'earn out' is pretty common, where they will require you contractually to stay with the business for a certain period and indeed they may make some of the consideration of the money contingent i.e. conditional on you hitting certain targets ... For this business (IT Solutions) I was happy to accept what is called a 'good will warranty' which states that I am technically an employee of the company for 2 years, I don't have to actually work for them, just to bring along the customer good will and the loyalty and the networks that I have built up over the last few years.

David of 'R-Ices Ice-Creams' also detailed another recurring network challenge during the take-over process in terms of salesmen/women targeting this stage:

> Another one with that salesmen will wait until the business changes hands before they contact you because they know that people will stay loyal to their suppliers and their well established networks. But they know that when someone else buys the business they are not loyal to anybody because they haven't built that relationship in their networks.

Thus, the owner-managers' identified that during a take-over it was critical to focus on maintaining existing networks; the difficulty was that these networks were not firm specific but were embodied in the previous owner.

5.4. NETWORK MORPHOLOGY (SHAPE): INTRODUCTION

This section will examine rationality in terms of network morphology. The literature associated with entrepreneurship and SME owner-management and network morphology is extensive and integral to a number of scholars' understandings of social capital. For example, Burt defines the theory as: 'The advantage created by a person's location in a structure of relationships is known as social capital' (2005, p. 4). However, this section will be limited to the two most significant morphological variables which emerged in the research. First, the research identified network density (the number and strength of connections between actors) as vital for managing social capital, with reference to the respective significance of strong and weak network ties. The second variable is concerned with network range (the extent and heterogeneity of a network) and highlights the significance of the number of network ties that the owner-managers' egocentric networks could sustain.

Regarding the first theme of density, social capital and network theory are replete with research confirming the benefits of tie strength, usually with reference to the respective returns of bonding/strong/tight and bridging/weak/loose ties. Further these different tie strengths are invariably taken as complementary, in that they each confer a different range of benefits. For instance in Burt's brokerage perspective: '... bridges are valuable for creating information variation, while bonds are valuable for eliminating variation and for protecting connected people form information inconsistent with they already know' (2005, pp. 11–28). In addition, in Burt's view strong embedded ties are associated with reputation development and social bonding, whereas weak ties confer 'vision' or entrepreneurial advantage: in his terminology with reference to brokerage opportunities in 'structural holes' to gain scarce resources (2005). Burt has also noted that: 'Contacts are redundant to the extent that hey lead to the same people, and so provide the same information benefits' (1982). In contrast, the weak ties' literature argues for compensating effects: 'More novel information flows through weak ties than strong ties' (Granovetter, 2005, p. 34). Thus in theoretical terms both network types are understood as having resource payoffs.

However, in this research the owner-managers were convinced that the optimum networks comprised strong embedded ties, to the detriment of assigning any substantial value to weak tie connections. Moreover, in their interpretation weak ties were not understood as networks, but rather as a set of random connections that consequently could not be rationally developed. In synopsis, the owner-managers' viewpoint and actions demonstrated economic rationality in recognising the value of strong ties, while conversely they were deficient in rationality in their under-acknowledgement that weak ties could also confer economic returns. Further, in the owner-managers' perspective they were rationally motivated to plan and cultivate strong connections with individuals who possessed valuable resources in a manner consistent with Granovetter's observation:

> ... the strength of a tie is a (probably linear) combination of the amount of time, the emotional intensity, (mutual confiding), and the reciprocal services that characterise the tie. (1973, p. 1361)

In contrast, the research highlighted that the owner-managers were convinced that weak tie networks were accomplished due to non-rational phenomena such as luck, or from these networks developing organically in an undirected, unsystematic, unstructured manner. In sum, weak tie networks were viewed as primarily driven by low or non-rational phenomenon.

5.4.1. Network Density: Strong Tie Strength

This section will then examine network range in terms of the owner-managers number of network ties, as the research identified that though advances in technology have led to the prospect of countless connections, in reality networks are subject to human factors that place limits on the number of ties (strong or weak) that any individual can maintain. This section will also detail that these human limitations on egocentric networks relate to traits that owe little to abstracted reason or ends-means economic rationality.

Moreover, the owner-managers emphasised that they purposefully cultivated, and placed a premium on embedded networks connections comprising close ties. In their view this was a rational approach to networks: within their understanding they targeted key individuals and subsequently constructed reiterated interactions to cultivate resource-rich network ties. Maria of 'Int' for example, typified this ends-means rationality motivating the establishment of ties when she stated: 'I don't enjoy networking with people who don't have the required funds to invest in the products that we offer'. Julia of 'H.T.S.' also offered another representative example of the owner-managers' emphasis on nurturing strong embedded network ties, for economic pay-offs:

> So what I found from another entrepreneurial friend of mine who is actually quite successful, he said look Julia you don't need to join every single social group, what you need to have is a few key people who are networked. I don't need to go to all these other social groups, I just need to have contact with him and from him I can bounce off to other people. So its on a needs basis, so whenever I need something I can always ring him up and say look I need this expertise, I need that, who would you recommend?

Aftab of 'Easy Tech', also recounted the commercial benefits of a strong tie connection:

> He has got a heck of a lot of pragmatic business acumen, the way he deals with businesses, the way he is going about his businesses. We have just known each other through other mutual friends. When I was trying to explain to him that we have business interests in Dubai and Saudi and he helped us there and more importantly he helped us in the UK as well. He said if you need a contact in IT, web developing here is another guy I can put you in touch with and who is very competitive. If you need your literature printed out, here is a friend of mine that does all my printing. He has literally become one stop shop for us ... To me he is probably the most strategic asset that I have got and that the company has, because we can just go to him and because he is a friend we can trust and rely on, he can pinpoint who to go to.

The research also confirmed a characteristic of these close ties was a preference for embedded connections to be horizontal, or non-hierarchical (Maak, 2007, pp. 329—343). For instance, Karl of 'K.T' elaborated that he favoured embedded strong network ties with individuals whom he regarded as peers:

> Some groups or networks it is nice to be associated with, because you have the same perception about the socio-economic, and/or the business environment ... Entrepreneurial behaviour ... Business Leaders ... You need to be part of a network, so

you can get something back .... You give something to them, and they give something
back to you ... It has to go both ways ...

The homophily principle was also evident in Nils of 'POGO' description
of a formal network:

I am also part of network called Dialog (Dialogue), which consists of managers/leaders
that meet and talk about different themes and subjects. It has not been the biggest
success, but it was fine, you get to meet a lot of new people who share your outlook.

In theoretical terms these findings are consistent with literature that
argues that there is a preference for homophilious interactions in networks,
which accords with the aphorism that 'birds of a feather will flock together'
(Lin, 2001, pp. 46–54). This homophily bias also reflects the view that
asymmetrical power relations undermine strong ties and social capital
(Foley & Edwards, 1997; Fukuyama, 1995a; Putnam, 1973). Conversely, it
is also worth noting there are negative interpretations on horizontal ties for
promoting collusion and tending towards inefficient monopolies (Casson &
Della Guista, 2007, p. 237), which may be true of the corporate sector,
although there was no evidence in this research supporting this viewpoint.

In summary, the owner-managers were resolute in their view that strong
ties offered considerable benefits and therefore it made rational economic
sense to cultivate strong ties. The research also identified that the owner-
managers preferred to cultivate homophilious connections, as well as
focussing on a limited number of ties as they assumed their facility to manage networks decreased in relation to the network size: the bigger the network the less it was subject to their control (see section below on tie
number).

5.4.2. Network Density: Weak Tie Strength

In contrast to the willingness to attribute self-directed rationality to as the
motivating force for strong ties weak, the owner-managers were far less
forthcoming in discussing their motivations and accomplishment for
weak tie networks. In their view weak ties were subject to fortune or were
understood as a by-product of work interactions developing in an
unpredictable and uncontrollable manner. In consequence the majority of
the owner-managers understood weak ties as not being subject to rational
planning or any significant degree of purposeful management. However,
the research conclusion is that the owner-managers' accounts of weak tie
processes underestimated their extent that they did rationally direct and

manage these weak tie interactions. For illustration, Darren of 'P.X.' pondered:

> However, in business you tend to meet someone coincidentally, at a conference for example. That happens a lot. To be 'out there and talking to people' is always very important in terms of business. When I work with people, however, I talk with them a lot to develop our idea and to take the 'project' further, together.

Nils of 'POGO' adopted a similar approach:

> Yes, being a part of 'The Viking Sponsors' could be one of them (Viking is the local football team). We used to sponsor Viking, however, we found that the amount of money we spent on sponsoring them maybe was a bit too much compared to what we got in return. However, it is a very good forum, if you use it to your advantage. We have met several customers this way, by taken part in social activities like this.

Reflecting this approach, David of 'R-Ices Ice-Creams' also stated:

> I would agree in that's how things come to you. One would be, I mean it nearly didn't happen, but in the Metro Centre I was told that the ice cream company had gone out of business and their places were empty so I contacted them and we looked very closely at expanding into there. That wouldn't have happened if someone hadn't have told me.

> I would say virtually all the time it's the distant relationships that you tend to find an go exploring and I think that's what I guess I do as a business anyway. I explore the extremities all the time of options and ways forward and it tends to come through a conversation I have had with somebody.

Nick of 'S.L.' also shared this interpretation of weak ties:

> With it being Skye are these people all connected, do they all know each other? I would have thought you would get a good or bad name very quickly there. Oh yes. It is contagious. The good thing is that because I am bolted into the system I know who is a good plumber and I know who is not a good plumber. For example I was advised on a painter, one of the joiners was saying if you want big industrial type stuff this is the guy to do it because he is fast, but if you want a detailed piece of paintwork doing on your property or you need internal stuff this is the guy to go to. It becomes very, one job you need, this person, so it's not just a painter; this is a painter with a specialism. The painter probably wouldn't tell you that but the joiner will.

Thus the predominant view was weak ties were resistant to any significant extent of rational planning or calculations, while at the same time there was evidence that these connections were not entirely random, rather the owner-managers' targeted and manipulated contexts to exacerbate the facilitation of weak tie connections. For example, a typical understanding of weak ties as being loose and un-systematic was articulated by Rob of 'F.B.':

> In general, when it comes to the contracts that we have, we very often get them based
> on the relation that we have. Someone who knows someone, who knows
> someone ... One of the contracts we got, we got through my relation with one of the
> employees by being connected to the same network. We don't have much control over
> these networks though.

Social events were also a common forum for establishing commercially valuable weak ties. Of course social events were attended for their intrinsic benefits, though the owner-managers did not view them just as leisure activities; rather they were understood as offering the opportunity to mix business with pleasure, which meant the owner-managers mixed rational and low and non-rational motivations. Moreover this interpretation is consistent with conclusions that argue that social events are instrumentalised for self-interest by entrepreneurs and owner-managers (Shaw & Conway, 2000, p. 370). This conclusion also agrees with research that identifies that: 'Socialising (i.e. diners and sporting activities) was an important activity in building social capital' (Bowey & Easton, 2007, p. 294).

In consequence, the research view is that the owner-managers, albeit at an under-acknowledged level, targeted these events to develop weak tie connections. For example, Steve of 'A.G.'IT' recounted:

> We have many social connections within business, culture, and many other sectors,
> which gives us the breadth in our networks which is very important, and we make sure
> to take care of these connections, by having social happening here in our offices, as an
> example, where we invite about 100–150 people once every 6 months, where both old
> and new social connections make us expand our network of relations continuously.

Kevin of 'Cogs' agreed:

> This is a bit of the network we build in our offices when we have or two annual social
> happenings. No one is trying to sell anyone anything, but saying, 'Hey, what you say is
> really interesting, what do you say about having a chat about this on Monday?' That's
> the way we do business.

> However, at the same time, we will never ever lose the human/personal aspects with
> what we do, because we have so much respect for people in general. NOT SELLING
> ANYTHING is the key to forming networks.

The research also identified the totemic role of the 'Christmas Party' for making connections and developing weak tie networks. Neal of 'IT Solutions' elucidated:

> The Christmas party, I always look forward to and for me it's a time to find out what
> people's other halves really think and I'm pretty sure I know people are reasonably
> happy or unhappy because they tell us. But, you wonder what their wife or husband's

perspective is, and I really believe in that by having a good relationship with peoples' partners that saved our bacon a few times. People have gone home and had a really hard day and p**** off for whatever reason and they have gone home and their husband or wife has said yes but it's a good company you are working for, they look after you and just think, how bad it could be if you worked somewhere else?, And I am convinced that has happened.

Steve of 'P.S.' also stressed the significance of Christmas socialising for establishing network ties:

We went to a Christmas party this one time, with a Local Bank, where a business chain where present, and were we got the opportunity to present our products, and they immediately became interested. After one formal presentation, the contract was signed. You don't get much business from sitting at home or just in your office! You need to go out and meet potential new customers, at one level or another! And you need to talk about business continuously, all the time! You need to be 'in the zone', to put it like that! And that's really fun.

Overall, the research identified that Christmas socialising presented immense opportunities for networking, even in the most unlikely of settings. For illustration, Robert of 'T.W.' detailed the network advantages of a sectoral seasonal event:

It gave us, good referrals from current clients and businesses I deal with. By being part of 'SAIF' (The National Society of Allied and Independent Funeral Directors) I am invited to the annual Christmas dinner which is an excellent networking opportunity. I also get to find out pretty quick what clients' expect of a quality coffin manufacturer and any new areas in the market i.e. themed coffins with bright colours, painted pictures, pet coffins etc. I remember at the SAIF Christmas dinner 2006 – through socialising at the event I gained 3 new clients.

Finally, there were also a few instances of owner-managers rationally cultivating network ties driven by forward driven utility maximisation combined with non-economic motivations. For illustration Neil of 'IT Solutions' valued his business angel role as a lucrative opportunity to network for economic gain, while at the same time he valued this role as a source of entertainment:

The Business Angel side is quite fun, kind of like the poacher turned gamekeeper and as I've been through it myself I'd like to think I know what I'm looking for. YABA (Yorkshire Association of Business Angels) meets every 2 months. 10 businesses come along and give an 8 minute pitch. To be honest you just have to have some money and that's why I say there are some numpties out there. I'm not naming any names. In YABA you pay £200 a year and to be honest I pay £200 a year for the comedy value. Most pitches are fantastic but some are ludicrous and some are absolute lunatics.

5.4.3. Network Range: Quantity of Ties

An emerging theme in the research concerned the number of network ties that the owner-managers could sustain in their networks. This research therefore identified a theme consistent with Granovetter's observation that network range is limited by innate human capabilities:

> Note that all things being equal, larger groups will have lower network density because people have cognitive, emotional, spatial and temporal limits on how many social ties they can sustain. Thus the larger the group, the lower its ability to crystallize and enforce norms, including those against free riding. (2005, p. 34)

Furthermore the anthropologist Robin Dunbar[4] has concluded that social capacity is limited to roughly 150 in terms of being able to maintain more personal, informal loyalties, which it has been oft reported is the favoured management of the owner-managers (Holliday, 1995). This understanding that there is human limit on the range of ties that humans can accommodate in networks has also recently been discussed by Malcolm Gladwell in terms of a 'tipping point'. Gladwell illustrates his point with reference to the 'Gore Tex' fabric company that limits its business units to 150 employees per plant (2000, pp. 182—187).

In this research, however, the owner-managers contended that network range was more restricted than the Dunbar 150 number. For example, Neil of 'IT Solutions' reflected on his experiences of managing expanding ventures:

> Absolutely, my number is 45. The first business we set up grew to 70 people and when we did a post-mortem after it was all over, everyone agreed we were happiest when we were at 40—45 people. Everybody knew everybody and knew everybody's strengths and weaknesses. We were big enough to have a big resource to mix and match to projects and a broad set of skills. We were all at our happiest then. So the people who used to work at the last business went into this business and said so what's going the happen when we get to 40—45 people? So absolutely, I subscribe to that, you cannot keep growing organically with a flat hierarchy until you are 2000 people it's chaos.

Nick of 'S.L.' also delineated the range of his external networks:

> I think I have got about between 20 and 30 people in different states of relatedness, some whom I value more than others. For example my cleaner is also an administrator for, well basically a sheltered housing agency, that's the one in Fort William, and her knowledge, she is far more valuable to me as a knowledge bank than she is a cleaner. So it may well be that these relationships are quite broad.

Further there was a theme that technological innovations were overloading the owner-managers with too many connections. For example, a typical understanding of the limitations of being overexposed to network ties was offered by Darren of 'P.X.':

> I think it's a curve, because you can have too many connections and end thrashing and just receiving and saying hello to the people and going to the events and keeping in touch can be too much. I am a member of LinkedIn and I'm very careful about who I link to in that you look at people that have 400 connections and you realise they are just going through the laundry list of people they have never met, and they are not valid connections. Whereas I have a genuine connection with everyone I know and want the outside world to see that connection there. We are probably talking 10's rather than 100's.

Kevin of 'Cogs' was also aware of the drawbacks posed by IT innovations creating connections:

> I think we are in an odd situation at the moment because it's easier to get nominally connected with so many more people than ever was possible before. You were saying there, what's the value and quality of that connection, possibly not so super, conversely a counter threat because of the lack of face to face exposure and people are opening up far too much via virtual networking sites.

In sum, the owner-managers favoured a limited network number of network ties, in terms of employees in their firms. Moreover, the research conclusion, based on observation, is that this restricted number was based on a preference by the owner-managers to preserve their typically spontaneous, face-to-face management style a characteristic of SME management. Therefore the owner-managers' favoured a management approach that relied on close relations, which aimed to avoid the bureaucratic, formal hierarchical systems that a higher range of network ties would entail. Moreover, this preference was motivated by rationality in the sense that the owner-managers' self-perception convinced them that they were most economically efficient operating in this style of management. Conversely, limiting the internal network tie number was also driven by non-rational motivations, based on the owner-managers' psychological character traits, unconnected to notions of economic rationality.

As for external ties there was a unanimity that IT connections were of limited value, and further in the majority of instances did not conform to the owner-managers' understanding of networks, which required a more robust personal or human contact to be considered as networks. Their view can be characterised as understanding IT networks as being akin to a telephone book and consequently IT connections were interpreted as offering no more than the platform to facilitate network connections.

5.5. CONCLUDING COMMENTS

The research confirmed that the owner-managers' networks were dynamic, unpredictable and evolved through phases (Jenssen & Greve, 2002, p. 263). For illustration, Steve of 'A.G.'IT' discussed his understanding of how networks evolved involving a process of repeated interactions:

> It's difficult to know when you start. It goes back many, many years. One of the most successful networks for us has been a technology user group associate IUA (Ingress Users Associate). For me it goes back to 1990 when I went to my first meeting there and then probably 1994 I did my first presentation there. Then in 1995 one of my business colleagues became Chairman of that group up until last year ... It's a very slow process going through those networks; it's very long sales cycles going through those networks.

It is also significant that the research identified the tendency of the owner-managers to overemphasise the importance of economic rationality in their accounts of networks and social capital. In consequence, research based on their descriptions including surveys, would inevitably report an exaggerated role for rational motivations and actions. For instance,

> ... so little of the social capital, which SMEs use in various ways, and to varying degrees, takes a non-monetary form. That is, everything (more or less) has its price. Friends do not expect a business to barter; they expect to pay for a service or product, and not necessarily at a discount. (Cooke & Clifton, 2004, p. 131)

In contrast, this research has identified the limitations of the rational paradigm in understanding owner-managers' networks. For illustration, viewed synoptically the primary characteristic of the owner-managers' networks is their unpredictable, dynamic nature, which in consequence means they are not fully amenable to rational planning and management. This finding is consistent therefore with Blundel and Smith's conclusions about small firm networks combining stability and turbulence, as well as for exhibiting, '... inherent uncertainty, which allows for unanticipated outcomes' (2001, p. 54).

Moreover, the temporal variable theme confirmed the process theoretical understanding (detailed in Chapter 1), that networks and social capital accumulate as a process that is self-generating, dynamic and subject to uncertain trajectories. This understanding is therefore also consistent with Burt's research into financial employees that: '... social capital can be said to accrue to those bankers who already have it' (Burt, 2006, p. 77). In addition, the temporal variable identified that within this fluctuating evolutionary process there were critical stages that either led rapid network cultivation or alternatively to regression and extinction.

As far as low or non-rationality is concerned the research highlighted the importance of the subconscious, for instance in terms of how owner-managers constructed prior start-up networks before the idea of the start-up was fully formed or articulated. For example, in many instances owner-managers were cultivating latent start-up networks in advance of any certainty that the business would be launched, which is consistent with psychological theories to do with entrepreneurial traits and cognition, in terms of non-rational, subconscious alertness to opportunities driven by instinct or intuition (Chell, 2008, p. 139).

The chapter also reported that owner-managers relied on their social connections as a business resource (Chell, 2008, pp. 137–139; Jenssen & Greve, 2002, pp. 254–255). The importance of social events, in particular the 'Christmas Party' has also been highlighted. In contrast, the research also identified the tension between the drive to rationally exploit social networks in the start-up stage, as opposed to the drive to preserve social networks by shielding these connections from economic pressures. The originality of this observation is to challenge the social capital and network orthodoxy of 'homo-economicus', rationally networking solely for self-interested instrumental economic benefits (Lin, 2001). Conversely, in this research the utility maximising approach to social connections was less prevalent than an approach that blended a fluctuating mix of rational and non-rational sociological/humanistic motivation. Accordingly, the majority of the owner-managers were anxious to limit, or to avoid the rational exploitation of non-economic social relations.

The significance of the non-rational social aspects of networking were also discussed in terms of the owner-managers' views on the futility of pursuing connections and business advantages via formal network events. In synopsis, these events were evaluated as being deficient in humanistic and emotional content, and in consequence there was an egregious unanimity among the owner-managers that start-up networking events yielded disappointing benefits.

The chapter further identified the significance of network morphology, which relates to the structure of networks and their impact on behaviour (Shaw & Conway, 2000, p. 371). The research identified significant morphological variables; first with reference to network density, in terms of strong ties and brokerage (Burt, 2005); network homophily (Lin, 1999, 2001; Putnam, 2000, 2004); closure (Coleman, 2000); and weak ties

(Granovetter, 1973). The second variable concerned network range in terms of tie number (Jenssen & Greve, 2002).

Moreover, the morphological theme confirmed that the owner-managers were rationally motivated to cultivate embedded strong ties, predicated on self-interested utility maximisation. The owner-managers' calculations were therefore consistent with an extensive literature which emphasised the value of close ties. For example, according to Jenssen and Greve dense, embedded network may provide better information and avoid information overload (2002, p. 263). Westerlund and Savhn (2008) have also argued that, '... some relations related to supply, distribution or supporting the business are more important than others, and companies thrive to focus on fewer relations with greater outcomes'. In their view, '... fewer relations with more outcomes are more valuable in the start-up stage' (2008, p. 492). Putnam has also noted the benefits of strong embedded ties: 'The denser such networks in a community, the more likely that its citizens will be able to cooperate for mutual benefit' (1973, p. 173).

In contrast, the counter-intuitive commercial benefits of cultivating weak ties were not as easily understood, with a number of owner-managers questioning the underlying logic of Granovetter's theory (1973) (see Kevin of 'Cogs' in this chapter). However, for the majority of owner-managers there was a recurring view that weak ties could be valuable, though less valuable than strong ties. For example, an illustration of this view of networks was articulated by Steve of 'P.S.':

> On the deep links and the many vague links I am seeing this within organisations I am working with at the moment, where they are like the Ant Hill mob running to where they think the sale is at the moment and not getting enough depth with any of their customers to actually make a sale. So you have to get the balance right of having lots of links with multiple organisations and recognising which of those you then want to make a lot deeper and then get into bed with that customer, supplier, or partner. You need to actually understand deeply how they work and to have that symbiotic relationship and make money.

Therefore the owner-managers' views were in part consistent with the literature emphasising the returns of weak ties, including Burt's conclusion that: 'Companies with a heterogeneous mix of alliance partners tended to enjoy faster revenue growth, and a dramatic advantage in obtaining patents' (2005, p. 76). Moreover, it is perplexing that the owner-managers were resigned to letting weak tie networks arise without any significant rational planning of action into their development, which is in stark contrast to their rational appreciation and planning of strong ties network.

There were also instances when owner-managers were prepared to characterise their networks as being driven by a mixture of rationality and low and non-rationality. For example: 'Sometimes to build networks it is just a case of empathising with them as well and saying yes, it's hard isn't it being your own boss?' (Terry of 'A.C.'). A further example was detailed by Neil of 'IT Solutions' who discussed at length his rational and non-rational appreciation of network phenomena:

> Was it luck or did we make happen? Don't really know. A certain amount of luck is required but I will go back to preparation meeting opportunity. You have to look for that luck, know where it could can be found and be ready because that chance conversation you have, which they often are, is usually the tipping point for winning a contract.

In summary, this chapter has examined the significance of rationality, non and low rationality and their interdependence in networks, and thus adds to literature that considers networks from other perspectives, as detailed by Nitin:

> Some have tried to explain the formation of networks on the basis of exchange theory; others have focussed on homophily and balance theory, with its emphasis on triad closure, still others have argued that networks are shaped by the control processes of agency, delegation and specialisation. (Nitin & Eccles, 1990)

CHAPTER 6

MANAGING SOCIAL CAPITAL – THE RELATIONAL DIMENSION

6.1. INTRODUCTION

This chapter will report on the research into the management of the relational dimension, which can be thought of as the qualitative component of social capital, with reference to the research questions.

In overview, the research confirmed that cultivating relationships was a core activity for owner-managers. For example:

> Everything in business relates to your relations. There is no business without any relations. Competing on price etc, is just something that is done to satisfy the needs of larger companies. Throughout history, you will see that all the business that is done is based on trust. Either you trust the one you do business with, or you don't. If you don't trust him, you don't buy from him or sell to him. Everything is like that, and in such a situation relations are Alpha to Omega. To find someone who is happy to buy the product or service you offer, at terms that satisfy you and your needs/wants, and that trusts what you are doing; it's what everything is about. In small businesses, you can never take someone to court over something. It would just be meaningless in small firms. Trust is everything! Relations are everything, to put it like that. (Nils: 'POGO')

Further, the chapter will report that in most instances the owner-managers were driven to cultivate relations, either to build a sustainable business and/or to overcome a particular business challenge. The research also highlighted that the owner-managers' understanding and statements of their consistent self-interested instrumental rationality were at odds with the reality of their day-to-day relational interactions. For example, the owner-managers' perspectives and approaches to relational interaction were driven in many instances by non-monetary motivations, relating for instance to more general business objectives of creating something of value, or most commonly of building a viable business. In consequence existing

149

literature that stresses instrumentalising relations, usually in terms of economic notions of value (reviewed in Chapters 1 and 2) is challenged by these research findings. In this research the relational interactions of the owner-managers could be characterised as being motivated less by the rational exploitation of work relationships, than by being driven by a focus, or 'zeal' born out of their 'passion for business'.

This chapter will also report on three related themes in the relational dimension. First, the research identified that although the owner-mangers were unwilling to discuss money, they nevertheless were enthusiastic to elucidate their credentials as 'realists'. This understanding was predicated on a market doctrine as a derivative of 'Social Darwinism', which understood that only the fittest survive in the marketplace. Further, being a realist meant that there was no room for sentiment, with all work-based relations being based on the strictures imposed by a competitive market. However, the research suggested that this perspective, despite being most readily discussed by the owner-managers, motivated only a minority of their relational interactions. The upshot of this research conclusion is that there is a considerable fissure between owner-managers' statements, emphasising the economically dictated rationality of their relationships, and the truth of their day-to-day relational interactions. It can be argued further that this gap is due to owner-managers feeling compelled to conform to an entrepreneurial archetype, embodying self-reliance of having to live up the view that the prototypical entrepreneur is, '… opportunistic, innovative/ imaginative, an agent of change, restless, adventurous and proactive' (Chell, Haworth, & Brealey, 1991, p. 154). As one owner-manager put it:

> Yes, it is very important to be open to things, because it might result in something. You never know which door will open. You need to take advantage of situations. (Mathew: 'D.G.')

Conversely, the research highlighted that the owner-managers were most concerned with the aforesaid 'passion for business', usually in terms of developing a sustainable business for the long term. This long-term approach entailed moving beyond both rational planning, as well as beyond the economic rationalism of utility maximising and self-interested short-term opportunism, in favour of a more holistic and nuanced understanding of relational interactions. This expanded understanding of relational interaction necessarily meant managing oblique and fuzzy humanistic factors, which were not amenable to a rational consistency in planning. Further, contradicting their statements on rationality, the owner-managers regarded these 'humanistic' factors as essential for developing the core business intangible, trust. Theoretically this long-term orientation to nurturing trust-based relational interactions accords with the socio-economic perspective that social relations overlay economic transactions: Granovetter also suggest these social relations as a non-economic explanation for the persistence of the SME sector (1985, p. 507). Therefore, the research is consistent with Granovetter's socio-economics perspective, with numerous examples of business relations being mixed up with social relations; the latter appreciated because these relations embodied vital business intangibles. For example, work-based social relations facilitate the settling contractual disputes without recourse to expensive legal remedies; and also in terms of buying patterns with suppliers being predicted to a greater extent on establishing social relations (in order to facilitate trust-based relational interactions) rather than on opportunistic relational transactions (*ibid.*, pp. 495–496).

Second, the research identified that to cultivate relations owner-managers had to be able to make credible commitments, which they described in terms of maintaining their 'integrity' or of being 'authentic' or 'professional'. Moreover, the research revealed that to make these credible commitments the owner-managers had to forgo opportunistic self-interest in favour of the longer term returns that would accrue from the development of trust-based relations. Cornell University Professor of Economics, R. H. Frank described this process in terms of opportunism faring badly when confronted with the 'commitment problem' (1988, pp. 1–19). The owner-managers' approach also confirms Coleman's insight that it is rational to decline short-term advantage, for the greater long-term social capital benefits: 'The function identified by the concept of "social capital" is the value of these aspects of social structure to actors as resources they can use to achieve their interests' (2000).

Third, the research findings identified that the ability to switch between intellectual paradigms; that is to move between the different logics of rational calculations and low and non-rational judgements were essential for managing work-based relations: too much of either would lead to failure (the rational fool at one extremity, who can't maintain relations, to the over socialised 'soft-touch' at the other polarity who will be targeted and exploited in the marketplace). Thus the successful management of social capital relations depended on an adaptive ability to switch between rationality and non-rationality, as well as being able to integrate them as circumstances dictated. This adaptive facility was necessary to allow owner-managers to tolerate and react to the ambiguity of complicated decision-making processes that are inevitable in a dynamic and evolving competitive marketplace: being consistently rational or driven by low or non-rationality would lead to below par outcomes.

This chapter will also be organised with reference to the research questions. Accordingly, the first section will consider the significance of rationality in relational interactions; the second section will consider relational non-rationality; and the third section will explicate the connections between rational calculation and non-rational judgements in the management of social capital relations. The chapter will then proceed to offer concluding comments.

6.2. RELATIONAL RATIONALITY: A MARKET FOR RELATIONS

This section will report on the first research question into the significance of rationality in the management of social capital relational interactions. At the extreme economic rationality can be characterised by a consistency in opportunistic and fleeting transactional relations, based on planning and cognitive reason with the objective to consistently maximise utility. Furthermore, this economic rationality strips relations of their non-economic content, reducing interactions to pure transactions, and there were examples of this emphasis on the primacy of rational notions of economic values in the research, as expressed by the following owner-managers:

> Good relations are not worth much, if you don't have a good product or service to sell. (Charlotte: 'H.P.')

> The most important thing is that you make money. And that your employees enjoy themselves at work and feel they are in a safe environment. And a safe environment starts by making money, so your employees can feel safe in the jobs they have when times are rough. (Karl: 'K.T.')

Further, the owner-managers were most enthusiastic to discuss economic rationality as underpinning their economic relationships. For example, a number of the owner-managers stressed that their relationships at work were forged under the competitive constraints imposed by the market. Neil's of independent freight operator 'HS' comments were typical:

> The problem with independents is just that, they are independent. I tried to develop partnerships, but they can't work together.

> I have given up after trying. Every contract, from a bloke in Nottingham to a national bid, always *** up, because you have 40 members with 40 different opinions. None of

them can be trusted: all of them have to make a penny more than you. They cannot be trusted; they could not split 50-50. They would have to make an extra penny 51p to 49p; they would rob each others' granny.

In overview, the owner-managers were convinced that in a competitive market, work-based relationships had to be based on rational economic imperatives: an understanding of the market consistent with theorists who argue that opportunity recognition is a defining characteristic or trait of entrepreneurs,[1] in terms of rationally calculating the costs and benefits offered by building relations.

Examples of this rational approach to relational interactions included a theme of being 'calculating'. For instance, Maria of 'Int' was explicit in her rational approach towards business relations, to build in her words, 'a favour bank'. However, even within this rational approach she admitted a non-rational physical/emotional motivation, in terms of being, '... energised by new contacts'. Further in her view the effective network relations took at least three years nurturing to reach a commercially valuable level, and consequently she emphasised that she would rationally evaluate whether relationships were worth cultivating on a cost/benefit analysis at the outset. Phil of 'P.B.' took a similar perspective on relational interactions, as he put it: 'Suppliers and clients would be considered just that. However I would want them to think that it was more to the relationship than this'.

Conversely, the researcher's observations were that owner-managers were far less driven by orthodox economic rationality than their words would suggest. The research reached this conclusion for two reasons. First, the investigation revealed that though there were examples when economic self-interestedness provided short-term benefits, based on economically exploiting transactions, this self-interestedness did not appear to contribute significantly to the much cited owner-manager aim of 'building a business'. On the contrary, the owner-managers emphasised to 'build a business', over the long-term required cultivating embedded, trust-based relations, which they acknowledged were the reverse of opportunistic transactional interactions. This long-term orientation also demanded a more nuanced approach to relational interactions than naked opportunistic self-interest. For example:

I would classify a lot of them as friends, not necessarily friends you go out with but friends you have banter with and pass the time of day. So it's not a deep meaningful relationship, but it is a relationship that goes beyond supplier or employee ... . You have got to have something that is much deeper. I don't get too hung up about much deeper but the idea is he will do something for me. (Nick: 'S.L.')

In synopsis, the owner-managers' viewpoint reflects the conclusion that just as firms who pursue rational economic utility (profits, shareholder value) are less successful than firms who aim to provide an excellent service or product:[2] being economically rational, somewhat paradoxically provided sub-optimal returns for the owner-managers in the long run. Furthermore, the research also established that while the owner-managers stressed self-interestedness, at the same time they understood the need for 'adding something on top' and 'going beyond expectations', to build relations for the long-term success of their firms. In consequence, the owner-managers held conflicting views on managing their relational interactions.

One can speculate that the owner-managers were desperate to avoid been taken as novices or unsophisticates, and this led them to over-claiming their economic rationality. In the researcher's view the owner-managers felt the need to stress their credentials as unsentimental business rationalists, to confirm their credibility both to themselves, and to others as serious owner-managers. One can further speculate that there is an expectation that successful owner-managers are economically rational to the exclusion of other motivations, and the owner-managers in the research were reflecting this view in their responses (see research questions).

6.2.1. Relational Marketing

The most transparent examples of a rational approach to relational interactions were based on marketing management techniques. In this approach relations were rationally planned and reviewed with reference to marketing methods. For example, POGO described how he rationally marketed and evaluated his firm's relationship:

> Personally, I also work with 'network marketing' ... Relations are everything, whether it is in terms of reputation and how the business is spoken of, or help of any sort.

> ... We market ourselves through relationship marketing, based on the things we have done for other companies previously ... From a one to six point scale, where one is the ones we refer to 'terrorists' who talks badly about your company, we want all our social connections to be at five +, talking only positive things about our company, and act as ambassadors for our firm.

In more general terms there were examples of owner-managers who rationally planned to create commercially valuable relationships. For example:

> When you are interested in other people, you seek their acquaintance, and they feel that you are interested. I was just in Copenhagen doing some work, and was part of

conference. At this conference I actively seek other people's acquaintance, by looking them in the eyes and walking up to them and introducing myself ... You need to be proactive towards other people. (Karl: 'K.T.')

Further, there was a recurring viewpoint that relationships could not be developed via computer technology, a view that contradicts web enthusiasts such as Nan Lin who have argued that the web has ushered in a 'golden age' of social connectivity and social capital (2001, p. 12). Thus although the owner-managers tended to be enthusiastic users of technology, they also took the view that relationships could not be mediated via computerised machine technology. This understanding therefore supports the conclusions of Cohen and Prusak concerning the 'Challenge of Virtuality' (2001, pp. 155–186), which is rooted in their belief that '... techno-utopians wildly overestimate the power of information technology to genuinely connect people' (*ibid.*, p. 20). In sum, computer contacts which were viewed as fleeting and superficial, for example:

I would say that we are much better with people than with computers. You can say that, in our industry, meeting new people and building relationships is the most important thing you do. So you won't need to pick up your phone, and start calling people you don't know, which is much more difficult, than getting to know new people based on leads and/or referrals. All of our employees are outgoing people, and are good at exactly these things ..., we will never ever lose the human/personal aspects with what we do, because we have so much respect for people in general. (Karl: 'K.T.')

The owner-managers' scepticism over the limits of computer connections also suggests that they realised that relationships require a 'human touch', or social engagement, which the web with its cold, impersonal IT-mediated communications could not generate. Accordingly, the owner-managers put a premium on 'face-to-face' and other social interactions over IT connections. Furthermore a number of owner-managers considered that the essential human element in relational interaction was lost on the web, but retained via phone communication.

6.2.2. Relational Management of Identity Intangibles

Without exception the owner-managers understood the importance of their own and their firms' identity intangibles, which were referred to variously as their 'good name', 'integrity', or in terms of 'goodwill', 'social status' or 'social standing', which collectively can be thought of the owner-manager's reputation. The research therefore confirmed that for owner-managers:

'Reputation is viewed as a valuable social resource, to be protected and promoted' (Lin, 1999, p. 55). For example, according to Phil of the eponymous, 'P.B.': 'The only thing that matters in my industry is reputation: it leads to increased work, leading to a higher turnover'.

The owner-managers were also most enthusiastic to delineate their understanding of reputation management from a rational perspective. For example:

> The problem here is reputation for what and with whom. I frankly do not care what people think or feel about me or my business image. The business has been created to generate income for a quality product. The only reputation that we will be measured by is customer loyalty. (Steve: 'P.S.')

In addition, the research highlighted that the owner-managers were driven by the understanding that their commercial identity, or reputation was a fluid business resource, which accumulated over time but could easily evaporate, for instance if crises were not correctly managed. Thus from this rational perspective reputation was understood as a fragile intangible asset, in that a single event could obliterate the kudos build up over the long term: as Neil of 'A.T.' succinctly put it: 'Reputation is brittle; you're only as good as your last job'.

Reflecting their avowedly rational view of the market, one theme expressed by the owner-managers emphasised that intangible identity assets could be planned and managed in the short term. The following statements give an indication of the planned rational approach to managing reputation and relationships based on this assumption:

> To build a reputation you have to constantly network and schmooze … Doing the best parties I could and improving every time … Handing out flyers so that every person I had contact with took home my contact details for the future. (Phil Burns: 'P.B.')

> I always aim to over spend time with client, even on modest contract. Also never point the finger a clients to highlight their problem areas. It's also a good idea to advise clients on issues outside our core deliverable, to make the decision maker appear valuable. (Steve: 'A.G.')

Thus there were a number of owner-managers who rationally cultivated their reputation by managing key relationships. Another example was Neil of 'A.T.' who emphasised that he concentrated on building, '… connections with fitters not with firms'. In his view fitters tended to be transient employees, changing employer on a regular basis and therefore it was vital to develop on-going relationships with fitters, which would continue when they moved to another employer.

In synopsis, this planned rational approach accords with the view that '... not all connections connect us to resources that matter' (Briggs, 2004, p. 152), in the sense that the owner-managers targeted the relationships which provided them with the most resources, to the detriment of avoiding connections with less resource-rich relationships. For example, George of 'C.W.' elaborated how he aimed to 'create a buzz' building word of mouth marketing, by identifying opinion leaders from his potential client networks. In his view the key people in nightclub promotions for students were the captains of university sports teams and entertainment journalists on student newspapers. To target these key individuals George had a range of calculative strategies towards fostering ties with these individuals, such as tempting them with free entry, free drinks and other incentives for his nightclub events. George reckoned these high-profile individuals would bring with them networks of individuals who would prove to be lucrative customers, both at the door and at the bar. He also argued that 'post event' these individuals would network and spread positive word of mouth about his promotions, thus enhancing his firm's reputation. George therefore was acting in accordance with the theoretical insight that the key to building a reputation is to establish a gossip chain, to build the right buzz (Burt, 2005, pp. 217–218).

Moreover, to a significant extent the research findings confirm Burt's first reputation hypothesis (2005, pp. 166–181). For instance, when the owner-managers argued that their actions were reflected in their reputation or social standing, they were consistent with Burt's 'bandwidth hypothesis', in which reputation reflects the ego's qualities and actions, in the sense that the individual owns and controls their individual reputation (*ibid.*, pp. 174–175) (see Chapter 2.14.2).

However, at the same time as emphasising the role of rationally in promoting their reputation, the owner-managers were also acutely aware that managing intangibles was subject to phenomena beyond their control. Thus they acknowledged the limits of rational planning and management. For example:

> You are subject to many things in business, and there are loads of crooks out there. You must not be naïve, and think that your position or reputation is on safe grounds. It can be attacked by anyone from anywhere, all the time. But this is one of the risks you take. (George: 'L.S.')

The research further highlighted that the relational rationality of managing identity or reputation were invariably tinged with human factors. For example, David of 'R-Ices' and George of 'C.W.' both commented that running a commercially successful business had given them a sense of recognition and self-worth, and these self-evaluations informed their approach to developing relations directed towards enhancing their firms' credibility and reputation. George, for instance stated he had grown in self-confidence, just as his firm had grown, and this newly acquired self-confidence fed into his assuredness in cultivating work relationships: George elaborated that he was more 'forward' in rationally identifying and then approaching individuals who he had evaluated as being potentially valuable for his firm. In his words he had developed, 'a lot more front about himself' as his firm prospered. George's understanding is consistent moreover, with Abraham Maslow's humanistic psychology, and with Cohen and Prusak's observation that: 'Most people derive a substantial part of their self-esteem from their work and work-life' (2001, p. 49).

6.2.3. Managing Relations and Gossip

The majority of the owner-managers could point to examples when rivals or disgruntled stakeholders had gossiped to the detriment of their firms. Maria of 'Int' summed up the most prevalent response to negative word of mouth: 'Just ignore it: it goes with the territory, there's nothing you can do about it so concentrate on your own business and leave them to it'. Another example was given by Carolyn of 'Alchemy':

> Local paper ran some articles which were fuelled by local competitors who didn't like what we were doing … . Its not a nice feeling, but when people come and visit and see what we are doing then they are usually really supportive.

There were also a minority of entrepreneurs who responded directly to negative 'word of mouth' with a rational focused retort. For example,

> Yes. Individual implied that our success was in someway underhand. Hit the accusation immediately, got a retraction. Limited/no long-term damage because it was so far from what our ethics shows how we operate. (Steve: 'A.G.')

Anthony of 'S.D.' also recalled during the start-up phase of 'S.D.' that:

> There were issues with an established competitor. Our close rival traded opposite (the high street) and didn't like us being a discounter – they clearly didn't like us being a discounter and reacted negatively and in a hostile manner – they were certainly down-grading our business, badmouthing us spreading the word that we couldn't survive charging such low prices.

> We responded that by informing our customers that we were here to stay, that we intended to stick around, but we didn't overplay it.

In summary, the overwhelming response was to either ignore negative gossip or to respond in a limited way. These responses were based on the view that individual owner-managers were almost powerless to stop gossip and that from a rational cost/benefit analysis it wasn't worth the resource commitments to respond. However, the instances when owner-managers responded to negative gossip were based on a mixture of motivations. For example, rational calculation motivated action when owner-managers evaluated that swift and restricted action would make an immediate impact to curtail the gossip. It is also notable that the owner-managers who had been subject to negative word of mouth associated these experiences with the start-up stages of their firms. To conclude, negative word of mouth was taken as inevitable in a competitive market and was only considered significant in the start-up stages before the owner-managers' firms had established their relationships and reputation.

6.2.4. Managing Relations, Identity Intangibles and the Limits of Rationality

In contrast to the rational premise that a firm's identity could be managed by cultivating the right relations, there were contradictory themes that stressed the elusiveness of this vital asset. This viewpoint reflects research over identity and reputation being dependent on an individual's freedom to make judgements: thus as being transcendently motivated (Pastoriza, Arino, & Ricart, 2008, p. 335). Further, this perspective is consistent with Burt's second reputation hypothesis in which reputation processes were beyond an individual's control, being sculptured by network actors concerned with establishing their identity with one another. In Burt's words: 'As we build images of people and events around us, we construct their reputation at the same time that we construct a sense of ourselves, making claims to a reputation of our own' (*ibid.*, pp. 174–175) (see Chapter 2).

The majority of the owner-managers also understood their identity as being multi-faceted and situational, depending on the relationship in question. This understanding also reflects the view that: 'The more groups that you are affiliated with the more alternative reputations you have' (Burt, 2005, p. 108). In the owner-managers case they associated with numerous stakeholder groups and thus there was an understanding that it would be impossible to rationally micro-manage all relational interactions with the objective of developing identity intangibles. The most prevalent response to managing the various relations was to regard it as a by-product of being professional (see below).

Further the owner-manager's perspective was that managing identity with rational planned objectives was futile. For example:

> Control its reputation? I would say that is difficult … You can do your best through good behaviour, but to control it … I am not to sure I am able to do that …? Yes, you can affect it, through good behaviour and by doing your best, but you cannot control it! (Nick: 'S.L.')

This view on managing identity intangibles accords with the view that the quality of relationships is based on stakeholder beliefs, as much as the actions of the owner-managers (Maak, 2007). Another example of this understanding was offered by Rob of 'F.B.':

> I would not say that you can control it, because you can't control people's minds and their way of thinking, however, you can manage it in a good way, and make sure that all the elements that needs to be present is present and so on, to have a good reputation. That's possible to do, but you can't decide what people are to believe. EG, I can't decide what you will think about me.

In summary, there was a distinct theme that managing identity intangibles was complicated, in terms of being both malleable by purposeful actions on the owner-manager's part, while also being resistant to micro-management by rational planning. For illustration, David of 'R-Ices Ice-Creams' was convinced that regardless of his efforts he would always be viewed by the villagers as the outsider, 'from three miles away' who had changed the much loved village general store into an ice-cream shop.

6.3. NON-ECONOMIC NOTIONS OF RATIONALITY

Granovetter describes non-economic notions of rationality as aiming at 'sociability, approval, status and power' (1985, p. 506). However, there was limited evidence that the owner-managers took these relational assets as significant in any aspect of their management, which supports the view that the entrepreneurial personality typically displays a scant interest in social approval (Chell, 2008, p. 167). This lack of concern for social approval is arguably because owner-managers lack what Shibutani has defined as a reference group, '… which serves as the point of reference in making comparisons or contrasts, especially in forming judgements about one's self' (1955, p. 109). The owner-managers in this research evinced no striking preference for any reference group, and in consequence cannot be considered as amalgamating to a sectional interest group: owner-managers were conversely characterised by their heterogeneity. Moreover, there was a tendency to view themselves as 'rugged individualists' who were content not to pursue any broader source of identification. Thus the owner-managers rejected or more commonly were uninterested in any process of: 'Identification whereby individuals see themselves as one with another person or group of people' (Nahapiet & Ghoshal, 1998, p. 256).

However, tentatively two examples can be offered of relational motivations that were motivated by non-economic notions of rationality, though both are contentious. First, a number of owner-managers had won industry awards and accreditation, which perhaps gave them status and wider approval. These awards included:

- R-Ices — Ice-cream retailer of the year (2008)
- IT Solutions — training scheme award and an Entrepreneur of the year award (2009)
- S.L. — 'VOWS' sector award
- H.T — Distributor of the year award (2006)
- S.L. and F.B. — Tourism Industry Awards

However, these awards and accreditations were not entirely valued as an end in themselves; rather the owner-managers also valued them as marketing material to promote their firms. For illustration, Neil commented that he had missed an opportunity to improve 'A.T.'s good name when the firm won 'Distributor of the year' at the NEC in 2006, '...with 900 in attendance, they announced the winner, started the applause but there was no-one from the firm to pick it up.' Neil also stressed that in his view awards were not that significant, but rather what mattered was a consistent process of building up their firm's intangible assets, which he emphasised depended on, 'consistently delivering what the customer wanted'.

Second, a small number of owner-managers discussed the significance of mentors. For example, David of 'R-Ices Ice-Creams' described the village's aristocrat (baronet), Sir Charles Inglebury as his mentor, while Kevin at 'Cogs' described at length the value of a mentor in offering advice, which he considered vital in the process of establishing his firm. The researcher did detect a note of prestige by association with these mentoring arrangements, however their pre-eminent purpose was understood by the owner-managers as being practical: in neither case were these mentoring arrangements socially based. A surprisingly large number of owner-managers also claimed literary sources as mentors (see Chapter 7 for a discussion of the owner-managers autodidactic style of reading).

6.4. RATIONALLY AVOIDING RELATIONSHIPS

The owner-managers demonstrated in a number of instances that they purposively managed interactions to thwart the development of relational ties. Their research identified four reasons for avoiding relationships, which were based on entwined rational and low and non-rational motivations.

First, a number of owner-managers reflected that they had declined to nurture relations and accept lucrative contracts or investment from investors due to their perceptions over power asymmetries. This reluctance to form relationships concurs with an extensive body of theoretical literature, which argues that vertical or asymmetrical power relations undermine social capital (Foley & Edwards, 1997; Fukuyama, 1995a, pp. 97–111; Putnam, 1993, p. 197). Moreover, another reason for avoiding these type of vertical relations, is that they, '… cannot sustain social trust and cooperation' and instead these, 'patron-client relations are characterised by dependence, opportunism and shirking' (Putnam, 1993, p. 174). In consequence most relations to external stakeholders are non-hierarchical (Maak, 2007, pp. 329–343), as there is a preference for homophilious interactions in networks; in Lin's words, 'birds of a feather will flock together' (2001, pp. 46–54). For example, Darren of 'P.X.' Applications Limited stated the reason for leaving his previous firm in which he had been a partner:

> We accepted a large investment from a supplier who we had develop a close relationship. But what I found is that it meant that our company was taken over by a bigger company, and it affects your possibility to affect the results, the entrepreneurial spirit inside you just disappears, which is why I left. I prefer to work towards my own goals, instead of other people's goals. It's just simply two different worlds for me.

Julia of 'H.T.S.' and Charlotte of 'H.P.' also reflected on their reasons for not developing relations with more powerful partners, to the extent that both had refused much needed investment and potentially valuable contracts. Moreover, in both cases the owner-managers were motivated by a combination of rational and low and non-rational factors, though as in other cases the owner-managers were more willing to stress economic rationality as their driving force. The rational aspects of their decision-making process involved wanting control over their firm based on the reasoning that: 'One of the risks associated with the pursuit of social capital through building commercial ties with larger firms is that the SME becomes, almost by osmosis, an echo of its larger partner, losing both its individuality and flexibility' (Thorpe et al., 2006, p. 56). Thus Julia and Charlotte were under no illusions that the relationship with a powerful partner risked placing them in a client or subservient position. The non-rational aspect of their decision-making processes concerned retaining control of 'their baby' that they had built up, even when it made financial sense to override these emotional attachments to their firms and form relations with more powerful commercial partners.

Second, a majority of the owner-managers were vigilant to avoid accepting favours from relational ties. More than one owner-manager expressed this viewpoint in the vernacular, 'there is no such thing as a free lunch'. This observation is consistent with Coleman's observation about favours carrying obligations (1990, p. 310). In overview, there was a widely held view that it was rational to avoid forming business friendships, due to drawback of being obliged to reciprocate favours and obligations, an understanding stated in the Ancient Sicilian motto: 'I don't do favours, I collect debts'. For example, Julia of 'H.T.S.' lamented that she had formed a business relationship with a leading Harrogate entrepreneur who owned a number of businesses in the town. Julia had sent her placement students to this local employer, based on an assurance that his firms would provide high educational and training standards. Instead the entrepreneur had exploited the students with long hours, poor training and low pay. Julia stated that she felt limited in her options, as this local employer was too integrated into powerful networks in Harrogate to confront without the risk of significant retaliatory actions with high costs to her college. On reflection, Julie wished that she had rebuffed the entrepreneur's initial contacts; in her evaluation he had exploited the relationship and consequently she wished that she had 'kept her distance', concluding that in future she would focus on short-term placement contracts, ideally with smaller sized firms.

Third, a number of owner-managers limited relational ties based on their sense of ethics, which can be thought of as a rejection of pure economic rationality. For instance, Karl of 'K.T.' stated that he had refused to join the Masons as it offended his sense of morality, even though he acknowledged that it would have provided a platform to develop valuable commercial ties:

> Yes, the Free Masons. I could never be a part of developing relationship like that. Free Masons or similar relationships, as that would be to sort of buying your friends.

> I choose my friends because I want to be around some certain people, and getting friends based on the way we are, is the most important things for us. In comparison to join into relationships and network with a lot of procedure and secrecy, and so on. I could never be a part of such a network, and I am very categorical on that.

Fourth, a number of owner-managers claimed to rationally select the development of their relational interactions in terms of a cost/benefit analysis, based less on financial than social and emotional motivations. In this instance the owner-managers preferred to form relations based on shared values and status attainment, especially avoiding interaction with lower status ties. This approach reflects the conclusion that individuals favour non-hierarchical relations (Maak, 2007, pp. 329–343). Furthermore, in these examples the owner-managers aimed at relational interactions with horizontal ties with an emphasis on discarding lower status relational ties. For example Nils of 'POGO' elaborated that his aim was to be able to form relationships with like-minded people:

> I try to identify the groups I attach myself to, to fit the sort of people I want to do business with.

Kevin of 'Cogs' was also assertive in contending that he aimed to be able to select his customers and other stakeholders: he regretted that in his start-up he was forced to be less selective, as his business had not been able to establish a robust enough customer base or general stakeholder relations. Kevin further questioned the value of maintaining weak ties, which he considered to be relationships with individuals, who: 'You don't really want to know – just exchange pleasantries and move on'. In his view the drawbacks of these relationships were in terms of them, '... taking more psychic energy to maintain, given that you do not share much in common with these individuals'. In Kevin's analysis these relations offered limited psychological support and consequently presented an unattractive trade off in terms of commitment of time and resources.

6.5. NON-RATIONAL FACTORS IN THE MANAGEMENT OF SOCIAL CAPITAL: THE ROLE OF CHANCE

The role of chance or serendipity was widely acknowledged with most of the owner-managers being able to recount chance encounters that were beneficial for their businesses in terms of developing relational ties. For example, Anthony of 'S.D.' recalled making a breakthrough during a social encounter over a coffee at a trade fair: he met a tin foil salesman who gave him an excellent contract to sell that product. Other examples of serendipitous encounters with business pay-offs in terms of forming relational ties included the following:

> All the time; everyone I meet is a potential client. I once got pulled over by the police late at night and after passing my 'breathalysing test' I sold them an event and did his (the policeman's) child's birthday party a few months later. (Phil Burns: 'P.B.')

> In Newcastle most people are discovered via personal relationship/social and references. Newcastle has a small village atmosphere, which enables this. Much harder in Leeds, no central location where key players meet, much lower social activity. (Stephen: 'A.G.')

> At the Mayor's Oscars we have made useful contacts and followed them up ... senior academics at the local university etc ... now also loyal patients, and they also are supporters of our social enterprise scheme.

> Also local charity for children with disabilities, we are now working with them to improve the oral health of the children. (Carolyn: 'Alchemy')

In overview, a majority of the owner-managers were able to point to unplanned encounters that benefited their firms, albeit in many cases offering only tangential returns. For example, Neil of 'IT Solutions' recalled how he was sold a good deal for office boilers and heating at a social event. Further this inclination to seize opportunities as they unexpectedly presented themselves can be understood as an entrepreneurial trait. It is also notable that though the interviewees aimed to separate business and social relations, the majority of them admitted that they were still willing to use serendipitous social opportunities to further their business objectives, which would further support the view that social and business activities are closely connected (Granovetter, 1985).

In summary, a significant number of owner-managers attributed their business success in part to chance encounters, which were also invariably linked to their instinctive 'gut' opportunity recognition that they acknowledged had nothing to do with rational calculation. For example, Sarah of 'S.W.' remembered that she had 'acted on the spur of the moment' at her own nuptials to begin a mentor type network tie with a kilt manufacturer for her wedding planning business. Thus, in many instances for the management of relational social capital: 'Frequently social encounters are the most productive' (O'Donnel & Cummins, 1999, p. 89).

6.5.1. Rationally Managing Chance

Chance by definition cannot be rationally planned. However the owner-managers did attempt to manage their exposure to serendipitous relational interactions, an approach that accords with 'The Strength of Weak Ties' arguments, as first espoused by Granovetter (1973, 2005). For illustration of this line of reasoning Granovetter stated that: 'More novel information flows through weak ties than strong ties' (2005, p. 34). Working in the slipstream of Granovetter's socio-economics, Ron Burt's developed the weak tie hypothesis in terms of his brokerage perspective (2005, pp. 11–28). Burt summarised this perspective as: '... bridges are valuable for creating information variation, while bonds are valuable for eliminating variation and for protecting connected people form information inconsistent with they already know' (*ibid.*, p. 25). Thus there is an extensive theoretical basis for arguing that while chance encounters could not be micro-managed, nevertheless by rationally planning to expose themselves to an extensive range of social interactions owner-managers were able to maximise their chances of serendipitous relational interactions. For example:

> ... in business you tend to meet someone coincidentally, at a conference for example. That happens a lot. To be 'out there and talking to people' is always very important in terms of business. When I work with people, however, I talk with them a lot to develop our idea and to take the 'project' further together. (Nils: 'POGO')

Another example was recounted by Aftab of 'Easy Tech', a scientist who prided himself on his reason-based logic. Nonetheless, he fully acknowledged that nurturing relational interactions was core to succeeding in the Middle East, and further he was adamant that these relations could not be rationally planned. However rationality did motivate him to socialise as much as possible on the understanding that this socialising would optimise his exposure to relational ties.

> I think for us the biggest positive thing is that we have met somebody in Dubai who got us notice within the education sector because they themselves had contacts. This contact came about through somebody else we had known. They said look this is an important individual, we recommend that you go and talk to them. The irony is we weren't even going to go to Dubai, we thought what is the point, but we went there, and because we met that one person they have got us acknowledgement now with the government, within Dubai etc. People know that these individuals, this is their skill; this is where they are pitching themselves at ... He is almost like introducing us, but because we are being introduced by somebody who has credibility in the industry and

the sector, its given us credibility, and that was just a chance meeting of one social contact knowing another. (Aftab: 'Easy Tech')

It is also worth stating that it was impossible to rationally plan the outcomes of developing these weak tie relational interactions; the owner-managers acknowledged that by socialising they would be presented with greater opportunity exposure, but they also acknowledged that the timing and nature of these opportunities were random and thus defied rational planning and management. In consequence these weak tie relationships should be considered broadly and in idiographic terms, as opposed to interpreting them with more specific characteristics, as is the case in theoretical literature where they are referred to as comprising bonding or bridging (Putnam, 2000) or linking (Woolcock, 2001) relationships.

6.6. RELATIONAL INTERACTIONS AND RISK TAKING

The owner-managers were prepared to admit that they had been less than rational in the past: in contrast they were less willing to admit present and potential future examples of their low and non-rationality. Moreover, this non-rationality was acknowledged as being most evident when the owner-managers described their risk profile during start-up processes. For example, Neil of 'A.T.' stated that 'buying out' his previous corporate division had been, '... a long-shot, a gamble', and Aftab of 'Easy Tech' regarded starting up in Dubai as being fraught with difficulties as: 'The odds were always weighted towards the locals'. Furthermore, managing relational interactions reflected the linking theme of non-rationality being bound with rationality. Aftab for example, recalled the significance of a chance encounter with a Dubai hotel owner that had been crucial for initiating network and relational ties, as: 'You need introductions in this [Middle-Eastern] culture'. He had then developed these introductions by rational calculations to form a personal rapport with key business connection; for instance Aftab recounted how he had studied books on falconry, as well as travelling into the desert in 'off-roaders' to camp, a Gulf custom popular for keeping locals connected to their nomadic roots. Thus, Aftab rationally built on introductions by researching local customs and interests to enable him to integrate more smoothly into Gulf-based business relations.

6.6.1. Relational Interactions and the Role of Emotions and Instincts

The owner-managers' emphasis on business-like (rational) calculations led them to underreport the significance of emotion and instinct. For example, Aftab of 'Easy Tech', an avowedly rational IT academic, with a penchant for reading his way to success, nevertheless admitted after probing by the researcher that:

> ... I'm going to be honest with you here; I go with my gut instinct. You always get a vibe about a person and I think that over there [Dubai] that is why they like to see us. If they get a positive vibe of you know what, this person is genuine. Sometimes you go into a meeting and think this doesn't feel right and whenever I go to a meeting I always think trust my gut instincts. That's where I told you we were given the opportunity to go into business with someone, but my gut instinct said this is not right.

The owner-managers also tended to introduce emotional words into their rational descriptions of their management. For example, David waxed lyrical on the 'Magic of the R-Ices brand', and Neil discussed at length the 'secret' of his firm's success as the 'IT Solutions Way', which took on almost mystical characteristics. Karl of 'K.T.' also described his management in terms of 'faith' and 'belief'.

> Ultimately, it is all about that you believe in the things that you can do, and that you in the end deliver as promised. If this is done, you are definitely doing business. You need to believe in what you are doing — its number one in fact. The expertise we don't have ourselves, we just bring in when it is required. We want the customer to have faith and believe in us, and we want to deliver accordingly.

Further, though most of owner-managers understood and described their firm's relational interaction in rational business terms, at the same time a number also stressed as an afterthought that they valued certain relationships for professional and social benefits. For example, these relational ties could serve to inform the updating of skills and for the social benefits of interacting with peers. For illustration, Roberta of 'Cosmetic Dental Services' described the social and professional benefits of: 'A peer group which met once a month in a pub restaurant which was organised by another dentist'. In part she joined this group for emotional support because in her words: 'I mainly worked on my own and felt isolated ... I felt trapped when working on my own'. Roberta's view was that although she worked with dental nurses and various dental technicians, as well as treating patients, nevertheless she felt isolated in terms of being cut off from other dentists. To counteract this sense of isolation Roberta maintained contact with the BDA (British Dental Association) to '... keep up to date with dental developments and for insurance purposes'.

Roberta's perception of being 'on her own' was also expressed by other owner-managers who commented on the social isolation and loneliness of managing their own business, regardless that they interacted with an extensive number of customers/clients and other stakeholders. Thus various stakeholder relational interaction were not enough to fend off a sense of isolation; to feel connected a significant minority of the owner-managers needed relational interaction with their peers, or other ties of the same status, which can be thought of as Lin's homophilious relationships (2001, pp. 46–52). For illustration Kevin of 'Cogs' stated that he valued the importance of relationships with his peers, for their emotional and psychological support. In his words these relationships comprised: 'A group of people you know well and trust gives considerable support to the entrepreneur who could potentially feel isolated'.

6.7. RELATIONAL RATIONALITY AND LOW AND NON-RATIONALITY

This section will address the third research question to consider the extent to which rational and low and non-rational motives and approaches to managing relational social capital were interdependent. The linking narrative of this section is that in the majority of cases motivations for developing relational interactions were complicated and integrated rationality and low and non-rationality. Moreover, this section will argue that owner-managers adopted this multi-layered approach as they considered it to be the best response to relational decision-making in the context of the uncertain, dynamic and often contradictory nature of the marketplace. These research conclusions therefore support Coleman's 'situational' understanding of social capital (1990, p. 302), as well being consistent with Chell's review of psychological research which contends that entrepreneurs have a high tolerance for ambiguity and a low aversion to uncertainty (2008, pp. 130–131).

This section will also emphasise that while rational self-interest, which in pejorative terms can be thought of as greed or a love of money was significant in relational interactions; more significant was the enthusiasm to establish a flourishing and sustainable business for the long term, which the owner-managers understood as a long-term orientation of 'building a business', combining rational economic objectives, for example to increase turnover, market share and profits, as well as in terms of building durable, embedded trust-based relationships. Therefore the owner-managers' views on managing relations reflect the following conclusion that:

> The motives that make for success in business are a commitment to, and passion for, business: which is not at all the same as love of money – a lesson that Lehman did not learn. (Kay, 2010, p. 37)

Moreover, the cultivation of relationships was perceived as a core growth strategy for developing intangible assets, which were universally understood as a vital commercial resource.

6.7.1. 'Being Professional'

The owner-managers approach to the cultivation of durable and embedded relationships was most frequently described as a by-product of 'being professional'. For illustration, George of 'L.S.' defined his understanding of being professional as follows:

> Do your job well, be in the game with the best solution. Take care of your customers and try to understand them, and be in dialogue with them. Be on the same level as the customer, and don't try to lecture anyone. Understand. Have respect for what the client/customer can do and what they know. Have respect for the things you are able to do and what you know. The things you can't do, is as equally important as the things you can in fact do. And don't try to act as something else than what you actually are, and don't try to make people believe you have a competence you don't have. We have seen too much of 'charlatans'. Authenticity, thoroughness, and quality, as I mentioned earlier, never goes off fashion. This is how you build relations.

For the owner-managers 'being professional' meant an expanded notion of economic rationality, so that short-term opportunistic paybacks were evaluated against the advantages of nurturing longer term, embedded trust-based relations. Underpinning this approach was an understanding that rational utility maximisation was a short-term orientation that could conflict and stifle a firm's success in the longer run. The owner-managers' view was that developing intangibles was not a straightforward process that could be rationally planned and strategically managed. Thus, there was an understanding that relational interactions could not be instrumentalised for opportunistic immediate gain; on the contrary it was assumed that trust-based relations would develop as a by-product of the owner-managers' attitudes and behaviour for being 'professional'. This perception reflects Coleman's view, '… that most forms of social capital are created or destroyed as by-products of other activities. Thus social capital arises or disappears without anyone willing it into or out of being' (2000). For instance, David of 'R-Ices, Ice-Creams' had cultivated relations with local suppliers, for the rational economic reason so that he could claim all of his ingredients were local and fresh, which he knew would provide his firm with an enhanced marketing profile. However, he also admitted that these supplier interactions had over time and repeated interactions moved beyond rational transactional arrangement into trust-based relationships:

> I'd say I have a good, trusting relationship with my suppliers because they are partners aren't they? I can't deliver if they don't supply and if it's not consistent quality.

David also stressed his commitment to being professional, in terms of the generous portions and the enhanced presentation of his ice creams. Further, he admitted that the customers tended not to notice generous portions and his expensive cone sleeves, and consequently he reckoned that could have saved money by cutting the size of the portions and by omitting to include a sleeve on the cone. However, in David's view the generous portions and attractive sleeve, regardless of the costs, were worth including as they made the firm more professional. This understanding of being professional therefore relied less on the opinions of his customers than with David's self-evaluations:

> … I sourced the ice-cream sleeves from Germany and Italy, 500,000 for each site. It cost me £10,000, which came straight out of my profits. The reason I had to get so many was because they were foil, they were the best quality and it was to create that professional brand so you come across as a bigger, more credible company than just somebody running an ice-cream shop.

Another example was Neil of 'A.T.' who argued that in his business keeping suppliers happy was far more important than keeping customers happy. Neil based this view on the reasoning that there were thousands of customers, but only a few suppliers. In consequence, though Neil contended strongly that he didn't network, nevertheless he was prepared to socialise to develop embedded relations with the managers of his key suppliers: he elaborated that it took time for these suppliers to 'take you seriously' and it was only be establishing that you were 'professional and there for the long term' that they would 'develop any trust in your credibility to deliver'.

Further examples of this view of the nature and benefits of being professional include Robert of 'T.W.':

> You need to be taken as a serious business-person and you need to act professionally.
> You cannot do much more than that. Behave, act professionally, and make sure you
> know what you are doing, and that you are perceived by the environment as
> trustworthy.

Darren of 'P.X.' Applications Limited' also held similar views on the
importance of being professional:

> The benefits to our company lay in the fact that, if you make one company satisfied,
> this customer will talk positively about your company and the business that you do to
> others. When other firms see that what you delivered works well, with 'a little extra on
> top', it generates more business.

The commitment to being professional was also manifest in the owner-
managers' responses to setbacks. Charlotte, for example recounted what
she regarded as the most egregious crisis in her retail business. 'H.P.' had
built up over a number of years a thriving 'Christmas Club', in which customers reserved and made payments for Christmas presents. Charlotte
characterised these customers as 'her regulars' and also with a tendency to
be less affluent; better off customers just bought items in one-off transactions. The disaster was that, '... on the 18th December, burglars tunnelled
through a double brick, reinforced wall into the stock room and stole all of
the reserved presents stored for the Christmas Club'. Charlotte recalled
that she had been mortified, the financial loss for the business was significant; but more important in her view that her customers would feel let
down, and that consequently trust in her firm would collapse. In response
Charlotte described how she worked non-stop to find replacements for the
stolen reserved items. This was extremely difficult as most of the reserved
items were toys, which had sold out in the warehouses by late December.
Charlotte agreed that legally she wasn't sure whether or not she was
responsible for replacing the items, however in her evaluation legal considerations were not the priority or even germane; what mattered was maintaining the trust of her customers. Charlotte concluded that thanks to her
unstinting efforts most of the customers were happy with replacement
items, or with a full refund along with an additional item. Charlotte also
recalled that she had subsequently reinforced the double brick walls of her
storage area with a metal plate, which served its purpose the following year
when burglars again breached the double brick wall but failed to penetrate
the metal sheet of her premises.

Aftab of 'Easy Tech' detailed another example of the extent that owner-managers valued their intangible assets for professionalism and their good name. Aftab recounted that a Saudi partner, 'made promises' for a substantial contract. Aftab recounted, 'with my over-trusting nature' took these promises at face value, and was crest-fallen when the contract was cancelled at short notice. Aftab elaborated by detailing his emotions of shame, embarrassment, as well as the fear that his good name for professionalism would be forever tarnished. Nevertheless, he forced himself to confront his sub-contractors, 'though acutely embarrassed' to offer profuse apologies, fully expecting these meetings to be confrontational and extremely unpleasant. In his words:

> I did go to everybody and say look I am genuinely sorry. I said look I genuinely took this person at face value that this was going to happen, and I said look if anything ever comes again, you know, but I will make sure that everything is signed now in tablets of stone before I come and see you again. Most people were understanding and said that's a shame, but good luck. I myself felt the embarrassment and to be honest now, with that individual, I don't take him at face value now.

> What my friend said was that over there they tell you half-truths and what you have to learn to filter out is; what is the key message? There is always a subtext. I am learning the skill, I wouldn't say I am adept at it yet but that is something that I need to learn that in a social setting there is subtext, and quite often that is more paramount than the verbal conversation you actually have. There are variables at play that neither party has any control over. I would love it if we lived in a world where people were a little bit more honest.

The lesson that Aftab took from the disappointment was that Saudi's deal in, 'half-truths and sub-texts' and that the only way to decipher these 'half-truths and sub-texts' was through social interactions over time, as Aftab put it: 'You have to learn the Middle Eastern customs'.

6.7.2. Managing Trust

The owner-managers' perspective on trust was to regard it as being closely related, or as a sub-dimension of being professional. Thus, there was a general viewpoint that being professional involved appreciating the importance of trust in relational interaction. Further, in most instances the owner-managers took an optimistic perspective on the human personality, reasoning that it was better to start-off from the understanding that most individuals could be trusted, as far as the context would permit. Conversely, to approach relational interaction from the viewpoint that individuals could not be trusted was considered 'bad business and un-professional' (Paul: 'S.I.' Property). At the same time however, the owner-managers' understanding of relational trust was nuanced and heavily context dependent, confirming Cohen and Prusak's observations that:

> Trust is largely situational: a particular person may be quite trustworthy in one set of circumstances, but not in another, where particular pressures, temptations, fears, or confusion may make him unreliable. (2001, p. 30)

For example, Kevin of 'Cogs' understood trust as a relative construct, emphasising the significance of situational or conditional factors, in terms of acknowledging that he was more trusting in his social life, as opposed to his relational interactions at work. Kevin was also typical in that he relied on his own judgement, without any obvious reference to any formal code or systematic reasoning in deciding how far to trust. For illustration of his nuanced approach to trust Kevin stated: 'Trusting someone to turn up on time is different to trusting someone with the keys of your house or with a £1000'. Kevin also stated that he didn't trust other owner-managers with commercially valuable leads, but he would trust his business neighbours, to the extent of leaving his office door ajar in a shared office building. Thus the entrepreneur considered that there are different degrees of trust.

It is also worth noting that though Kevin believed that most people could be trusted, he also stressed that he wasn't naive and knew that not everyone kept their word or behaved in a trustworthy manner. However, Kevin stressed that to approach each relational interaction from a position of distrust would be more taxing, and generally more disadvantageous (with the risk of creating resentments) than approaching connections from an optimistic assumption of trust. Nevertheless, Kevin was astute enough to limit his liability in what he evaluated as 'high risk contexts'.

Another example of managing trust was offered by Roberta of 'East' who described her interaction with customers as follows:

> Most of them could be trusted. However significant minority were bad debtors when for instance, cheques bounced. Pursued a number via a debt colleting agency that would pursue the debt through small claims court. One patient was made bankrupt and I was way down the list for payment.

Anthony of 'S.D.' held a similar nuanced perspective:

> Sometimes trust them, but had significant doubts about the integrity of one of our managers who I later dismissed.

Tom of 'S.V.' perspective on trust was also typical in that the owner-managers tended to approach their business interactions from a provisional or 'bounded trust' perspective; that is there understanding of trust rested on a valance of temptation. Further, to reiterate the extent to which individuals could be trusted was evaluated in an autodidactic way, without reference to any legal or moral codification. For example, Steve of 'P.S.' stated:

> Yes, you need to trust the people connected to your business, in order to make any business. If you don't trust your customers, you won't sell anything. And to not trust you employees would also be very sad … It would have been difficult to go to work, if I felt I couldn't trust my employees and co-workers.
>
> Of course, if you look back at the bad experience we had with one of our partners who fooled us, it came as a surprise. Maybe it is a bit naïve … However, I have this self-fulfilling prophecy; if you live out your expectations that something positive is going to happen, it is more likely that it actually will.
>
> So, yes, I believe that they can be trusted.

In synopsis, in managing trust the owner-managers evaluated themselves as rationalist/realists interpreting trust as being contingent on circumstances, with an inverse relationship between levels of trust and levels of temptation: the owner-managers logically claimed to be less trusting when there was more chance of being cheated. Further a number of owner-mangers recounted how they had suffered for being too trusting. For example, Matthew of 'D.G.' claimed to have been too trusting to a number of arts and crafts lecturers who had, 'swindled him over their bills'. Matthew responded initially by 'blackballing' them and later by not supplying them with his best products, and also by demanding payment in advance.

Furthermore, there were a minority of interviewees who claimed that they found trust-based relations in the market context unrealistic. For example, George Wainwright of 'C.W.' stressed that with: 'Cash and an open till friendship meant nothing, you just couldn't trust anyone'. Neil of 'A.T.' held similar views on individuals being unable to resist temptation, and he argued that it was unrealistic to base work relationships on any significant levels of trust. This minority perspective on trust also accords with the research understanding concerning the heterogeneity of the owner-managers.

6.7.3. Cultivating Relational Trust

The owner-managers understood cultivating durable embedded trust-based relations as a key component of being professional. Thus being professional and developing trust were interpreted as being integrated. The most prevalent view was that trust-based relations would develop over time generated from a consistency in relational interactions, which reflects Putnam's conclusion that social capital has a historical or path dimension (1993, p. 179).

For illustration Nils of 'POGO' maintained that building trust-based relationships took time and resource allocation:

> The other thing I do is to build trust through long-term processes. You work together with people, and build trust in a way that people speak of me as a person who is good to work with, and I tell them that I enjoy working with them.

The emphasis on trust-based relations developing over time was also noted in terms of the owner-managers purposefully de-selecting relationships that were not considered trustworthy, based on their evaluations of these on-going interactions. The owner-managers were characterised by the view that it took time to develop and then to evaluate which relational interactions were untrustworthy and potentially exploitative to their businesses. However, the learning from experience approaches of the owner-managers was based on often idiosyncratic, judgements which contained an eclectic mixture of rational and low non-rationality. For illustration, a typical approach to trust-based relations was expressed by Rob of 'F.B.':

> Earlier I tended to be a bit scared about being 'fooled', but not that much today. I believe that we have been able to get rid of that sort of business relations. Today I trust most people I do business with, but it took time to develop these relationships.

Further, the majority of owner-managers understood trust-based relations as comprising a valuable intangible asset. For example, Lee of 'W.Y.' (body art supplier) was consistent in the view that in his sector what differentiated 'Wearyours' from its rivals was that it had developed a name that it could be trusted. Lee's opinion of his rival suppliers was uncomplimentary, '... they were all very shady', and he placed emphasis on his firm being known for its integrity, as he put it: 'My customers know I won't rip them off'. Daren of 'P.X.' also held similar views:

> The most important thing in business is trust. If the market doesn't trust you and have faith in you, it is time to pack your bags and go home. You will not ever make any business out of it. It's all about different variations of trust and distrust, and your success in business will be dependant on this.

> The optimal situation would be that the market trust you and have faith in you. Then you would have solid ground to build your business on and to succeed, I sincerely believe this to be the secret of success.

In synopsis the research confirmed that the majority of owner-managers placed a premium on developing trust-based relations. This approach to relational trust as a valuable resource taking time to develop is also analogous with Granovetter's observation that actors rely on knowledge of relations as:

> They are less interested in general reputations than in whether a particular other may be expected to deal honestly with them – mainly a function of whether they or their own contacts have satisfactory past dealings with the other. (1985, p. 491)

It is further notable that social capital scholars have contended that levels of trust are related to levels of social capital (Fukuyama, 1995; Putnam, 2000). Thus one benefit of developing trust-based relations, which the owner-managers implicitly understood, was that these relations would be replete with wider resource benefits that are synonymous with the returns associated with social capital.

6.8. CONCLUSIONS

6.8.1. Research Question One and the Rational Interpretation of Relations

Most of the owner-managers were strident in expressing the view that friendship and business did not mix. For example, the views of Anthony of 'S.D.' were typical: 'I haven't made any friends at work, but I never set out to: its business, I'm there to make a living'. Matthew of 'D.G.' held a similar viewpoint: 'The firm does not have social connections, only business connections'. Further, as already stated Neil of HS-Atic; Maria of 'Int'; and Phil of 'P.B.' also all stressed that work relations were predicated on rational economic calculations, which precluded the development of close social ties or friendships. These owner-managers argued firmly in favour of the view that connections at work were different from social or personal friendships, accordingly they were also at pains to keep the two separate.

This perspective can be understood as reflecting Albert Carr's view that business and private affairs followed different 'rules of the game' (1964), with the owner-managers preferring to keep the two 'games' separate. Further, the owner-managers tended to stress that the instrumental use of social relationships was borne out of necessity, with most of these owner-managers being uncomfortable using their social friendships in this way. Consequently, these owner-managers stated that they had striven to establish work-based connections as quickly as possible, so that their friendship relationships could revert to their previous exclusively social role. For example, Tom of 'Student Vinyl's: Driving Advertising Forward' admitted that he regretted his dependence on his wide circle of social relationships for generating business leads. In his words: 'Business and pleasure don't mix'. However, he stated that in his case he had no choice as it was only by tapping into his social connections that he could establish a client base. He also elaborated that a core business aim was to establish a robust enough client base so that his firm would not have to rely on his non-work friendships for generating leads.

In sum, a majority of owner-managers admitted that they had relied on previously established social friendships to establish their firm in the start-up stages, including Neal of 'IT Solutions' who commented, '... that he didn't know how you could start a firm in the IT sector without experience and social contacts'. This viewpoint was common to the owner-managers, who tended to admit that they had relied on pre-start-up business friendships to launch their firms: the prevalent approach was to use social connections in the start-up phase, with the majority of owner-managers also depending on family connections to launch their ventures. However, at the same time there was unease at the blurring of social friendships with work-based relations. For illustration, most of the owner-managers in the research confirmed that they aimed to limit the time that their social friendships would be subject to business purposes.

The owner-managers were also enthusiastic to state that they understood work-based relations from a vantage of critical market rationality. For instance, the most common adjective chosen to describe relationships was, 'colleague', which the owner-managers took as falling well short of being a friend, though perhaps more than a transactional interaction. Examples of the owner-managers' views on the nature of their interactions include the following views:

> Acquaintances, sent Christmas card and later letters which I suspect were related to me writing a reference. (Roberta: 'East')

> I see them mainly as colleagues. Owner is probably a professional friend. Always stay in touch. Mix with work socially, but not at a family/personal level. (Stephen: 'A.G.')

> Closer to suppliers than customers as no big customers. (Neil: 'A.T.')

> Not as friends but want them to be happy. (Paul: 'S.I.' Property)

In sum, the owner-managers were most ready to discuss their understanding of work-based repeated relational interactions within the parameters of rational calculation. The viewpoint of these owner-managers therefore stressed that it displayed a lack of reason to regard work-based interactions as anything other than economic transactions.

6.8.2. Research Question Two: Low and Non-Rationality Views on Relational Interaction

For the second research question the research highlighted that the owner-managers were unwilling to discuss the low and non-rational characteristics of their relational interactions. Further this reticence reflects a 'reason'-based view of the market in which success was overwhelmingly ascribed to talent rather than luck, though contradicting this viewpoint the owner-managers were willing to attribute failures to non-rational phenomena such as bad luck. In summary, the owner-managers tended to underplay the humanistic and sociological characteristics of their business interactions, in favour of rational economic realism in which rational 'market values' prevailed.

Conversely, in contrast to the owner-managers' emphasis on their ends-means rationality, the research confirmed that low and non-rational factors though scarcely acknowledged, were influential in the management of relational interaction. For example, a minority of owner-managers, after reflection agreed that they maintained relationships that had no economic utility, including the most successful owner-manager researched, Neal of 'IT Solutions' (a self-made multi-millionaire), who stated that he 'moved in different circles' from when he launched his business. However, he reflected that he still stayed in contact with the start-up owner-managers he had met at Leeds Met's incubator, even though he realised: 'There was no financial reason for him to maintain these contacts'. On further questioning by the researcher he mused that he maintained these contacts out of loyalty to the incubator, and also because he had made an emotional attachment, based on shared start-up experiences with these less successful owner-managers. In Neil's words these relationships had turned into 'habitual friendships'.

In terms of theory these non-economically motivated social ties reflect Fukuyama conclusion over the significance of 'spontaneous sociability' (1995), which functions as an economic asset for facilitating trust-based relations, based on cultural evaluations that are not derived from economic notions of utility maximisation.

6.8.3. Research Question Three: Rationality and Low and Non-Rationality in Understanding Relational Interaction

The previous sections have reported that the owner-managers were effusive in emphasising their rationality, while at the same time underestimating the significance of their low and non-rationality in their relational interactions. Further when these interpretations were investigated and explored in depth, most of the research population were prepared to volunteer the perspective that their rational motives were inseparable from their intuitive, emotional and other humanistic and instinctive motivations. One example of this duality of rational and non-rational motivations, was stated by Matthew of 'D.G.', who described a work relationship with reference to being a friend; but also with reference to a rational-based view of interaction:

> Me and one other person founded the business. He is partner, a colleague, and a friend; but we don't have a personal relationship. He is like an acquaintance. And it is the same way with the others as well. No one has anything to do with each other on a personal level.

Another example of an understanding of work relations that involved rational and non-rational perspectives was offered by Steve of 'A.G.' IT Limited, in his view:

> Some customers become your friends, while others are acquaintances, and some of them are just business relations. It is all very different in our profession. Of course, some of them you get to know better than others ...

> In fact, there are many expressions that cover our work relations.

Nils of 'POGO' also acknowledged that he understood business relationships as different from social friendships, at the same time though he didn't just interpret these interactions as rational economic transactions; there was a concurrent human, non-rational element present:

> We use the word collaborator, and in fact, on some occasions the word friend. This is about permitting you to work well together on a business level, but having room for a good story and a good joke, and having a glass of wine or two without crossing any borders. It is room for talking about private and personal things, without getting personal.

Whereas, Karl of 'K.T.' detailed how he understood his business relations, with a focus on friendships:

> Because, the ones you can be friends with, you can also be business partners/associates with. If you have a customer, who you are really friends with then you have a good customer! And if you are not friends with a customer, than things are not the way that

they should be! And to be friends with a customer, you need to work on how to be one. You need to take care of your customers, just like you take care of your friends. They all need care!

This focus on work relationships being a form of friendship, although not the equivalent of a social friendship was a recurring theme, for example, George of 'L.S.' opined:

I would describe them as colleagues, not exactly as friends ... Well, not in a general term though. We were all good friends, but we were not friends on a personal basis. They were my colleagues or collaborating relations. There is a difference between personal lives and business. I feel it can be good to differentiate between those ... It's two different things. Although I respect them and treat them nice, I do not necessary call them my friends if they are my colleagues ... They all come and go.

Julia of 'H.T.S.' also described the nature of work friendship in terms of her views on her firm's employees:

I would describe my work colleagues as friends, which in turn might cause some troubles on occasions, while you at the same time are trying to be their boss. This is all about balance, and to make sure that your employees know that the things you say as their boss; it's the way it is. You are their boss. While on other occasions, you are just their friend. But you know ... Working as close with people as you do here, you become friends with them eventually, many of them at least.

Moreover, though rationality was emphasised, on further investigation the most prevalent understanding of the owner-managers was to acknowledge the importance of both rational and low and non-rational factors in understanding relational interactions. This dual perspective is highlighted in the ambiguous use of the word 'friends' to describe these work-based relationships; something less than a social friendship, but more than a purely economic transactional arrangement. Theoretically this understanding accords with the Aristotelian-based interpretation that, ... business friendships are instances of 'incomplete friendships for utility' (Schonsheck, 2000, p. 897). Moreover, according to Schonsheck Aristotle assumed a hierarchy of friendships ranging down from complete to incomplete friendship. From this perspective therefore business friendships can be interpreted as: 'Incomplete friendships for utility ... [which] are not based on reciprocal love of character; the basis is reciprocal utility, reciprocal value' (*ibid.*, p. 900). Put another way: 'In a utility friendship, a relationship is externally useful to both people' (Spence, 2004, p. 5).

Furthermore, it can be argued that on occasion the owner-managers' business friendships were more substantial than that suggested in this Aristotelian understanding. For illustration, despite the fact that most of the owner-managers categorised their work-based relational interactions primarily in rational economic terms, at the same time they also stressed that they valued professional and work-based relationships for updating skills and for the social benefits of interacting with fellow owner-managers and peers. For example, Roberta of 'East' previously discussed perception of being 'on her own', was expressed by a number of owner-managers who tended to comment on the social isolation and loneliness of being an owner-manager, regardless of their interaction with an extensive number of customers/clients and other stakeholders. Thus connections were not enough to fend off a sense of isolation; to feel connected the owner-managers needed to interact with like-minded individuals that they could identify with on a certain emotional, non-rational level. This conclusion therefore accords with Michel de Montaigne's presumption that friendship is the result of 'the correspondence of manners, parts and inclinations'.

Thus, the owner-mangers' perception was that to form deeper relationships they needed to interact with same status individuals, so that they could forge 'homophilious', relations (Lin, 2001, pp. 46–52). Further, it can be argued that these 'homophilious' relations were a form of friendship, as they provided a range of benefits as noted by Spence:

> Business friendships exhibit many of the characteristics of 'normal' friendship. Such relationships may not be the lifelong commitment to each other's character development necessary for true intrinsic friendship, they may be time and context restricted and not last forever, but they can be important dynamic relationships characterised by reciprocity, sharing information, non-substitutability, empathy, goodwill, liking and pleasure. (2004, pp. 5–6)

Finally, the importance of work-based friendships was also noted by Coleman in terms of the, '… information that inheres in social relations' (1990, p. 310). Thus Coleman drew attention to the returns of social relations. This information is an important resource, providing contemporary and contextualised information, which are key intangible assets that facilitate the development of tacit, experiential knowledge. In the vernacular '… the information that inheres in relations' can offer advantages in terms of 'learning the ropes'. This return on work-based friendships also corresponds closely to the skills based, difficult to codify, insider knowledge as described by Polanyi (1958). Therefore from this perspective developing relations to be more than pure economic transactions, towards a type of friendships had the potential to provide the owner-managers with significant intangibles, in terms of commercially valuable knowledge.

6.8.4. Concluding Comments

There are four key conclusions of this chapter. First the research identified that the owner-managers' viewpoints and words expressed an overly rationalist view of the market and consequently of their management of social capital. In contrast the research revealed that their management of social capital was characterised by a fluctuating (context specific) interdependence of rationality and low and non-rationality. Thus the research is consistent with the following conclusion pertaining to greed, which is arguably a pejorative term for calculated, self-interested, opportunistic utility maximisation:

> Everyday experience tells us that while greed is a human motive, it is not, for most, a dominant one ... Greed is not generally an overriding motive, even for the very wealthy. For them, money is a mark of status, a register of achievement — or the by-product of a passion for business. And while there are people who are obsessive in their greed, that obsession frequently destroys them or the organisations that attract them. (Kay, 2010, pp. 37–38)

It is also significant that there was a considerable gap between the owner-managers' statements empathising their rational credentials, and their experiences and more reflective understanding of their relational interactions. This is a significant finding because it suggests that research based exclusively on owner-managers' words and viewpoints, for example in surveys, will only reflect the surface rational perspectives of the owner-managers. In consequence, this research questions the validity of research into social capital based on surveys. For example, Clifton and Cooke have written extensively on social capital and SMEs, drawing conclusions based on survey methodology (2002, 2004). One of their key findings being that: 'It was only after considerable prompting that the SME's could offer any examples, usually to do with advice, that were not financially based' (2004, p. 112). However, drawing conclusion from this research it can be argued that owner-managers in the aforesaid surveys would overemphasise their economic rationality, thus offering a distorted perspective of social capital processes. In contrast this research has highlighted that owner-managers are driven by a variety of motivations as far as relational interaction is concerned: including emotional (the motivation to avoid loneliness) and sociological factors (the motivation for peer recognition). For example, the owner-managers in this research were driven by the motivation for, '... the human need for membership and identification, the satisfaction gained from recognition of peers, the pleasure of giving as well as getting help'

(Cohen & Prusak, 2001, p. 7). The owner-managers were also driven by sub-conscious motivations, which perhaps explained why they were at a loss to explain why they maintained certain business friendships that offered no business advantages.

Second, the chapter has identified the importance of being credible in order to facilitate trust-based relationships. Moreover, to nurture these trust-based relationships, the owner-managers volunteered the view, albeit reluctantly, that they had to expand their rational perspective beyond transactional relational interactions. Most frequently the owner-managers referred to this process as being 'professional', or in terms of being 'authentic'. In social capital theory Maak has expressed this viewpoint:

> For social capital to emerge a certain level of trust and sociability need to be established. This is only possible if stakeholders believe they are not being instrumentalized, for the purpose of maximizing profits but engaged instead to contribute to balanced values creation. Thus in contrast to the dominant assumptions in social capital research that actors are driven by instrumental reasons in exploiting resources for individual benefit, I argue that stakeholder social capital ... will emerge only if an organization and her leader engenders and communicates a moral motivation based on normative commitment to normative business practices. (2007, p. 338)

The third conclusion is that to optimise the accomplishment of relationships, owner-managers had to display flexibility, in terms of an adaptive capacity to switch seamlessly between rational and non-rational paradigms: thus, to be able to artfully manage rationality, non-rationality, as well as being able to integrate these different drivers of purposeful actions. For example, the adept management of social capital relational interaction involves rational calculation, in terms of a cost/benefit rational calculation on the returns of cultivating a relationship, together with the charm or other humanistic factors to cultivate key strategic relationships. Moreover, this ability to switch between paradigms is an on-going process, with rational calculations and low and non-rational judgements being dynamically interdependent. Thus the owner-managers had to be adept at paradigm shifts, between rational calculations and low and non-rational judgements. Further this conclusion is consistent with Granovetter's views on, '... business relations being mixed up with social ones' (1985, pp. 495–496). A perception he illustrates with a quote from a businessman about the 'give and take' needed in business. This chapter's view is that this 'give and take' encapsulates the flexibility needed to manage relational interaction. In synopsis, Granovetter's 'give and take' is another way of expressing the understanding that the successful management of relational social capital requires the adaptive capacity to weave together rationality and low and non-rationality, as well the ability to judiciously apply a mix as circumstances dictate.

The fourth conclusion concerns the owner-managers' viewpoints on their work-based relations, which were inconsistent and contradictory. For illustration, the majority of the owner-managers stressed the rational, transactional nature of their relational interaction. In contrast, on closer probing and also from conclusions drawn from the researcher's observations, the theme emerged that the owner-managers' more considered view was based on an expanded understanding of their relationships at work. This expanded understanding acknowledged the priority of building relations in order to 'build a business'. Moreover, this process required cultivating embedded trust-based relations, which in turn relied on humanistic non-rational judgements. Thus:

> Being known to experience certain emotions enables us to make commitments that would otherwise not be credible. The clear irony here is that this ability, which springs from a failure to pursue self-interest, confers genuine advantage. (Frank, 1988, p. 5)

Thus the research agrees with the conclusion that, '... we face important problems that simply can't be solved by rational action' (*ibid.*, p. 4). Furthermore, developing trust-based relations necessitated moving beyond rational transactional relational interactions, and this chapter has argued that these relations can be considered a form of friendships in Aristotelian 'friendship of utility' terms as already discussed. This understanding also reflects Ben Johnson's view that: 'True friendships consists not in the multitude of friends, but in their worth or value'.

To conclude, this chapter has highlighted that the rational choice framed theoretical perspective, which assumes an instrumental approach towards relationships has important but limited applications. It follows therefore that rational choice assumptions are not universally applicable to the relational dimension of social capital and hence the rational perspective needs to be applied with greater parsimony. In synopsis this chapter has demonstrated that owner-managers' social capital relations are too complicated to be reduced to a rational choice framework, being also characterised by a shifting and situational blend of rational and low and non-rationality.

CHAPTER 7

SUMMARY OF RESEARCH QUESTIONS AND EMERGING THEMES

7.1. INTRODUCTION

This chapter will present the key research findings with reference to the research questions. In synopsis the first question confirmed that the economic, rational approach offers a compelling yet narrow method of analysis for framing understanding into social capital processes. In contrast the second research question drew attention to the crucial role that low and non-rationality plays in social capital processes, which is considerably under-acknowledged in theoretical literature. However, question three's findings were most significant, indicating that the social capital processes were characterised by deep and often integrated connections between economically rationality and low and non-rationality. These finding are consistent with the view social capital is more complicated and integrated than suggested by the rational, self-interested method of analysis that currently frames theoretical research.

The linking narrative of the chapter is that rationality, which encompasses a family of theories (Kelly, 1995, pp. 96–97), is an incomplete theory of human motivation and method of analysis, and hence the rational perspective inhibits explanations of behaviour, by virtue of its claims for universality, which this research confirmed are overstated. Further the research identified that the owner-managers felt compelled to emphasise their rational credentials, in terms of economic notions of rationality which have been summarised as emphasising: 'Material self-interest, usually financial, [tending] to be a privileged justification' (Abelson, 1995, p. 32). In consequence, the owner-managers' self-awareness was stymied by their belief that the primary, indeed the only realistic and legitimate approach to economic interaction had to be expressed as being predicted on self-interested economic rationality.

This chapter will also detail two emergent social capital themes, which relate first to the owner-managers' business ethics, and second to their approaches to reading. The chapter will contend that these emergent themes are distinctive because they offer an original perspective on social capital processes, revealing the owner-managers' autodidacticism, which fastens onto and filters out phenomena in a distinctly idiographic manner. The chapter will further demonstrate that this autodidactic approach is driven by an interdependence of rational and low and non-rationality.

7.2. SUMMARY OF RESEARCH

7.2.1. Summary of Research Question One

The cardinal theme from question one is that the economic interpretation of rationality, derived from Coleman's instrumental theory of teleology (1990, 2000), offers a penetrating, but partial lens for understanding social capital processes. Therefore economic rationality's explanatory power is restricted to a narrow and significant area of social capital processes. Consequent of this conclusion is the view that claims for rationality's universal scope (which this book has argued are the framing assumptions of economic social capital literature) are erroneous: in social capital processes economic rationality is merely one explanatory paradigm or social construction, coexisting and interdependent with motivations and phenomena that can be characterised as being of low or non-rationality.

Further, the first question highlighted that economic notions of rationality were overemphasised by the owner-managers. For example, there was a considerable amount of a 'post hoc', 'Franklin's Gambit', hindsight rationalisation of decision making; that is finding rational reasons for decisions already made from other motivations (Kay, 2010, p. xiii). In this rational perspective the owner-managers' propounded the view that self-interested, independent, personal responsibility and initiative were the only way of surviving in the market. At the same time however, the owner-managers contradicted this economic rationality by acknowledging that their survival and success was significantly based on establishing networks and relationships predicated on low or non-economic phenomena such as trust and ties of mutual reciprocity. In consequence, though not explicitly expressed, rather than dependence on networks and relationships (suppliers, employees and partners) being viewed as a weakness, the owner-managers understood these connections as a source of commercial strength – which contradicts the core economic rational nostrums of atomised, utility maximising individuals. Thus there was a considerable gap between the owner-managers' statements of rationality, which stressed consistency in their utility maximising motivations (a component of rationality is consistency), and the reality of their management of social capital processes which were characterised by an interdependence of motivations, as well as by a pragmatic flexibility to adapt and exploit situations on an 'ad hoc' basis.

In theoretical terms this theme identifying the significance of economic rationality in social capital is consistent with Woolcock's summary:

> Rational choice theorists, for example, regard social capital as an informational resource emerging as a result of interaction between rational agents needing to coordinate for mutual benefit. (1998, p. 155)

The research also highlighted that there were occasions when owner-managers would deliberately avoid forming social capital relations and networks to avoid obligations. For example, a number of the owner-managers quoted the adage at the heart of economic rationalism, that 'There is no such thing as a free lunch', coincidentally a book title by arch economic rationalist Milton Friedman (1995).

Moreover, in terms of economic rationality being significant the first question findings are consistent with Granovetter's evaluation that:

> ... while the assumptions of rational choice must always be problematic, it is a good working hypothesis that should not easily be abandoned. What looks to the analyst non-rationalist behaviour may be quite sensible when situational constraints, especially those of embeddedness, are fully appreciated. (1985, pp. 505–506)

It is also worth noting that Ahn and Ostrom who are critical of the economic way of understanding life have argued that:

> Unlike first generation theories of collective action that presuppose universal selfishness, second generation collective action theories acknowledge the existence of multiple types of individuals as a core principle of modelling human behaviour. (2008, p. 79)

However, they also caution that these theories do not assume universal selfishness (economic rationality) is any more realistic than universal altruism (2008, p. 78). Further Frank who has argued in favour of the 'Strategic Role of Emotions' has also concluded that: 'Uncritical charity leads to failure' (1988, p. 34). Thus critics of economic notions of rationality have acknowledged that a degree of rational self-interest is evident and indeed necessary in economic behaviour.

The research also revealed that broader notions of rationality were insignificant, a finding that challenges the relevance of Granovetter's non-economic goals such as, 'approval, status and power' in the workplace, which he labelled in historical terms as the 'passions' (1985, p. 506). In this research, in contrast to the emphasis placed on economic rationality by the owner-managers, there was no evidence that broader notions of rationality motivated behaviour. Therefore, Lin's view that individuals are motivated to rationally pursue resources, which he describes as valued goods that correspond to wealth, including reputation and power (2001, pp. 55–77) were not evident. One can speculate that this lack of concern towards these historical 'passions' is connected to the owner-managers lacking a common and dominant reference group (Shibutani, 1955) as discussed in Section 5.2.

7.2.2. Summary of Research Question Two

You have to be a Little Bit Crazy to be an Entrepreneur. (Nils: 'POJO')

The second question confirmed that economic rationality explanatory power was curtailed by the owner-managers' motivations and actions, which were broader and more complicated than supposed in rationality's over-abstracted 'homo-economicus'. For example, non-rationality was evident in the owner-managers prior start-up networking, which was instinctive (Chapter 4), and low rationality was apparent in the role of intuition, encompassing both M. Polanyi's tacit, skill-based knowledge (1958), as well as other less rational evaluations: for instance the owner-managers invariably relied on intuition to select which start-up network events to attend.

Further the conclusion that economic action is not always driven by economic motives has considerable theoretical support. For example, Fukuyama's concludes that: 'Not all economic action arises out of what are traditionally thought of as economic motives' (1995b), arguing in favour of the economic significance of, 'inherited ethical habit' (1995b). Fukuyama view is that economic efficiency is a consequence of an embedded, 'pre-existing moral community working together' (ibid., p. 22). Burt has also commented on the various non-economic driving forces of entrepreneurs.

Motivation is often traced to cultural beliefs and psychological need. For example, in 'The Protestant Ethic and the Spirit of Capitalism', Weber describes the seventeenth-century bourgeois Protestant as an individual seeing – in religious duty, in Calvinist 'calling' – the profit of sober, thrifty, diligent exploitation of opportunities for usury and trade. Psychological need is another motive. McClelland (1961) describes the formation of a need to achieve in childhood as critical to later entrepreneurial behavior .... (1902/1992)

In entrepreneurial theory Schumpeter also drew attention to the non-pecuniary motivations for entrepreneurship:

First of all, there is the dream and the will to found a private kingdom, usually, though not necessarily through a dynasty ... Then there is the will to conquer: the impulse to fight, to prove oneself superior to others, to succeed fro the sake, not of the fruits of success, bit of success itself ... Finally, there is the joy of creating, of getting things done, or simply of exercising one's energy and ingenuity. (Schumpeter, 1912/1934, p. 93)

It is also notable that the owner-managers approached the majority of their network and relational interactions with distinct lack of planning, preferring to rely on previous experience of interactions (trial and error learning) for guidance rather than forward-looking calculation. Thus in most instances the owner-managers were inspired by past experiences, rather than forward-focussed calculation to drive their interactions. This backward, experiential wellspring for action therefore contradicts the calculative, rational planning approach, which is a core nostrum of economic rationality.

7.2.3. Summary of Research Question Three

The test of a first rate intelligence is the ability to hold two opposed ideas in the mind and still retain the ability to function. (Fitzgerald, 1945/1960, p. 69)

The research emphasised that in the majority of social capital processes, so-called soft phenomena were interdependent with 'hard', self-interested, rational utility maximisation. Therefore the prevalent approach among the owner-managers comprised a situationalist (context specific) entanglement of rational calculations and low and non-rational humanistic motivations and judgements. Further the relationships between economic rationality and low or non-rationality were complicated and dynamic.

In overview, there are two conclusions that can be drawn from this inter-dependence of economic rationality and low or non-rationality. First, the research indicated that managing social capital processes required that facility of owner-managers to switch between rational calculation, and low or non-rational judgements. Furthermore, though the owner-managers put an emphasis on their rational credentials, the research identified that they were also flexible enough to use their experiential knowledge and humanistic characteristics (such as intuition and instincts) to evaluate network and relational interactions on a case-by-case basis. Moreover, the research also highlighted that though the owner-managers were opportunists, rationally seizing opportunities as they arose ('ducking and diving' in common parlance), they were also pragmatic in this opportunism, tempering this own self-interest with longer term considerations. Thus the owner-managers did not exhibit the absolute consistency supposed in economic rationality: absolute consistency in any case can be understood as a form of fanaticism, a quality not especially associated with owner-management.

Theoretical support for this conclusion can be found in Granovetter's assertions over the erroneous assumptions of exclusively focusing on individual motivations without regard to broader societal forces:

> Economic action (like all action) is socially situated and cannot be explained by reference to individual motives alone. It is embedded in on-going networks of personal relationships, rather than carried out by atomized actors. (1992)

In addition the view that the market is embedded in broader society has been expounded at length by Fukuyama, most significantly in his 'Trust, and the Social Virtues' (1995a), which argues for the primacy of culture and ingrained ethical habit for economic success. Moreover, Woolcock has also summarised the established perspective that individual motivations are subject to broader factors than the economic rationality's assumptions of atomised individuals pursuing material rewards as follows:

> Edmund Burke, on the other hand, had a much more pessimistic view, arguing that markets could not function at all unless they were supported by the "prior existence of 'manners' ... 'civilization' and ... what he called 'natural protecting principles' grounded in the 'spirit of a gentleman' and 'the spirit of religion'. Adam Smith took a more ambivalent stance in both The Wealth of Nations and The Theory of Moral Sentiments, arguing, on the one hand, that the market did indeed require certain moral sensibilities but on the other, that there were serious limits to the market's self-regulating capacity and its ability to produce equitable welfare-enhancing outcomes. (1998, p. 160)

The second conclusion for question three concerns the orthodox understanding of rational and low or non-rationality as being binary, drivers of action. In contrast in this research the relationships between rational and low and non-rational motivations were more complicated than a simple, impermeable separation, and in many instances were interdependent. Thus in social capital process discrete rationality and low and non-rationality motivated the management of social capital, while there were also many instances when these motivations were fused together.

7.3. EMERGING THEME ONE: MANAGING SOCIAL CAPITAL AND ETHICS FROM A RATIONAL PERSPECTIVE

One emerging theme that laced through the research concerned the owner-managers' understanding and approach to business ethics. First, the research identified that ethics was considered as significant by a majority of owner-managers from a rational perspective in that it brought business advantages and economic benefits. For example, Neal of 'IT Solutions' was convinced that his firm won business directly as a direct result of legal attempts to improve ethical behaviour in the market:

> In post Enron and Guinness types of scandal you are probably aware that Directors can now go to prison if they can't demonstrate that they are in control of their systems and their organisation so a lot more focus has been put on being Sarbanes-Oxley compliant etc. Any UK companies quoted on the stock exchange would be subject to Sarbanes-Oxley ...

> But most big corporations have got Heinz 57 varieties of technology and at Board level they just weren't in control. Typically a MD would be getting a report from one system, which didn't tally with a report from another and so the long term objective was to build a regulatory compliance system which did integrate management reporting.

Neil also stated that to preserve the 'authentic' business culture of 'IT Solutions' (which relates to firm's social capital) he was prepared to accommodate his staff's deeply held ethical beliefs. For example:

> We did have an incident recently with our customers 'William Hill', the bookies. They are growing in terms of being important to us; but we have a member of staff whose past was in law and he had worked for William Hill in a legal capacity. Morally, he believed what we were doing was wrong, and on the basis developing our staff being one of the most important things we do, we agreed to pull him out and have done and have found someone else to put in to replace him.

Ethical behaviour was also understood as being linked with rational economic benefits, on the reasoning that it facilitated the creation of vital intangible assets, such as developing a 'good name' and also for assisting in the development of a reputation for integrity and professionalism. For illustration, Steve of 'A.G.' stated that ethical behaviour was integral to developing a commercial reputation, with benefits in terms of more: 'Word-of-mouth referrals and less client churn'.

In sum, the preeminent perspective was that what seemed ethically reasonable to the particular owner-manager was also understood by them as being moral, which highlighted that the owner-managers viewed themselves as ethical, based on their own self-evaluations. The owner-managers could therefore be described as autodidacts, interpreting ethics primarily with reference to their own, self-taught understanding and perspective on morality.[1] In consequence, the owner-managers were inclined to follow their own judgements, which led them to ignore, to focus and to elaborate on whatever appealed to their individual evaluations.

Consistent with this view of the idiographic nature of the owner-managers' ethics there was also a tendency for their morality to be made with reference to two opposing perspectives. First, the majority of the owner-managers interpreted business ethics in terms of 'norms' or 'conventions'. This perspective can be understood as a rational approach to business ethics, and closely accords with Albert Carr's view of business operating under its own ethical standards, or 'rules of the game' (1964). Thus, in this perspective pursuing rational self-interest was considered ethical. This view of ethical behaviour also accords with Fukuyama's conclusion that rejects the view that the rational 'instrumental' use of relations is intrinsically unethical as follows:

> Market exchange promotes habits of reciprocity that carry on from economic life into moral life. Moral exchange promotes the self-interest of the people who participate in it. The sharp dichotomy that is often drawn between self-interested and moral behaviour is in many instances difficult to maintain. (2000, p. 261)

In contrast the owner-managers second understanding of ethics was predicted on the view that social, non-business morality was fungible to the marketplace: in this perspective social and non-business ethics were interpreted as interchangeable with business morality and ethics only operating in different contexts. This understanding of business ethics, incorporating non-economic perspectives, can be understood as incorporating a low or non-rational approach consistent with Polanyi's (1944/2001) and Granovetter's (1985) embedded understanding of the economy. For instance, the embedded nature of this ethical perspective was evident in a number of owner-managers who approached business morality with values taken from their religious beliefs (including Aftab of 'Easy Tech' and

David of 'R-Ices Ice-Creams'); or with ethical values derived from professional standards, grounded in expertise and conventions (including Roberta of 'East' and Julia of 'H.T.S.').

Further a significant minority of owner-managers managed to hold conflicting ethical viewpoints at the same time, in most instances without being aware of any contradictions. For example, David of 'R-Ices Ice-Creams', combined a deeply held business morality based on his religious faith, together with an opportunistic rationality in which he consistently sought to maximise his economic outcomes. For illustration, David did not consider it unethical to claim his business was world famous and had existed for generations, though he had only bought the firm in 2005, as he recounted:

> Trading Standards came and we discussed this about the world famous, so they were fine with it, because what's world famous? I ran it past my lawyer and he said as long as it doesn't change the actual impression of what the goods are it doesn't matter. You see if you called it much better than Walls, well then I'd be in court.

The majority of the owner-managers were also willing to volunteer accounts of rivals who had fallen short of the minimum ethical standards, as defined by their own individual moral frameworks. These owner-managers adjudged these rival entrepreneurs as miscreants, who would pay the price for their deficiency of morality in the long run, as they would be marginalised in the marketplace for lacking credibility. Thus they took a rational view on the cost of a lack of morality, in the sense that it would undermine the creation and maintenance of intangible assets (goodwill and reputation), which confirms the conclusion that opportunistic behaviour is antithetical to trust-based relations (Frank, 1988, pp. 1–19). For example, a number of owner-managers expounded at length on how they had been swindled by fraudsters, including Nils of 'POGO':

> The idea that we had was that we wanted to establish a network of flat screens all around Norway. We went with this idea, and signed contracts with various businesses around Norway, but we ended up getting burned by our partner who swindled us.

> When I worked in the Oil and Gas Industry, all of the contracts were very extensive, and at that time I found this to be a sign of distrust towards us and our business; but as a result on the experience I just mentioned, I now see that it is a necessity.

Another example of the owner-managers' proclivity to understand and describe unethical behaviour in terms of being the victims of moral malfeasance was offered by David of 'R-Ices Ice-Creams'. As already stated David recruited from his network of religious connections forged in 'His

Church'. In David's view the value of employing staff via church connections was fully justified, not only for providing trustworthy staff, but also as an efficient relational network for exposing dishonesty, as the following account details:

> I got this lady from church and later I was given an anonymous tip off from someone else in church, which was be very, very careful, something is about to come out of the woodwork. Then one day the takings were written down for the ice cream of £1500 and I thought that never, ever happens, it would always be £1489.01, so alarm bells started ringing. So I went to this person and you could tell they were being dishonest. Anyway, it came out about 2 weeks later that she went to court and has now gone to prison for stealing £130,000 from a lady she cared for. So I immediately suspended her on the court case and when it came to court, it was just in the paper the other day actually, she was sent down for 3 years. ... Sometimes I have got £17,000 in the drawer. But it wakes you up a bit: do you really know people?

Furthermore, to an extent the owner-managers' ethical viewpoints placed an emphasis on rationality, consistent with Albert Carr's, 'Game Ethics', as expressed in the statement that: 'The ethics of business are not those of society, but rather those of the poker game' (1994, p. 28). Moreover, these 'rules of the game' were more implicit and unarticulated than explicit, but revealingly when transgressed were noted and acted upon. For example, Neil of 'IT Solutions' recalled being furious with an interviewee for what he regarded as an outrageous and unethical breach of his privacy, as follows:

> About 4 years ago we were looking for a Sales Director and this guy had found my 'Friends Reunited' profile. When I wrote that profile back in 2001 I had no idea that somebody in a business context would even think to access that today, it sounds like a stupid idea, but this was 6 years ago and I thought nobody would be interested in that so I put some stuff in there but this person quoted it back to me during the interview. Well I was incensed and I was furious because he had overstepped a mark and shown me he had done that. That was my lesson.

However, despite the owner-managers' emphasis on rational motivations towards managing business ethics, there were a greater number of examples which could be most accurately characterised as involving an interdependence of rational and low and non-rational approaches: a conclusion that matches a pattern throughout the research. For example, for a significant minority of owner-managers professional and ethical values were understood as being integrated and mutually reinforcing. This approach encompassed rational motivations, for example in terms of maintaining standards to justify high prices. Thus professional standards could be rationally justified as these standards attracted a professional level pricing structure.

However, being professional also involved low and non-rational factors, to do broader notions of tradition and cultural values associated with the profession in question. Professional values were also tied up with the professional's sense of self-worth, and their self-perceptions over upholding their 'good character'. For example, a typical example of the owner-managers' views was expressed by Clare of 'P.G.' in her evaluation: 'You have to show character to maintain professional standards'.

Roberta of 'East' also ruminated that because she offered a 'professional' service it would be: 'Difficult to turn anyone away because it would be unethical and unprofessional'. Further, Roberta stated she had lost money through not having enough time to concentrate on orthodontics; instead she had registered difficult patients: 'Who didn't bring in much in the way of fees'. Roberta justified this uneconomic and therefore non-rational action, as she considered it unethical (based on her professional values) to turn away patients in genuine medical need. Julia of 'H.T.S.' also commented that she: 'Tried her utmost not to turn any student away', as it would contradict her ethical and professional values of giving students a 'second chance', and not writing them off for having failed in the state education system. Julia further stated that she had lost a considerable amount of money, as she wouldn't send her students to McDonalds: Julia was adamant that this firm was unashamedly exploitive towards her student trainees. Thus, there was a theme among the owner-managers who regarded their professional values as being interdependent with their ethical values.

There were also a minority of owner-managers who were vocal and forthcoming in emphasising that their motivations and actions were informed with reference to a set of religious values. For example, the aforementioned David of 'R-Ices', considered himself to be highly ethical as a direct result of his high-profile role and commitment to his church. Moreover, this understanding of the role of non-economic religious relations (in cementing trust-based interactions) has also been noted in theoretical literature in Coleman's vignette on trust-based relations in an orthodox Jewish community in the New York diamond trade (2000, pp. 20–21), which can also be connected to 'Reference Groups as Perspectives' (Shibutani, 1955). It is also worth noting that according to Putnam: 'The denser such networks in a community, the more likely that its citizens will be able to cooperate for mutual benefit' (1995a). David, for illustration commented that he was at ease in working with fellow church-goers, as they shared his values. The researcher also observed that David was teased by his employees for the clerical aspect of his management style.

For example, on one occasion when business was slow, the researcher observed David advising an employee at great length on a theological matter. In David's words:

> ... interestingly enough it's my family that run the church and I pastor a church. So it's all sorts of things relying on it, which creates all sorts of interesting dynamics, including trust and commitment, and also giving people slack. So I really understand business as an extension of social networks now because of that really.

There were also other examples of owner-managers who emphasised that they approached their business relations, based on a finely tuned moral orientation. For example, Phil of 'P.B.' emphasised his commitment to an ethical supply chain, to the extent that he had visited factories in China to inspect conditions for employees: Phil was in the process of sourcing toys for a venture to supply party bags to UK supermarkets at the time of the research.

7.3.1. Ethics and Social Obligations: Does Rational Choice Allow for Philanthropy?

It has been argued that: 'Fairness violates the normal maximising principles of rationality' (Lane, 1995). And the research highlighted that the majority of the avowedly rationally owner-managers were oblivious of any expectation that they should shoulder social obligations. On the contrary, the majority of the owner-managers tended to emphasise that their obligations were limited to establishing and developing a viable firm, which in their view would meet their obligations, in terms of generating employment and taxes. Further, this view is consistent with a rational choice understanding of social obligations, as most famously espoused by Milton Friedman in the seminal article that 'The Social Responsibility of Business is to Increase its Profits' (1970).

However, while a majority of owner-managers stressed that while they felt under no social obligations, conversely there was a rational business case for accepting wider social responsibilities. For example, a number of owner-mangers' acknowledged the business case for donating to charity, including Julia of 'H.T.S.' who donated money to a local hospital (from a collection box) at Christmas each year. Julia described how the handover of money garnered welcome publicity: the informal agreement was that the 'Harrogate Post' would send a photographer and write a caption praising the students, to appear as 'a good news story' in the run up to Christmas.

There were also a minority of owner-managers who considered themselves to be under significant social obligations driven by a range of factors; but common to all of these firms was the view that social obligations were not a business handicap. For instance Carolyn of 'A.I.' stated, '... we have proactively recruited local people, and particularly where there are language barriers we have recruited staff who can speak a range of different languages'. Thus, in Carolyn's case the rational business case and the non-rationally driven ethical case were complementary. Charles of 'J.R.' also stressed that: 'There is a social obligation for the security of our customers and for users not to find content offensive, which can be a major problem in our sector'. In his view offering a secure site that was guaranteed free of offensive content offered both a rational business advantage and an ethically desirable operating strategy.

A number of owner-managers also approached social obligations from a rational perspective, considering that broader social obligations could garner significant economic returns, in terms of enhancing their firm's 'good name', which is consistent with social capital theory that contends that reputation is tied up with social obligations (Burt, 2005, pp. 173–174). Burt's insight is that it is rational to support social obligations, for the economic benefits of developing vital intangible assets. In consequence, the extent that these rationally motivated social obligations could be considered as philanthropic is open to question: for illustration, the classical economist Francis Hutcheson (Adam Smith's teacher) '... argued that benevolence motivated by vanity or self-interest was not benevolence' (Ridley, 1996, p. 21). The most extreme example of social obligations being corrupted for self-interestedness was offered by Neil of 'IT Solutions', who recalled with disgust extreme unethical behaviour:

> I was working for (withheld) for some time and their massive sales pitches was the amount of work they were doing for 'Smile Train', which was a charity set up to help people in underdeveloped countries deal with cleft lips. They literally had a train with a hospital on it and they sent it around Africa and they done some tremendous work for these poor kids born with cleft lips. It would appear, and this is now in public domain, that they actually used it as a front to do money laundering into directors' pockets!

In synopsis, the minority of owner-managers who considered social obligations important were motivated by professional values, in the case of the educational and health service firms; or by explicit reference to their religious or self-generated personal business morality and ethical values.

However, reflecting the heterogeneous nature of the owner-managers Neil of 'H.T.' bemoaned that charities, 'hounded and harassed' his firm. One can speculate that this view perhaps reflects the investment background of this firm, which received private and government equity backing, on the proviso that 'H.T.' would employ the long-term unemployed in deprived areas. In consequence, Neil's attitude was influenced by the belief that he was already burdened by more than his fair share of social responsibilities.

7.3.2. Managing Social Capital and Bonding Capital

Chapter 5 has already discussed that the majority of owner-managers had no obvious reference group identity. Thus, identification, which can be understood as 'the process whereby individuals see themselves as one with another person or, group of people' (Nahapiet & Ghoshal, 1998, p. 256) was not evident among the owner-managers. However, while the owner-managers did not self-identify themselves as a distinctive economic or social grouping, paradoxically they had a tendency to be alert and wary towards Out-groups or individuals. Thus the owner-managers did have a reference identity at one level, though this identity was not connected with being an owner-manager, but related to deeply embedded cultural assumptions that were implicitly understood rather than being explicitly articulated. In synopsis, the owner-managers' collective identity was subsumed within broader culturally forged identities, which is consistent with Fukuyama's understanding on the significance of culture in the economy:

> As Adam Smith well understood, economic life is deeply embedded in social life, and it cannot be understood apart from the customs, morals, and habits of the society in it occurs, In short, it cannot be divorced from culture. (1995, p. 13)

Further, this research conclusion emphasising economic activity being embedded in cultural values, also relates to Putnam's caution over the promotion of social capital, in terms of it being, '... most easily created in opposition to something or someone else. Fraternity is most natural within social homogeneous groups' (2000, p. 361). In this research the 'homogeneous groups' were based on deeply embedded cultural and national affiliations. For instance, 'foreigners' could be excluded from membership as Out-groups,[2] which also reflects Putnam comments concerning race segregation as a drawback, of what he coined, 'bonding capital' (*ibid.*, pp. 362–363). For instance the owner-managers, while resistant to identifying with any economic reference group, were far more willing to identify and bond against outsiders who they perceived as possessing, or embody-ing, different cultural values. For illustration, the owner-managers made no reference to nationality, except when they had dealing with firms in other nations. For illustration:

> In terms of the Americans, I experienced that everything takes more time than you expect it to do. While you also need to be careful doing business with firms from other countries, when you as a small firm need to go through another countries laws and reg-ulations, which may cause you all sorts of liabilities. (Nils: 'POGO')

Further, while there were a minority of owner-managers prepared to admit the significance of their religious faith, the majority of the owner-managers made no reference to religious values. However, among the majority there were a number of examples when religious and cultural values were noted as being in opposition to the owner-managers' unspoken, but deeply embedded value systems. For example, bonding capital's Out-groups, in terms of religious and cultural values were described by the following owner-manager:

> We had an employee here a while back, who was a foreigner ... An immigrant ... and had a different perception than us on most things. It went well for a while, but in the end it did not work out ... We here very open with him, but it's all about having the same values, and that people have the same perception on things as you have ... People need to give the people around them a chance to prove themselves, but he couldn't or wouldn't fit in. (Rob: 'F.B.')

Religious/cultural values also could provoke this sense of the 'other' belonging to an Out-group. For example:

> I felt it was a social obligation to hire a person with a non-Norwegian background. We hired a Muslim, and my partner is in fact a Christian. I found this very exciting and interesting, but in the end it did not work out that well. It was in fact a very strange and unfortunate and sad experience. But, it had nothing to do with him being a Muslim; rather it was a culture shock for our business. I will not hire someone like that again. We first hired him because he was really competent, but he had a way in being which made him often to come in conflicts with people around us, and we had to ask him to do things in a very careful way, and he could just disappear sometimes, making excuses for his absence, and be hard to get in touch with by turning off his mobile phone etc. It was very difficult. (Karl: 'K.T')

In this instance the owner-manager could be interpreted as expressing views of 'the Other', or 'Out-group', which according to Edward Said's, 'Orientalism' hypothesis, understands that: 'The Orient exists for the West, and is constructed by and in relation to the West. It is a mirror image of what is inferior and alien ("Other") to the West'.[3] This view of 'the other' is also consistent with Coleman's view that social capital is most easily formed in opposition to an external threats (1990, p. 319): in this instance external cultural values can be understood as a threat to the dominant value systems of the owner-manager, which made him more aware of his own embedded cultural values.

To conclude, in this research the owner-managers' 'bonding capital' which tends to 'bolsters our narrower selves' (Putnam, 2000, pp. 22–23) or 'radius of trust' (Fukuyama, 2001, pp. 8–9) was based on sociological and cultural factors. Thus there was an assumption that there would be ease at interacting with ties that shared their cultural and ethical values, and conversely unease when interacting with relational ties with different cultural and ethical values. In negative, this viewpoint was expressed by Aftab of 'Easy Tech', who was astonished and disappointed by what he viewed as the duplicity of the Middle East's business culture, even though in his words 'they were fellow Muslims'.

7.3.3. 'Situationalist' Ethics: Managing Social Capital and the Recession

The final theme identified by the research concerned ethics being subject to situational factors in terms of the recession. This emerging theme highlighted the owner-managers' view of the economy as becoming more competitive in recessional conditions, and in this accentuated 'survival of the fittest' environment, less ethical than in more prosperous times. This understanding reflects earlier research, which noted:

> Relatively speaking, the recession is likely to have a greater impact on small firms than on large firms, as the survival of the firm is paramount. Consequently, ethical behaviour in small firms may be influenced and so fluctuate through times of recession and boom. (Vyakarnam et al., 1997, p. 1627)

In overview there were two broad understandings of the ethical effects of the current recession. First, the majority of the owner-managers' considered that the market was perpetually in a process of intensifying competitive pressure. Thus, these owner-managers claimed that levels of competition had never decreased, even in the boom times: the viewpoint was that levels of market competition, regardless of booms or busts would intensify, as this was the nature of the market. For example, Neil of 'H.T.' argued that technology developments had rendered his firm's previous competitive advantage (of stocking a wide variety of parts) obsolete, as with the advent of the Internet, 'anyone could order anything'. Neil responded to these technological changes by adapting and in his view sharpening his competitive profile to the intangible of being: 'Completely reliable; we always get the job done. The customers know they can trust us'.

Moreover, from a theoretical perspective the perceived increase in competition has been noted by Putnam, in terms of 'declensionist narratives' (2000, p. 24), which he characterises as arguing that contemporary market developments have led to less trust and fewer social connections in the workplace (2000, p. 88).[4] From this perspective a number of owner-managers argued that business ethics had remained unaffected by economic vicissitudes: in their view the recession had not changed their ethical behaviour, as the downturn's significance was a matter of degree rather than ushering in any fundamental change in competitive conditions. For example, Rod of 'D.G.' was adamant that his sector (arts and crafts) had always been unethical, for instance with customers deliberately damaging glass to claim discounts, in his words. 'It's a bitter business', which persisted without reference to general boom or bust conditions.

Further examples of economic conditions failing to significantly affect behaviour, ethical or otherwise, were identified in terms of informal, owner-manager partnering for mutual advantage. For instance to reduce transaction costs there were numerous cases in the research when the owner-managers would work collaboratively for greater efficiencies, oblivious of general economic conditions. Charlotte of 'H.P.', for illustration stated she would give other retailers leads for warehouse offers: in return she expected them to reciprocate favours. However, this reciprocity was framed by a rational business case, as these instances of cooperation were only conducted with firms who traded outside of her customer base. In her words: 'It was the right thing to do', to give fellow retailers leads, as long as these favours did assist her competitors: an understanding that characterised her views on business ethics, which mixed rational and non-rational motivations. In a similar approach, Neil described the complicated nature of 'IT Solutions' competitive bids, in that his firm would often put in its own bid, at the same time as mounting a joint bid with a rival firm, and the rival firm would also put in their own unique bid. Neil stated this was a difficult process to manage, in terms of ensuring that commercially valuable secrets would not be divulged in the joint bid. However, Neil evaluated that it was worth sharing a bid to reduce costs associated with bidding processes. It is also worth noting that Neil elaborated that he wasn't interested in destroying the opposition, even though the recession presented opportunities to target rivals, but that his aim was to develop 'IT Solutions'. In

Neil's view the IT sector had a set of values that disapproved of targeted manoeuvres against rivals, as he put it:

> A major competitor is (withheld) and there is a dozen reasons why I wouldn't want to use (withheld) in certain circumstances, but you feel you can't go to town ripping them to shreds because then you start to lose credibility because you have ripped a competitor to shreds.

In contrast, the second and minority owner-manager understanding of the recession was that raw competitive pressures had intensified due to the economic downturn. In the latter groups' view the downturn had resulted in stakeholders acting more cautiously and becoming less trusting in their interactions. For example, David Thompson of 'R-Ices Ice-Creams' commented that his suppliers, especially his farm suppliers, had drastically cut their payment times: credit was therefore severely restricted when compared to pre-recession transactions. David also noted the following effects of the recession:

> ... with some of our suppliers because we are now a relatively big ice cream producer and seller, we have been able to negotiate downwards on price to some of our suppliers. The reason I did that is I guess going into a recession and I don't know what is going to happen to us, let's see my cost savings. I was able to negotiate a significant percentage added onto the bottom line because I managed to tweak some of the prices to us. Now I wouldn't necessarily do that to the Estate [R-Ices] – because I'm not in a position to do it. But I haven't put the prices up on the ice cream this year because of the credit crunch as well. So I guess the answer to that is its multi layered isn't it?

Thus David was using the recession to improve his bottom line by rationally calculating that his supplier 'partners' would not be able to resist demands for cost cutting in these straitened trading conditions. David did not consider these actions to be exploitative, in the sense of unethically taking advantage of stakeholders' weaknesses: in his view he was just acting as a business rationalist promoting his own firm.

Moreover, in social capital theory a number of scholars have considered the effects of economic conditions on social capital. For example, the recession with its harsh economic conditions, relates to Coleman's notion that social capital is destroyed in unstable structures (1990, p. 320). In this research there were a number of examples when owner-managers were prepared to sacrifice trust-based relations and their social capital to ensure their firm's survival. Another theoretical reference to the effects of the recession and difficult trading conditions is in Burt's assertion that social capital is more significant in 'extreme network conditions' (2005, p. 225). Thus, these 'extreme network conditions' can be taken as the effects of

the recession, which according to Burt would witness an enhanced significance for social capital. For example, a number of owner-managers
commented that in these straitened economic conditions they had grown
more wary and less trusting, as there was increased evidence that their
interactions would be subject to less ethical behaviour. In Paul, of the 'S.I.
Property' words: 'The sharks out there are more hungry'.

Further, the research did not find any consistency in terms of the owner-
managers relying more heavily on their embedded social capital relations;
rather the reverse, with the owner-managers displaying a proclivity to being
more reliant on rational business approaches as a response to times of recessional competitive pressure. Thus, while it has been argued that in times of
stress people become less rational (Lane, 1995), for this research the contrary conclusion was emphasised by the owner-managers; that is economic
rationality focussing on economic notions of value was the surest way to
survive the recession. The sub-text was that trust-based relations comprised
owner-manager's long-term objectives, whereas financial imperatives were
an immediate, short-term response to ensure business survival.

To conclude, the majority of owner-managers understood the market as
in a cycle of accelerating competitiveness, with all the attendant downward
pressures on business ethics, which the recession had merely accentuated.
This perspective reflects long-term theoretical debates over the nature of
capitalism, for example in terms of the ethical effect of Schumpeter's
entrepreneurial creative destruction (endogenous economic change). For
illustration of this debate Fukuyama has considered the issue in a chapter
entitled: 'Does Capitalism Deplete Social Capital and Undermine Moral
Life?' (2001, pp. 249–262).[5] Further, while a majority of owner-managers
argued that they had not allowed the recession to alter their ethical
approach, there was also a significant minority who acknowledged that
these difficult trading conditions had deleteriously affected ethical behaviour in the economy in general terms, as well as in their social capital
interaction in more specific terms. As in the case of fraud, however, these
owner-managers stressed that they had been the victims of unethical
behaviour rather than that they had adopted lower ethical standards as a
survival strategy in response to the recession.

7.3.4. Concluding Ethical Comments

The research illustrated that social capital processes have an ethical
dimension because all network and relational social interactions have

the potential for moral components. However, the ethical aspects of social capital have been described as 'under-conceptualised' (Preuss, 2004, pp. 154–164), and the explicit literature examining the social capital and ethical interface in SMEs is limited (Anderson & Smith, 2007; Spence et al., 2004; Spence & Schmidpeter, 2003).[6]

The research also highlighted that ethics was significant for managing social capital processes in terms of the research questions. First, the rational approach to business tended to be most prevalent if the owner-manager took a short-term approach to business survival. Building social capital in terms of cultivating relations and being professional were understood as secondary for a struggling firm, with opportunistic ends-means utility maximisation taken as critical for survival. This understanding also reflects more critical views on owner-management which highlight the negatives associated with entrepreneurship, including Brenkert who has noted the, '... common motivational roots shared by entrepreneurs, criminals and juvenile delinquents. Deception, manipulation, and authoritarianism are often said to be behaviours exhibited by entrepreneurs' (2002, p. 6). The research further suggested there were 'situationalist' aspects of business ethics, with a number of owner-managers noting that the recession had heralded a decline in the ethical quality of network and relational interactions.

Second low or non-rationality underpinned perspectives on ethics and morality that derived from non-economic social constructions, including religious value systems or from personal ethical frameworks. For instance Charlotte of 'H.P.' recounted how she felt no compunction about selling bundled goods separately even though they were marked 'not to be sold individually'. In her moral code this was not dishonest, as she had bought the products and therefore it was up to her how she retailed the products.

However, the majority of the owner-managers interpreted business ethics with a mixture of rational and low and non-rationality, as well as an interdependence of these motivations. Further, the preeminent owner-managers' ethical perspective was that for long-term business prosperity it was essential to establish trust-based relations: from this perspective it was economically rational to be ethical, as the unethical 'opportunist' would lose out in the long run as they would be unable to cultivate intangible assets. Therefore, to develop intangible assets required a commitment to being trustworthy, as well as to maintaining standards of behaviour, for example in terms of meeting the expectations of reciprocal obligations. However, this perspective on business ethics was also driven to a substantial extent by non-rational motivations, which can be understood in terms of 'process benefits' (Lane, 1995, p. 113). In this research the owner-managers' statements and the researcher's observations indicated that the satisfaction of being ethical, regardless of maximising outcomes, financial or otherwise, was a critical driver of ethical behaviour. Thus in most instances, owner-managers were ethical for nothing more than the intrinsic satisfaction of being ethical: being ethical was its own reward.

7.4. EMERGING THEME TWO: MANAGING SOCIAL CAPITAL AND OWNER-MANAGER READING

The second emerging theme in the research concerned the majority of the owner-managers refining their management of social capital with reference to biographies, and guides to small business success, which had been written by successful entrepreneurs. In Kevin of 'Cogs' words: 'I want to read about someone whose been there and done it', in preference to more academic works which were regarded as too theoretical to be of any practical value. It would be going too far to say that these books were valued in terms of how great a fortune the respective authors had accumulated, though there is an element of truth in that assertion. However it is accurate to state that the owner-managers were not swayed in their choice of reading by academic credentials. Moreover, the owner-managers' reading style was autodidactic, thus replete with all the limitations that a self-taught approach entails.

7.4.1. Does Owner-Manager Reading Lead to Learning?

The majority of the owner-managers sought to reflect and refine their management of social capital from reading books written by financially successful entrepreneurs. In their view this was a rational approach to learning, as who knew more about being an owner-manager than self-made millionaire entrepreneurs? For instance the researcher observed that David of 'R-Ices Ice-Creams' had a shelf of books by 'Ben and Jerry'. Another example is Aftab of 'Easy Tech', who enthused over his (literary) mentor:

> To be honest, one of the people who inspires me, I don't know if you remember him, is Victor Kiam, of Remington Steele. He loved it so much he bought the company! He has such passion and drive and determination. Whenever I read his book I thought my god this is amazing, and it gives you that desire and that passion. You have got to have a role model, to me my greatest tragedy is that he has died, I would have loved to have

met him, because he has inspired me in so many ways ... To be honest I have read his books and articles and analysed his business and though you know what, I know what he is trying to say. He is very generous with his advice and looks at it from a very practical and pragmatic perspective so you know these are the mistakes I made, but here are some ways you can overcome them.

Aftab had also rationally planned to read books that he considered would enhance his firm's chances of success, for example, Aftab had read books on falconry for business purposes

One thing I can understand from working out in the Middle East is relationships. At the same time I have had to read up and learn, well falconry, because some of the people that you deal with you have to have something in common with them that you can discuss, I would love to talk to them about Liverpool Football Club, but you know ...

In broad terms, Aftab's rational approach to reading was summarised in this statement:

One thing I have developed, because I read a really good book on it, is listening skills. Listening to what they [Middle-Eastern clients] are interested in and then actually going out and researching about it.

Karl of 'K.T', also stressed his self-avowed rational approach to reading:

In addition, I read everyday. It can be everything. It's all true. I'm not joking. We don't have extensive network around our business, and large sales team. It is just me and my colleagues, and we need to make sure ourselves that we all deliver.

Yes we have learned loads. We need to make sure that we don't make the same mistakes that others have made before us! It is very interesting to read about other entrepreneurs that have succeeded before, and learn about what they did and did not do.

Thus, there was a theme that owner-managers', bereft of the guidance and training often available in larger organisations took charge of their learning in terms of reading biographies and management tomes written by financially successful, self-made entrepreneurs. However, the owner-managers' interpreted this reading from their own individualistic perspective, and hence their rational appreciation of their reading was subject to idiosyncratic and often low and non-rational evaluations. For example, Neil of 'IT Solutions' commented on one of his favourite business books[7]:

There is a famous book called E-Myth by Michael Gerber which is a text about the American dream of being an entrepreneur and becoming a multi millionaire. The myth is if you are very good at doing something then just by taking a risk with some money you will have a successful business. Just because you are good at something does not mean you are a great business person. There are lots of businesses out there where the operations side is quite weak and more of a sales and marketing machine and their delivery is weak or completely outsourced to somewhere else. You have got to apply yourself as an entrepreneur to each area with equal importance. If you don't then you will come a cropper. If you just focus on sales and marketing and get some fantastic leads coming through then you can't deliver and at worst you end up in court and your customer says you are a charlatan, I'm going somewhere else.

Neil also stated that he was deeply influence by 'Ricardo Semplar's' approach to building organisational culture and talked at length about 'Maverick!: The Success Story Behind the World's Most Unusual Workplace' (1993). In addition, Neil was typical of the owner-managers in that he filtered his learning and reading through his own evaluations:

I don't think you should turn away any advice or information from books at all, as you then assimilate and come up with your own way through. I was overwhelmed with all the advice and books available. ... the advice I give to start ups, is go to these events, listen to the advice and read about successful entrepreneurs, but don't assume that these business 'gurus' and millionaires know it all.

In summary, the owner-managers claimed to be either too busy, or just not interested in seeking out external feedback or expert guidance and consequently they were prone to draw conclusions based on any number of methods of analysis, though prominent among them were 'gut instincts' and other non-rational analytical evaluations. In consequence, just as relying on experience as a guide for learning could lead to mistakes being repeated, self-directed reading could also provide erroneous guidance. Further this research finding on the autodidactic approach to reading is consistent with observations on the idiosyncratic nature of entrepreneurial learning (Chell, 2008, pp. 259, 264–65; Lee & Jones, 2008, pp. 564–566). The same personal approach to knowledge has also been identified by Anderson, Park, & Jack who contend that new business creation, '... must also be inductive, requiring leaps in perception, and the ability to see things in a different way' (2007). In this research the owner-managers' reading style was characterised by seeing things in a different way.

In terms of the research questions the owner-managers reading style was in part predicated on economic rationality. The authors selected were always financially successful and the owner-managers were explicit in their aim of emulating this financial success, by identifying any key lessons to be learnt to forward their own financial returns. The role of low and non-rationality was more pronounced however, with a number of owner-managers' relishing reading about business 'mavericks' that had acted on their own judgemental decisions to 'do their own thing'. This reading was based on the archetype of the heroic individual who triumphs over more powerful forces/organisations. In terms of the integration of rationality and low and non-rationality the typical owner-manager reading style also combined this interdependence. For example, Aftab was rational in taking note of Victor Kiam's proven success with marketing, but his reliance on this source for as a fount of knowledge can be characterised as being of low and non-rationality.

CHAPTER 8

CONCLUSIONS AND RECOMMENDATIONS – EXPANDING THE SOCIAL CAPITAL PERSPECTIVE

8.1. INTRODUCTION

This chapter will draw together the threads of the preceding seven chapters to conclude on the book's distinctive contributions to literary, theoretical and empirical knowledge. The chapter will also identify areas for future research, which have been suggested by the research.

The book has already discussed in Chapter 6 its contribution to knowledge in terms of the identification of two emergent themes for the management of social capital. Furthermore, this chapter will present three additional contributions to knowledge, first in terms of a literary contribution, second in terms of its theoretical contributions and third in terms of its empirical contributions.

The chapter will continue by contending that the book has presented a distinctive literary contribution, as it has explicitly examined the economic form of social capital's intellectual antecedents (through which social capital developed), as well as the theory's relationships to broader socio-economic and political debates. The book has thus presented a single source review of the economic meaning of social capital.

The chapter will then present its second contribution to knowledge with reference theoretical perspectives, to argue for an expanded and process-driven understanding of the economic form of social capital. This under-standing contends that economic rationality is predicated on a false individualism, which overestimates the power of reason and misunderstands how individuals (owner-managers) make sense, experience and shape social capital processes. Further in this understanding, social capital's rational framing assumptions, which are based on the logic of consequentialism, will be interpreted as just one of many social constructions. Thus, social capital processes are not only subject to economic rationalism but also to low rationality (culture, morality, professional values) and non-rationality (idiosyncratic learning by doing, gut-instincts, avoiding loneliness, risk taking or gambling and process benefits).

The theoretical contribution will also argue for a new understanding of social capital's ontology, challenging the orthodoxies of dis-aggregation, and also of the subsequent framing 'econometrics' (applied neo-classical economics) and its consequent research bias towards quantification. The theoretical contribution will further contend that there is a flaw in the prevalent empirical method, in terms of the social capital research orthodoxy of breaking down and building up approach to the theory, as this research revealed that social capital processes are not readily disaggregated. Thus the research orthodoxy, which is driven by a Newtonian science approach that assumes it is more analytically rigorous to break something down into constituent parts, will be contested in favour of an ontological understanding that contends that social capital is more accurately understood in terms of interconnected, dynamic forces or fields rather than as discrete sub-dimensions. In addition, this new ontological understanding will argue that the prevalent levels and types of social capital sub-components are in any case one-dimensional and overly focussed: to reduce human interaction to bonding or bridging capital, or weak or strong ties is simplistic and ignores the nuances, as well as the dynamism of network and relational interaction.

The third and empirical contribution to knowledge relates to the research understanding that the economic form of social capital is 'situational' (Coleman, 1990, p. 302), and will elucidate these situations in terms of generic social capital management processes. Further, while these generic processes are not proposed as a blueprint, they nevertheless offer guidance for managing social capital processes. This contribution will therefore challenge the viewpoint that social capital is entirely subject to contextual variation, as suggested by a number of theoretical scholars (Rothstein, 2004), as being overstated.

Finally the chapter will offer a number of recommendations for future research, before concluding by weaving together its key themes, with an emphasis on the distinctiveness of the book.

8.2. FIRST CONTRIBUTION TO KNOWLEDGE: LITERARY CONTRIBUTION

The book has contributed to social capital literature by examining the theory's intellectual antecedents; its connections to contemporary socio-economic and cultural debates; as well as grounding social capital in contemporary interpretations of rational systems of thought (Chapters 1 and 2). This is a significant contribution as most literature reviews of social capital are limited to a narrow focus on current applications and to reviewing recent theoretical scholars.[1] Further, Woolcock is correct to assert that social capital lacks consensus (1998, p. 155) and consequently the validity of social capital can be buttressed by both identifying and reviewing its historical roots, and also by contextualising the theory's development to prevailing intellectual debates.

Moreover, there are a number of scholars who have attempted to eluci-date the intellectual antecedents and relevant theoretical traditions of social capital in the standards of social theory, though this literature is limited to publications by Portes and Sensenbrenner (1993), Woolcock (1998), Portes (1998), Patterson (2000, pp. 39−55) and Castiglione (2008, pp. 177−195). These scholars approach has been characterised as:

> … linking different aspects and sources of social capital to some of the main currents of sociological thought, and to modern social theory in general. (Castiglione, 2008, p. 180)

In consequence, this book has added to the underdeveloped literature examining social capital's intellectual history: the literature review is also novel in identifying the significance of earlier scholars as the precursors of the key social capital scholars. This contribution is therefore to add to social capital's theoretical coherence by identifying its roots, and by review-ing influences on the key theoretical scholars. For example, the literature review highlighted the influence of:

- de Tocqueville on Putnam and Fukuyama's social capital treatments, who both lament the passing of a 'Golden Age', when 'Americans played by the rules' in the immediate post-war WW2 period (Fukuyama, 1999, pp. 3−26).
- Etzioni (1988) and the American communitarian tradition on Putnam's social capital interpretation.
- Putman and Fukuyama's misunderstanding of Italian social history based on the flawed research of Banfield (1958/1967). Social capital

research in Italy has also been identified as significant in the development of the theory (Fukuyama, 1995a Huysseune, 2003, pp. 211–23; Putnam, 1993).

- Becker's human capital (1961) in Coleman's rational choice social capital framing assumptions.
- Polanyi's (1944/2001) socio-economics and embedded perspective on Granovetter, which is under-acknowledged in the literature that claims the latter as a social capital scholar.
- The philosophers of the Scottish Enlightenment (primarily Adam Smith) on the social capital ideas that economic activity is morally constituted and subject to mutual dependence.

Further critical viewpoints were examined that interpret social capital as a disciplining or consensual theory. In this interpretation social capital is understood as essentially conservative in nature, supporting the status quo in terms of rendering prevailing paradigm more efficient rather than offering a challenge to the core nostrums of:

> ... neo-liberal initiatives [which] are characterised as free market policies that encourage private enterprise and consumer choice, reward personal responsibility and entrepreneurial initiative, and undermine the dead hand of the incompetent, bureaucratic and parasitic government, that can never do any good even if it is well intended, which it rarely is. (Chomsky, 1999, p. 7)

Chapter 2 also established that social capital is in vogue as it complements a view of society that omits class analysis, while acknowledging the inevitability and superior efficiency of neo-liberal markets. Thus: 'It simultaneously obscures and legitimates wider social inequalities, and provides a lens through which the rich become virtually invisible' (Levitas, 2004, p. 49). In consequence, if neo-liberal markets are about 'getting the incentives right' then social capital is about 'getting the social relations right'. The review further identified that social capital can be understood as a deficit theory; that is it's up to the individual to acquire their own social capital. Moreover, the literature review identified the theory's intellectual origins, most transparently in its antecedents in the 'Scottish Enlightenment', in terms of moral sentiments balancing self-interest in the economy (Patterson, 2000, pp. 39–55).

In summary, the book has presented a literary contribution by offering an original review of the theory's intellectual origins, and also by contextualising social capital contemporary prominence to cultural and socio-political debates on the role of the state and the individual.

8.3. SECOND CONTRIBUTION TO KNOWLEDGE: THEORETICAL CONTRIBUTION – AN EXPANDED PERSPECTIVE ON THE IMMEASURABLE COMPLEXITY OF MOTIVATION AND ACTION

The author's prior experience as an owner-manager led him to doubt the validity of economic rationality as a universal method of analysis and explanation for motivation, and the research confirmed this viewpoint. Accordingly, the theoretical contribution is based on the research conclusion that economic rationality is highly idealised and abstracted. Furthermore rather than rationality being bounded (Jones, 1999; Simon, 1979, 1986) it is usually integrated with low and non-rationality. This contribution is predicated on the research informed conclusion that economic rationality's intense, but limited focus posits an overly simple and extremely individualistic and materialistic account of human personality and motivations. The rational method of analysis also assumes an unending process of opportunistic and self-interested competition that does not accord with this research, in terms of the owner-managers' experiences and more reflective understandings of economic interaction. Thus, rational theoretical assumptions give a distorted methodology and general perspective for analysing social capital processes. It can also be argued that rationality needs a social context to develop (see Section 7.2.3), and therefore rather than being a universal theory at the heart of the universe, it is more accurately understood as a social construction, among many other social constructions.

Another research-based conclusion is that social capital processes are paradoxical, in that conscious pursuit of rational utility is often detrimental to its accumulation: thus for cultivating social capital there can be advantages in foregoing opportunistic self-interest. For example, in contrast to their rational statements, the owner-managers' actions reflected an under-articulated understanding that naked self-interest led to sub-optimum outcomes: a conclusion consistent with Frank's insight that a self-interested person can't develop trust or commitment-based relations as:

'... the ruthless pursuit of self-interest is often self-defeating. As Zen masters have known all along, the best outcome is sometimes possible only when people abandon the chase ... self-interest often requires commitments to behave in ways that will if triggered, prove deeply contrary to our interests. (1988, p. 11)

Therefore the theoretical contribution is to offer an expanded dynamic and process understanding of social capital theoretical framing assumptions. The contribution is that to appreciate and analyse social capital processes requires an acknowledgement of the ongoing, dynamic and usual interdependence of rational and low and non-rationality in the context of the complicated, process-driven and interactive nature of economic behaviour. This is also a timely contribution, as it is no coincidence that the 'rational nineties' (Kay, 2010, p. 81) was the decade that social capital began its exponential growth (see Section 7.2.3).

8.3.1. The Limits of Economic Rationality in Framing Social Capital Processes

It is reasonable to assume that rational motivations would be accompanied by the rational planning of networks and relationships, however in the research there was only one example of formal rational planning of relationships (see Chapter 5). In contrast the majority of the owner-managers were characterised by their pragmatic ability to adapt their motivations and their decisions, with reference to contextual variables. Thus the owner-managers disregarded rational planning of social interactions and network interactions, as being unrealistic in constantly evolving and disorganised markets. Another reason for this lack of interest in rational planning, was the owner-managers' perception that social capital could not be planned or willed into existence (Pastoriza, Arino, & Ricart, 2008), thus they implicitly rejected the method that directly links plans to outcomes (to anticipate or plan the future is to attempt to shape it).

This scepticism over the efficacy of rational planning for social capital processes also has extensive theoretical support. For instance, Jane Jacobs, an oft cited founding scholar of social capital, elaborated at length in her *The Death and Life of Great American Cities* (1961) that rational planners never fully understand the complexity of human environments, and concomitantly that they were unimaginative in pursuing certain ideas and ignoring others. In her view individuals (especially rational planners) have less control and knowledge over their lives and events than they commonly think, and further they tend to misapply 'organised complexity' solutions to problems that require far more subtlety. Jacobs also stressed the difficulties of creating a community: 'Only an unimaginative man would think he could: only an arrogant man would want to' (*ibid.*, p. 350). This view is germane to this research, as creating a community and creating social capital involve connected processes of social interaction. Nicholas Hayek also argued against, '… the organisation of our activities according to a consciously constructed 'blue-print'' (1944/2001, p. 37).

Moreover, this expanded framing perspective is also consistent with the complicated, iterative processes of entrepreneurial heuristics and learning from experience processes (Chell, 2008, pp. 264–266; Jack & Anderson, 1999; Lee & Jones, 2008). In this research the owner-managers' perspectives, motivations and actions were often driven by their autodidactic, experiential learning processes (Chapter 6). This contradicts the rational paradigm because this learning was predicated on past experiences, as opposed to economic rationality's forward calculation of costs and benefits and utility maximisation. Further the owner-managers were usually unable to express how these ongoing experiences shaped their motivations and actions, which reflects Michael Polanyi's conclusion on tacit knowledge, relating to difficult to articulate, context specific, work-based skill (1958). Kay has also remarked on the significance of this difficulty to express, but vital knowledge in motivating behaviour:

> By lumping a bundle of things together under the headings of instinct and intuition, and contrasting them with a particular kind of rationality, by failing to acknowledge the central role that tacit knowledge plays in everyday human activities, we fail to recognise how good judgements are arrived at. (2010, p. 168)

For example, in this research the owner-managers were unable to articulate how to network effectively, all they could say was that it was an eclectic trial and error process, and that the more network events attended the better one became at filtering out futile meeting from the more lucrative events.

To conclude, the rational paradigm was contradicted in this research as the owner-managers were not consistent in their motivations, reflecting Karl Jung's conclusion that: 'Not only is "freedom of will" an incalculable problem philosophically, it is also an misnomer in the practical sense, for we seldom find anyone who is not influenced and indeed dominated by desires, habits, impulses, prejudices, resentments, and by every conceivable type of complex' (1983, p. 246). For example, one contextual variable was that of opportunities creating their own motivations, for instance in terms of a 'lucky break' serendipitously presenting an opportunity (see Chapter 5). This understanding is therefore consistent with Burt's view that motivation and opportunity should be treated as 'one and the same' (1990, p. 80). In summary, there is considerable research evidence that flatly contradicts the universal claims of economic rationality, both in general terms and in particular in terms of social capital processes.

8.3.2. Expanding the Social Capital Perspective: The Human Factor

This book has contended that social capital is best understood as a process (Chapters 1 and 4). The implication for the expanded framework of social capital is that motives and viewpoints are also subject to processes and consequently are not fixed, as they dynamically interact with the marketplace. Further, the understanding that motivations and viewpoints develop in interaction with the environment is consistent with Charles Lindblom's, 'The Science of Muddling Through' (1959) and Kay's arguments about 'Obliquity [which] describes the process of achieving complex objectives indirectly' (2010, p. 3). Thus, 'muddling through' and 'obliquity' relate to drivers of action shifting in relation to ongoing changes in the environment.

The limitations of rationality have also been discussed in a number of academic disciplines, for example behavioural economics has overturned the assumptions that people will behave rationally to price incentives to promote their self-interests (Chapter 5 on owner-managers maintaining relations that have out-lived their economic utility); and with Darwinian observations that humans have social instincts which compel them to socialise without reference to forward looking calculation (see Section 4.2 on the owner-managers' pre-start-up networking); as well as with intuitive observations that economic behaviour is often economically disinterested: for instance Karl of 'K.T.' shunned invitations to join the Free Masons due to ethical values overriding economic self-interests (see Section 5.3).

Moreover, in the prevailing rational choice background assumptions of the economic form of social capital, rational motivations are interpreted as being the only legitimate wellspring of action. Conversely, if mentioned at all low or non-rational motivations are dismissed as being detrimental to utility maximisation; thus to be so distinct as to be set against rational motivations. In contrast in this expanded framing perspective there is an acknowledgement that though motivations may be exclusively rational or of low or non-rationality, in most instances drivers of actions are fuzzy and interdependent. This theoretical contribution is therefore more consistent as a method of analysis with the immeasurable complexity and integrated nature of human perspectives, motivations and actions.

8.3.3. Statement of First Theoretical Contribution

The first theoretical contribution is to expand the framing notions in the economic form of social capital beyond their current rational theory assumptions. Moreover, this is not a new method of analysis, but rather argues for a reinstatement of previous perspectives on economic activity, which have been forgotten or jettisoned, in the recent 'rational' past. This suggestion is therefore consistent with the viewpoint that economic rationality has been overextended in contemporary analysis. Frank, for instance has drawn attention to the significance of compassion and morality in Smith's view of the market, which is absent from contemporary understandings of economic rationality (1988, pp. 21–23). Further, according to Fukuyama:

> ... the totality of the intellectual victory of free market economic theory in recent years has been accompanied by a considerable degree of hubris. Not being content to rest on their laurels, many neo-classical economists have come to believe that the economic method they have discovered provides them with the tools for constructing something approaching a universal science of man. The laws of economics, they argue, apply everywhere ... These economists believe in a deeper epistemological sense as well; through their economic methodology, they have unlocked a fundamental truth about human nature that will allow them to explain virtually all aspects of human behaviour. (1995a)

Reflecting this view that the economic view of rationality has been overextended Midgley has also recently written about our age being obsessed by individual competition, with social atomism as the prevailing myth of the time. For illustration of her views:

> Today, as in the nineteenth century, individualist propaganda is phrased in economics terms drawn from the spectacular financial gyrations of the time. The fantastic idea of 'the bottom line' − money as the final arbiter of reality − grew up then and is prevalent again today. (2010, p. 115)

It is also worth noting a common criticism of this rational overextension, that in economic rationality the assumption is that, '... people maximise whatever it is they choose to maximise, a tautology that robs the model of any interest or explanatory power' (Fukuyama, 1995a). In consequence, in economic rationality utility merely describes whatever ends people pursue, which has led to highly dubious claims of rationality, including the view that self-harming behaviour such as drug addiction is rational, if understood from the drug addict's perspective.[2] It is also surprising that Coleman, who identified that his 'variant of methodological individualism' was perhaps closest to that used by Karl Popper's in 'The Open Society and its Enemies' published in 1963 (1990, p. 5) made such strident claims for rationality's universal application claiming that, '... much of what is ordinarily described as non-rational or irrational is merely so because the observers have not yet discovered the point of view of the actor, from which the action is rational (*ibid.*, p. 18). This is a surprising assertion because it directly contradicts Popper's primary contribution to philosophical theory in terms of his 'refutability principle'. Thus:

> If a hypothesis 'explains' every possible hypothesis, Popper argues it explains nothing; it must be incompatible with some possible observation if it is to explain any observation. (Passmore, 1957, p. 407)

Therefore Coleman with his rational choice social capital treatment can be criticised from Popper's perspective (along with every advocate of economic rationality's universalism), on the grounds that if all behaviour is by definition utility maximising (from the actor's perspective), then the assumption is rendered non-falsifiable.

In consequence, based on these limitations of economic rationality there is a need to present an expanded perspective for framing social capital literature reinstating earlier insights concerning the nature of economic behaviour. For illustration:

> Even before Darwin, the scholars of the Scottish Enlightenment and thoughtful conservatives such as Edmund Burke had sensed that social organisation emerged through iteration and adaptation and was not the product of a serene or lucid mind. (Kay, 2010, p. 152)

This expanded perspective is also consistent with Fukuyama's emphasis on the importance of culture in determining economic outcomes:

> The problem with neoclassical economics is that it has forgotten certain key foundations on which classical economics was based. Adam Smith, the premier classical economist, believed that people are driven by a selfish desire to 'better their conditions' but he would never have subscribed to the notion that economic activity could be reduced to rational utility maximisation. Indeed, his other major work besides 'The Wealth of Nations' was 'The Theory of Moral Sentiments', which portrays economic motivations as being highly complex and embedded in broader social habits and mores. (1995b)

Social capital therefore needs to be framed by assumptions that expand the economic rational perspective beyond the extant market doctrine of heroic independence, at its extreme of 'Randian individualism',[3] 'laissez-faire' capitalism and its faith in the market to produce efficiencies out of disorder. In synopsis, the proposal is to expand this framing perspective to incorporate economic rationality, but also to contend that there is no simple bisected division between rational motivations and low or non-rationality; for instance between reason, and intuition and emotions. Thus, in this expanded explanatory framework of social capital, reason-driven rationality can be a distinct motivating force, but it is more commonly integrated with low or non-rational drivers.

Furthermore, in this expanded perspective of the motivating drivers of social capital processes the following observations are also significant:

- The expanded framing assumptions of social capital are consistent with the views of Scottish philosophers of the Enlightenment who had 'a well developed sense of mutual entitlement' (Patterson, 2000, p. 39). Adam Smith's insights on 'political economy', for example were achieved from his vantage as a moral philosopher with a firm belief that individuals were morally bound to have a regard for their fellow individuals, as they were all part of a common moral community. For illustration, in his *Theory of Moral Sentiments* (1759) Smith wrote: 'Kindness is the parent of kindness; and if be to be beloved by our brethren be the great object of our ambition, the surest way of obtaining it is by our conduct to show that we really love them'.[4] In summary this expanded perspective does not assume a Utopian market of individuals working together for mutual advantage, as rational self-interest will always be significant in the economy; but it does assume the adoption of Smithian moral insights on the economy in the modern context.
- Motivations and actions driven by economic rationality are less frequent than motivations and actions motivated by an integration of rational and low and non-rational motivations. Reflecting earlier conclusions this is not a novel observation outside the rational choice perspective. For example, Hayek contended that the drivers of economic action are not due to the 'pecuniary motive', arguing against:

> ... the erroneous belief that there are purely economic ends separated from the other ends of life. Yet, apart from the pathological case of the miser, there is no such thing. The ultimate ends of reasonable human beings are never economic. Strictly speaking there is no 'economic motive' but only economic factors conditioning our striving for other ends. What in ordinary language is misleadingly called the 'economic motive' means merely the desire for general opportunity, the power to achieve unspecified ends. (1944/2001, p. 92)

Further, the significance of emotion integrated with reason has also been long noted, for instance in the much quoted observation of Blaise Pascal (1623–1662) the French mathematician and theologian that: 'The heart has its reasons which reason knows nothing of'. There are also well-established criticisms of the view that there is a sharp distinction between reason-based rationality and low or non-rationality; that is, between consistent calculation in contrast to emotional drivers of action. For example, the view that there is no sharp division between reason and emotion has been expressed by Midgley that:

> ... Hume's sharp, simple division between Reason and Feeling still ignores the many kinds of thought by which people struggle to find their way between wild emotion at one extreme and pure abstraction at the other. It ignores reflection, rumination, contemplation, brooding, worrying, dreaming, reminiscing, speculating, considering and imagining. In particular, it ignores that deliberate re-directing of attention by which we can, if we please, gradually transform our feelings ...' (2010, p. 75)

There is also a considerable amount of management theory in favour of reframing the economic social capital perspective to acknowledge so called 'soft factors'. For example, Tom Peter's has recently asserted:

> ... The signature of my first book (written with Bob Waterman) as a six-word phrase 'Hard is soft. Soft is hard'. As Bob and I examined the problems besetting US corporations circa 1980, we believed they and their advisers had got things backwards. We said that in the end it was the supposedly 'hard numbers' so readily manipulable, as we have often seen of late, and the 'plans' that were soft. And the true 'hard soft' was that the business schools and their ilk undervalued as soft: people issues, character and the quality of relationships inside and beyond the organisation's walls.[5]

Daniel Goldman's influential 'Emotional Intelligence' (2006) with its focus on 'empathy' and developing 'flourishing relationships' also reflects the notions of this expanded perspective into framing social capital processes.

Thus the viewpoint that human rational and low or non-rational motivations are integrated is well established, and therefore support the research-based conclusion that social capital's framing perspective should be expanded.

8.3.4. Implications of an Expanded Social Capital Perspective

One implication of this expanded understanding is that the existing framing assumptions in social capital processes should be appreciated where they are relevant. For illustration of this important but narrow focus, it has been argued that people are more rational when their self-interest is obviously engaged (Lane, 1995, p. 121). However, there are also many actions for which reason and rationality are deficient as a means of analysis and for framing action. For example, according to Granovetter self-interest was less likely to explain the absence of fraud than the role of morality in the economy (1985).

Second, the reframing of social capital's background notions is consistent with Midgley's contention for a synoptic understanding of the human personality: 'In short, the sharp division between thought and emotion really doesn't work at this point. We need to drop it and talk of the whole person' (2010, p. 69).

This is a significant contribution as a synoptic view, which acknowledges the 'whole person' offers a more penetrating lens for investigating economic life (including social capital processes), than the current research orthodoxy that is distorted by rational choice theory. In summary, self-interested rationality, which is an extreme individualistic doctrine, is relevant in certain contexts, but to assume it as a universal method of analysis is a gross overextension. For example, in this research pure economic rationality conflicted with the core of being an owner-manager (and managing social capital), which is a social process requiring social empathy and competence, as much as self-interested forward looking utility (Chell, 2008, pp. 137–139). The implication is that the proposed synoptic framing assumptions offer the potential for developing understanding of social capital processes and more generally for developing understanding of owner-managers' social capital interactions.

To conclude, in this expanded perspective social capital processes will be viewed as subject to adaptive human agency forged out of interaction, with individuals interpreting and reflecting on shared, not atomised social reality. The contribution will offer a new theorisation of social capital processes as mediated by interactive actors, in which economic rationality is understood as just one of many social constructions. For illustration in this expanded framework it would be equally valid to understand the management of social capital as being driven by end-means notions of utility, as it would be to be motivated by other social construction to do with being professional, or in terms of perspectives on risk taking.

8.3.5. A New Ontological Understanding

This section will present a new ontological understanding of social capital that argues against the theoretical orthodoxies of decomposition into constituent parts and quantification in favour of a holistic and qualitative ontology.

This ontological understanding is based on the research process that emphasised the difficulty of maintaining the integrity of any discrete social capital sub-dimensions. Thus in this research the two sub-dimensions, which in any case were always understood as porous and overlapping, were difficult to maintain as distinct as evidence generated tended to seep into both categories, indicating that these network and relational sub-dimensions were deeply interdependent.

It is also worth evaluating this holistic understanding of social capital with reference to recent literature examining levels of analysis and the contemporary orthodoxy for 'rational' scientific methods of decomposition. For example, according to John Kay the danger inherent in over-focussing is one of perspective, of seeing the trees but not the wood:

> You cannot necessarily deduce the properties of the whole by adding up the properties of the individual parts. This is true of many biological systems and of all social, economic and political systems. (2010, p. 83)

This understanding is also directly relevant to the research questions into rationality, as recently identified by the philosopher Midgley (2010). In her analysis:

> ... the reductive thinking that theorizes about large-scale behaviour from analogy with behaviour of small parts is not reliable or scientific. (2010, p. 8)

Further she eloquently argues that the, 'reductive shift from organisms to genes' (*ibid.*, p. 23) is driven by pseudo-Darwinism and a competitive individualism, predicted on rational 'egoist doctrines' of economic self-interest. In her view these 'reductive strategies', which she contends are the contemporary orthodoxy, can be characterised as:

> ... a combination of the deep individualism of the age ... and a prejudice about method: a general idea that it is always more scientific to consider separate components that the larger wholes to which they belong. Indeed, it is often believed that those larger wholes are actually less real. ('There is no such thing as society'). (*ibid.*, p. 19)

The connection to this research is that the decomposition of social capital into conceptualised constituent parts or dimensions (discussed in Chapter 3) is an example of these rational reductive strategies. Further, in Midgley's analysis these rational 'reductive strategies' are derived from pseudo-science, based on a misreading of Darwin that, '... avoids complexity by breaking organisms into smaller units, dropping the thought patterns that were useful for understanding them as wholes' (*ibid.*, p. 23). For this research it is a short step to relate the decomposition of social capital to this contemporary trend for social atomisation, which Midgley argues relates to our 'age obsessed by individual competition' (*ibid.*, p. 115). Thus the orthodox decomposition of social capital can be understood as an example of contemporary pseudo-scientific rationality, which takes putative rigour ahead of an accuracy.

In addition, the research suggested the orthodox subdivisions in social capital literature are in themselves sterile modelling, being too blunt and reductionist to capture the intricate nature of social capital networks and relationships. This conclusion is therefore consistent with Bill Jordan's conclusion on social interactions:

> These are far more complex, diverse, and ambiguous than the inadequate categories of 'bonding' and 'bridging' capital can allow. (2008, p. 669)

Jordan illustrates this conclusion by considering the significance in social interactions of intimacy, obsession, power and exploitation, respect and belonging. Further in this research the owner-managers were nuanced in their network and relational interactions, implicitly acknowledging that the human personality is multi-varied and not subject or responsive to rational (economic or otherwise) consistency. Thus the owner-managers were driven by the understanding that there are different types of people, in different types of environments, which are a commonplace assertion, and contrary to the nostrums of rational economics. For instance a novelist has recently mused, '... there's no such thing as a coherent and fully integrated human personality, let alone consistent motivation'.

The conclusion is therefore that Putnam's bridging and bonding social capital (2000, pp. 22–24); Woolcock's linking capital (2001, p. 13); Granovetter's weak and strong ties (1973); Fukuyama's 'radius of trust' (2000, pp. 17–18); Lin's heterphilous and homophilous interactions (2001, pp. 46–52); and Burt's *Brokerage and Closure* (2005) are neither realistic nor predictive. Further these understandings of interactions also tend to suggest a binary choice: in contrast the research confirmed that social capital's interactions are integrated, complementary and complicated. For example, a social capital tie can at the same time be both weak and strong, as well as having characteristics of bonding, bridging and linking capital. For illustration in this research the owner-managers' relations with their suppliers (detailed in Chapters 4 and 5) were on occasion dynamic enough to fit into all of these categories.

It is also worth noting Midgley's comments on the selection of the level of decomposition, a selection that has never been adequately justified in social capital literature:

> If smaller units are always more informative than large ones, we might expect that it would be more scientific to start from physical particles – the quarks, and so on ... However, this choice of a particular level is not exceptional. Scientific enquirers

always concentrate their thinking at a particular scale because it interests them, often for reasons that have nothing to do with science. (*ibid.*, p. 24)

The validity of these comments is arguably supported by leading social capital scholars who have constructed levels of social capital to reflect their research interests: Putnam's bonding and bridging capitals (2000, pp. 22–24), for instance sit comfortably with his long established political and sociological research interests (Manning, 2010b).

Furthermore, the research confirmed the view, that social capital is deeply qualitative (Coleman, 1990, pp. 305–306). The significance of this observation is to challenge the theoretical orthodoxy of measuring social capital, usually with reference to 'Putnam's Instrument' (see Chapter 3). The research conclusion is that this measurement approach is an attempt to quantify the unquantifiable, which reflects a contemporary interpretation of rationality, linking measurement to understanding and management (originating in Lord Kelvin's viewpoint), to the exclusion of other explanatory approaches,[6] which is consistent with the view that:

Kelvin's approach leads directly to the modern curse of bogus quantification. (Kay, 2010, p. 71)

8.3.6. Implications of New Ontological Understanding

This new ontological understanding is a significant contribution to knowledge, as there remains a significant degree of theoretical confusion and disagreement (Woolcock & Radin, 2008, pp. 411–412). This new ontological understanding will contribute therefore to a more convincing understanding of the essence of the theory. Further, the implication of this ontological understanding is that research based on decomposition will inevitably create a false divide, as there is a flaw in the empirical method of breaking down, followed by building up. Conversely this research indicates that social capital processes do not work in that way, but rather are integrated in an ongoing dynamic manner, subject to situationalist variables. In consequence, the decomposition and usually enumeration of social capital in its supposed sub-components is misleading, resulting in the measurement of phenomena without regard of how these sub-dimensions interact to form the wholeness of social capital. In summary, the implication is to challenge the validity of the research orthodoxy of decomposition. For example, in this ontology Putnam's bonding and bridging (2000, pp. 22–24) capital have meaning only if they are examined together. For research into owner-managers the implication is that to develop understanding of social capital a holistic, integrated perspective is required.

8.4. EMPIRICAL CONTRIBUTION TO KNOWLEDGE

> The accumulation of social capital, however, is a complicated and in many ways mysterious cultural process. (Fukuyama, 1995b)

The empirical contribution is to present guiding assumptions for the management of social capital. This contribution is based on the research conclusion that though situationalist variables are vital, nevertheless there were a number of generic approaches adopted by the owner-managers that were effective in managing social capital processes. Further this contribution is consistent with Coleman's situationalist theoretical treatment (1990, p. 302), as well as with the book's viewpoint of social capital being a complicated and dynamic process. Moreover, given social capital's dynamic and fuzzy nature its generative mechanisms and management will inevitably rely on a blend of measures, rather than a single 'magic bullet'. Thus the following points are best understood as offering a guiding focus, rather than as a blueprint of rigid prescriptions. This empirical contribution is also consistent with the research conclusion that appreciates the significance of low and non-rationality in the management of social capital processes and consequently this empirical contribution will serve to rebalance the theory away from the overblown and unrealistic rational transactional orthodoxy, towards an understanding that acknowledges the integrated, nuanced, humanistic and relational essence of social capital processes.

First, the optimum approach is to actively cultivate social capital. In Coleman's view, '… social capital depletes if it is not renewed' (1990, p. 321), and the research confirmed that managing social capital requires continuous renewal and efforts to establish and maintain networks and relations. This vigorous approach is also consistent with Burt's concluding words of *Brokerage and Closure*: 'There is a simple, moral here: when you have an opportunity to learn how someone in another group does what you do differently – go' (2005, p. 245). In sum, social capital increases with use and therefore can be enhanced by actively developing and maintaining networks and relations: adapting Burt's syntax, 'stay plugged in'.

Second, network and relational interactions should be predicted on a view of interaction that emphasises relational cooperation and not opportunistic transactions. Of course rational self-interest is significant, but should not be assumed to dominate motivations and action, as the ideal social capital individual is not calculating (Frank, 1988, p. ix). Instead, the optimum approach is to settle on a pattern of mutual cooperation in which it is advisable to initiate the cooperation and to embody cooperative social attitudes, while using judgement to assess situational variables to avoid being exploited.

Third, ignore the sterile sub-components prevalent in social capital literature. In this research the majority of relational ties were multidimensional and hence not consistent with the crudely drawn and flat understanding of interaction described in theoretical literature.

Fourth, interpret social capital as integral to being in being an owner-manager and attempt to manage it from the perspective that it is an unavoidable and pleasurable activity. From this perspective, managing social capital attains the level of 'process benefits' (Lane, 1995, p. 113), in which activities are pursued because individuals enjoy the activity in themselves. Thus the optimum approach is to develop a passion for business, with an understanding that this passion involves cultivating networks and relationships. This approach is also consistent with Darwin's conclusions on social instincts conferring advantages, for illustration in 'The Descent of Man' he wrote: '... the fittest are not necessarily the strongest, nor indeed the cleverest, but the most sociable: those whose temperament inclines them to friendly cooperation' (quoted in Midgley, 2010, p. 490).

Fifth, in theoretical literature, there is a notion that social capital develops over time and therefore has a path dimension (Anderson, Park, & Jack, 2007, p. 249) (see Section 4.2). In consequence this guiding step for creating social capital is not to destroy the existing stock. For this point, the medical maxim of 'first do no harm' should apply, which is given greater credence by the observation that social capital is easier to destroy than create (Fukuyama, 2000, p. 258).

1. The research confirmed in Section 5.4.1 that though serendipity cannot be managed, individuals could maximise their exposure to opportunities favouring social capital processes.
2. The research has also identified in Section 4.3 that social events, particularly Christmas parties were often key for developing new social capital.

3. Social capital requires a human touch, usually with face-to-face contact, though telephone communications can be effective. However ICT mediated interactions are ineffective in social capital processes (see Section 5.1).
4. Opportunistic, rational interactions are more likely in times of extremity as survival strategy. For instance, the current recession has led to more rational self-interested approaches to transactions. In consequence firms in a parlous state are more likely to adopt this approach to interactions (see Section 6.2.3), which should be appreciated by all of those involved in these interactions.
5. The research has also identified that there are critical recurring temporal events that are significant for social capital processes: Section 4.2 noted the importance of the prior start-up stage, start-up stage and change of ownership stages.

8.4.1. Implications of Empirical Contribution

The implication of these guiding assumptions is that social capital can be managed, not precisely but nevertheless to a significant extent. Thus the guide offers owner-managers the opportunity to reflect and adapt their management of social capital with reference to the 10 listed points. In sum the implication is that there are generic social processes, subject to purposeful actions that stimulate and enhance the management of social capital.

These guiding assumptions are also deliberately imprecise to reflect the disorder and fuzzy, dynamic nature of human group life and consequently of social capital processes. Further, one could characterise these guidelines as emphasising flexibility and pragmatism, which is an appropriate response to social reality that is resistant to rational planning (Jacobs, 1961). This flexibility and pragmatism is necessary to enable owner-mangers to switch between different systems of thought, or paradigms as circumstances dictate: thus to be able to move between rationality to low and non-rational, or to an interdependence of these intellectual paradigms dependent on the particular situational variables. The implication is that to manage social capital owner-managers have to be dynamic, flexible and pragmatic. In the author's experiences these were also the characteristics associated with financial success in owner-management.

8.5. AREAS FOR FUTURE RESEARCH

There are a number of recommendations for future research that have been indicated and/or generated by this research. These recommendations are organised into three research areas. The first area recommended is aimed at developing the book's focal point into rationality and social capital; the second focuses on further research into various stakeholders and social capital; and the third recommendation is in terms of further investigation into the emergent themes identified in Chapter 6.

Moreover, the first area for future research is based on the conclusion that the contemporary understanding of economic rationality is a recent and arguably Western obsession, with a narrow and unrealistic understanding of economic activity. Accordingly, the focus of the research suggestion is to investigate the current obsession, as exemplified in this research by the owner-managers' fixation on stressing their self-interested, rational credentials, which defied their own day-to-day experiences. The research suggestion will aim to develop insights into the economic interpretation of rationality, for instance to examine why this perspective has such a firm grip over contemporary economic perspectives, including the social capital perspective.

This is also a timely area for future research as economic rationality, which is one of a number of contemporary 'egoist doctrines', has been described as the orthodoxy of the age (Midgley, 2010, p. 39). However, these 'egoist doctrines' have recently been questioned, following the financial crisis of 2008, as the economic rational perspective can be understood as integral to a triumph of economic ideology justifying a particular set of (neo-liberal) economic views. In Lane's words: 'I think rationality is inserted to justify not explain the market' (1995). Economic rationality can be understood therefore as a legitimising rhetoric to vindicate economic orthodoxies and these economic orthodoxies are at present subject to intense criticisms. For example, Nicholas Taleb recently enjoyed a best seller, *The Black Swan*, which analysed these economic orthodoxies, arguing that rationality has become a 'strait-jacket' and that optimisation has, 'no practical (or even theoretical) use' (2007, p. 184). In sum, economic rationality can be understood as a doctrine used to justify prevailing socio-economic and political views and ideological choices, including the market doctrine of self-reliance, frugal self-discipline and the maximising of profits.

It can also be contended that rationality of any stripe is at least in part learned, and therefore not an expression of an innate human proclivity to self-interest, but rather is a social construction. For illustration, it has been observed that individuals who study economics become the most economic-ally rational:

> ... the only group for which the strong free rider hypothesis received even minimal sup-port in the vast experimental literature turns out to be a group of economics graduate students. (Frank, 1988, pp. 226–227)

It can also be suggested that the elegant models of optimisation modelling (originating in Paul Samuelson's, 'Foundations of Economic Analysis') which stress consistency,[7] are either learnt or accepted as the dominant orthodoxy, often at an unconscious level. In this research, for instance the owner-managers were characterised by their unconscious and un-reflective assumptions on the legitimacy of economic rationality (see Section 6.1), which is consistent with the view that economists are realists, whose theories are: 'Not recommending selfishness just recognising it' (Ridley, 1996, p. 145).

However, even among cheerleaders for free markets there have always been cautions over the extent that economic rationality can be universally applied, for example:

> We can think of neo-classical economics as being, say, eighty per cent right... But there is a missing twenty per cent of human behavior about which neoclassical economics can give only a poor account. (Fukuyama, 1995b)

Fukuyama further elaborated this observation by contending that social capital requires a 'moral community' that can't be acquired through, '... a rational investment decision' (*ibid.*, p. 26).

More strident critics of economic rationality have also come more to the fore following the recent financial crash, which has led to direct challenges to neo-liberal assumptions. For example, Midgley has recently argued for an alternative zeitgeist, or spirit of the age, to reflect the, '... recent wide-spread interest in the social brain: that is, of natural human cooperation and mutual suggestibility' (2010, p. 39). For instance in terms of putting an emphasis on the significance of cooperation as opposed to individualism, and also in stressing the role of the multitude of human motivations in con-trast to the economic rational view, which relates to an Hobbesian extreme account of human motivation.

It is also significant that the only owner-manager in the research operat-ing outside the West (in the Middle East) drew attention to the different cultural approaches to business interactions: in the United Kingdom Aftab of 'Easy-Tech' attempted to be as rational as the other owner-managers, whereas in the Middle East he adapted to a less rational and more rela-tional ways of doing business.

Research questions to be addressed could include the following:

1. If economic rationality is applicable to certain narrow conditions why is it assumed to be universally applicable? Further, why is this attachment to economic rationality so entrenched that it is still cleaved to despite contradicting everyday experiences?
2. Is the interest in rationality in forming social capital networks and relations a Western fixation that has yet to permeate into non-Western cultures? For example: 'In the modern West, it is widely assumed that personal gain is the legitimate goal of economic activity, while it is thought to be illegitimate in other spheres, such as political and personal life. Indeed, the economic realm could be defined as the arena in which selfishness is regarded as legitimate' (Friedman, 1995, p. 4).
3. Is economic rationality self-fulfilling in social capital processes? Thus if an individual is motivated and acts in accordance with self-interested utility maximisation does it provoke an equal economic rational response from network and relational interactions?

The second recommendation relates to this research being limited by its focus on owner-managers. In consequence, to achieve a broader perspective, research into additional stakeholder groups has the potential to contribute to further knowledge and understanding of social capital processes in owner-manager and entrepreneurial contexts. These stakeholders can be detailed as follows:

1. The research noted that owner-managers understood social capital as an individual level endowment and therefore it would be worth investigating how SME employees understood, experienced and shaped their social capital. It is also worth noting that extant research into social capital processes has focussed on entrepreneurs and owner-managers, to the exclusion of SME employees (see Section 2.3).
2. The research identified the role of 'shadow' (usually female) owner-managers. In the researcher's view the owner-managers' spouses often possessed more power and entrepreneurial drive than the putative owner-manager of the firms. However, because these 'shadow' owner-managers operate implicitly in the SMEs, their role as hidden partners or owner-managers has been under-acknowledged. The recommendation is therefore to research these shadow owner-managers, to investigate these shadow owner-managers' role in managing social capital processes.

3. Related to point two the research has already identified as a limitation that the owner-managers were selected without reference to gender (23 male to 7 female owner-managers). The third recommendation is therefore to examine whether there are any gender differences in the way women and men manage social capital processes.

4. This research selected the owner-managers from the service and retail sectors and the recommendation would be to add to the literature that considers sectoral variations in social capital processes (Soetanto & Jack, 2010). As already stated there is a developing literature focussing on the IT sector (Anderson & Jack, 2008; Liao & Walsh, 2005) and social capital, and it is worth investigating further the extent that sector variations are a significant variable for social capital processes.

5. Fifth, the role of family firms was not considered as selection criteria. Only four of the owner-managers described themselves as working in a family SME. Further, it is commonly assumed that family firms are characterised by a long-term focus and relational approach to management and therefore it would be worth investigating whether family firms manage social capital processes differently than non-family firms.

6. Sixth the research identified (see Section 4.2) that social capital is subject to temporal variables in terms of its network dimension. The research suggestion therefore is to investigate social capital's time-framed variables. Moreover research in this area would be consistent with Putnam's conclusions on the power of the past, with reference to his 'path dependency' theory; that is, '... where you can get depends on where you're coming from, and some destinations you simple cannot get to from here' (1993, p. 179). For example, research could investigate the issue of time in relation to 'buy outs' or other change of ownership and could examine the best approach to ensure that the social capital of the firm is not dissipated by the departure of the previous owner-manager. For illustration, in this research Neil of 'IT Solutions' 'Earn Out' arrangement (see Section 4.2), was very expensive, and future research could focus on a more cost effective way of maintaining social capital resources.

The third general area for future research relates to the emergent themes identified in Chapter 7 and accordingly these research recommendations can be detailed as follows:

1. There is a considerable body of research into entrepreneurial learning and education (discussed in Chapter 7). However, research into entrepreneurs and owner-managers' reading styles is deficient. Accordingly,

the recommendation is to research owner-managers reading, for example in terms of: their selection of material; the length of time they devote to reading; their evaluation of reading; and their approaches to putting their evaluations into action.

2. The research also identified the emergent theme of ethics and social capital processes. Further in the research the concept of 'reference groups' (Shibutani, 1955) was discussed with reference to ethical values associated with religious affiliations (see Section 6.2), and also in terms of Putnam's 'bonding capital' (2000, pp. 22–24), (see Section 6.2.2). The research recommendation is therefore to investigate the role of religious beliefs and practices in the management of social capital processes.

Furthermore, in social capital literature there are extensive references to religion and social capital. For example, Putnam has argued that 'amoral familism' (Banfield, 1958/1967) has been self-reinforcing in Southern Italy from the Middle Ages as:

> Membership rates in hierarchically ordered organisations (like the Mafia or the institutional Catholic Church) should be negatively associated with good government; in Italy, at least, the most devout church-goers are the least civic minded ... Good government in Italy is a by-product of singing groups and soccer clubs not prayer. (pp. 175–176)

Putman further contends that the Southern Italy was caught in a self-perpetuating 'vicious circle', which, '... reproduced perennial exploitation and dependence' whereas, the North had greater stocks of social capital due to its 'virtuous circle' (*ibid.*, p. 162):

> Any society ... is characterised by networks of inter-personnel, communication and exchange, both formal and informal. Some of these networks are 'horizontal', bringing together agents of equivalent status and power. Others are primarily 'vertical,' linking unequal agents in asymmetrical relations of hierarchy and dependence ... Protestant congregations are traditionally thought to be more horizontal than networks in the Catholic Church. (*ibid.*, p. 173)

Putnam's concluded that there is an inverse relation between levels of Catholicism and social capital in Italy (1993, p. 107), though this is a controversial interpretation, not least among Italian scholars: Mario Diani, for instance, reaches the opposite conclusion that high levels of social capital are predicted on high levels of Catholicism (2004, pp. 137–161). Fukuyama also claims: 'Social capital is frequently a by-product of religion, tradition, shared historical experience and other factors that lie outside the control of any government' (2001, p. 18). Thus, Fukuyama considers religion to be a source of social capital (1999, p. 17), asserting that Protestant conversions in South America have led to great social and economic gains due to the intrinsic values of Protestantism (1995b). Conversely, Portes and Sensenbrenner reach a contrary conclusion arguing that converts exploit existing social capital resources and that consequently there are no wider social gains:

> By shifting religious allegiance, these entrepreneurs remove themselves from a host of social obligations for male family heads associated with the Catholic Church and its local organisations. The Evangelical convert becomes, in a sense, a stranger in his own community, which insulates him from free riding by others who follow Catholic inspired norms. (1993, p. 1339)

Coleman also considered that Protestantism encourages individualism, which in his view inhibited the creation of social capital (1990, p. 321). In contrast he evaluated the educational advantages offered by Catholic schools to be significant for creating high levels of social capital (*ibid.*, pp. 32–34).

In synopsis religion features prominently in the work of Putnam and Fukuyama who are broadly critical of Catholicism, while conversely Coleman and Portes are broadly critical of Protestantism. Accordingly, to add to and complement existing social capital research into ethics and religion this research recommendation is to examine the role organised religion plays in managing social capital processes. For example, in this research a Muslim was ascribed the role of Edward Said's 'the other', by the respective owner-manager; that is as someone outside normal social interactions (1990) (see Section 6.2.2). This research would also add to literature into entrepreneurship in the social context concerned with *Entrepreneurship and Religion* (Dana, 2010) therefore complementing research into 'how entrepreneurial ventures are created in a religious milieu' (Anderson, 2010, p. x).

8.6. CONCLUDING COMMENTS: OWNER-MANAGEMENT AS A SOCIAL ACTIVITY

The research has identified a lacuna between the rational framing notions and the day-to-day reality of the management of social capital processes. This book has also concluded on the desirability of an expanded framework of analysis, as well as a new ontology that acknowledges the value of rational choice explanations and method of analysis yet is not overwhelmed by claims for economic rationality's predominance and universal application. Thus in this new theoretical perspective owner-managers (and any economic agent) are more than the idealised rational calculating machines in fixed task environments interacting under conditions of certainty.

The conclusion of the research is that the background assumptions of the economic form of social capital, grounded in economic notions of rationality, offer a penetrating and at the same time narrowly focussed method of analysing social capital processes. Moreover, the rational framing assumptions of social capital are based on a false belief that reason and rationality are universally applicable as a method of analysis to human actions and motivations. This research has also identified that in social capital processes there doesn't need to be a bisected division between untamed emotion and pure rational abstraction, as more often than not motivations and actions are driven by a complicated and ever changing integration of rational and low or non-rationality. In sum, in social capital processes economic rationality is not bounded, but more frequently is integrated with low and non-rationality.

Social capital has also been interpreted as a process with no sharp distinction between means and ends, which consequently means it is not a linear theory subject to linear cause and effect explanations, but rather is characterised by nuance, dynamism and complexity. This is why its rational framing assumptions are inadequate: social capital is not reducible to an elegant framing theory of universal economic rationality; rather it is consistent with the lived world of human networks and relations, which are immensely complex and paradoxical. Thus criticisms of the type recently discussed by Putnam are misplaced, as at its core social capital is subject to rationality and to low and non-rationality:

> Putnam recently stated in his 1999 'Marshall Lectures' that social capital is accused by economists of smuggling soft concepts into economics and criticised by sociologists for smuggling 'rationality' into sociology'.[8]

Finally, the spark for this research was first ignited by the author's experiences as an owner-manager, which convinced him that managing an SME was a social activity. Researching the management of social capital processes has strengthened this viewpoint.

END NOTES

CHAPTER 1

1. For a comprehensive review of rational choice theory see Friedman (1996).
2. See the following for an overview of entrepreneurship teaching: Jack and Anderson (1999).
3. See the following book review: Manning (2009).
4. See Chapter 2 for a full discussion of the limitations of Putnam's analysis and Manning (2010b).
5. The significance of rationality to social capital is also discussed in Chapter 2.
6. For example rational choice has been described as '... one variant of a much larger research programme of nineteenth century energy mechanics ... Indeed, virtually every discipline that aspires to the mantle of science does so by adopting the paradigm of classical mechanics' (Murphy, 1995, p. 157).
7. Fine notes that Becker, Grossman, and Murphy ran a joint bi-weekly seminar to consider the economic approach to the social sciences (1993).
8. Coleman claimed the closest variant to his methodological individualism was in Karl Popper's, *The Open Society and its Enemies* published in 1963 (1990, p. 5). Popper's methodological individualism can be summarised as taking the ultimate constituents of the social world as individual people, and in consequence as obliquely stating that there is no such thing as society.
9. Abelson (1995, p. 34) has criticised the following article for gross theoretical over-reach: Becker, Grossman, and Murphy (1993). For a more general criticism of rational choice theory see Bohmam (1992).
10. Granovetter further discussed how clever institutional arrangements, such as implicit and explicit contracts, including deferred payment, had evolved to discourage the problem of malfeasance. However, Granovetter considered that these arrangements, '... do not produce trust but are a functional substitute for it' (*ibid.*, p. 489). Further, he

noted that conceptions that have an exclusive focus on institutional arrangements are, '... undersocialized in that they do not allow for the extent to which concrete personal relations and the obligations inherent in them discourage malfeasance' (*ibid.*, p. 489). He also cautioned that if malfeasance was controlled entirely by clever institutional arrangement then a malign cycle could develop in which economic life would; '... be poisoned by ever more ingenious attempts at deceit' (*ibid.*, p. 489).

CHAPTER 2

1. For a comprehensive overview of entrepreneurship theories see Chell (2008).
2. For an overview of ethics and entrepreneurship see Hannafey (2003).
3. Brenkert has listed representative examples of sometimes conflicting accounts of entrepreneurship as:

   ... an alertness to profit opportunities (Kirsner); the exploitation of a new technology (Schumpeter); a bet, gamble or chance on some new idea (Brenner); the exercise of control over means of production (McLellan); a management discipline (Drucker); the creation and ownership of a new business (Drucker; Reynolds et al.); purposeful task practice (Drucker); and the acceptance of risk and/or uncertainty in the pursuit of profit opportunities (Cantillon). (2002, p. 9)

4. See *International Small Business Journal* 2007, *25*(3) which was devoted to social capital and entrepreneurship.
5. A large-scale research's sampling frame, moreover, was constructed on a regional basis to create an index of area performance based on 12 standard regions. Then a postal questionnaire was followed by sample face-to-face and telephone interview. In total 3,600 postal questionnaires and 40 social capital interviews were conducted (2004, p. 110) The response rate was 14% to the survey, which the authors evaluate as being in line with response rates for other postal surveys of UK SMEs.
6. See Chapter 4 for the limitations of adopting this decomposition.
7. Granovetter's extensive list of publications is available at sociology.stanford.edu/people/mgranovetter/ and reveals that he has never published an article with social capital in the title, accessed on 23 January 2009.
8. The extent of social capital literature can be gauged by considering the diversity of theoretical literature at the following websites:

   http://www.ksg.harvard.edu/saguaro

http://www.socialcapital.strat.ac.uk
http://wwwlworldbank.org/prem/poverty/sccapital
http://www.socialcapitalgateway.org/eng-websitesocialcapital.htm
http://www.BetterTogether.org
http://www.worldbank.org/poverty/scapital/index.htm

CHAPTER 3

1. Six years after the original 'Coleman Report' was issued, Coleman published a re-analysis of data using 'regression' procedures ('regression' procedure is a one-step analysis that estimates the net effect of each variable while controlling for the effects of the other variables). Based on the re-analyses, Coleman concluded that the original report gave an inflated estimate of the influence of home background due to unexamined effects of school characteristics. These later conclusion were however over-shadowed by the earlier controversies.

2. Becker's theories on 'utility maximizing individuals' are complementary to Coleman's social capital treatment. It is no coincidence that they both held tenure as professors at the University of Chicago and they ran a: '... a joint seminar together on the application of rational choice to social sciences from 1983 when Becker took up a joint appointment in the Department of Sociology' (Fine & Green, 2000, p. 80).

3. Fine comments on Coleman's conservative family values and 'scary worldview' (2000).

4. The most significant communitarian scholar of recent times is Amitai Etzioni, who achieved considerable academic and popular success with 'The Spirit of Community' (1988).

5. For a contending analysis of Silicon Valley, see Cohen and Prusak, who argue: 'The main networks of social capital are not dense networks of civil engagement but focussed productive interactions among the following ... the great research universities, US government policy, venture capital firms, law firms, business networks, stock options and the labour market. This trust is based more on performance than anything else' (2001).

6. An influential social capital debate concerning Putnam's use of social capital was conducted in 'American Prospect' from issue no. 26, May–June 1996, which is available at: www.prospect.org/authors/putnam-r.html

7. See introduction for a defence of this processual theoretical understanding of social capital.
8. See the following article for an in-depth analysis of Putnam's politics:
   Manning (2010b).
9. See *The Dark Heart of Italy* by T. Jones which gives an account of
   the 'Clean Hands' revolution targeting Northern endemic white collar
   corruption (2004, pp. 131–158).
10. For a review of the Whig view of history see Burrow (2007,
    pp. 472–473). Marwick defines this approach to studying the past as:

    > ... a spoken or unspoken assumption that the central theme in English history was
    > the development of liberal institutions: thus in the study of remote ages they greatly
    > exaggerated the importance of 'parliaments' ... they tended to interpret all political
    > struggles in terms of the parliamentary situation ... in terms, that is, of Whig refor-
    > mers fighting the good fight against Tory defenders of the status quo. (1970, p. 47)

11. For example to blame the Norman Kingdom, and by association its
    feudalism, for contemporary low levels of social capital in South Italy
    is to misunderstand the nature of feudalism, a social system based on
    land ownership common to parts of Europe, Egypt, China, Benin and
    Japan (Bloch, 1961, p. 441). Further, reinforcing the previous criticism
    over there ever being a 'prime determinant', experiences of feudalism,
    produced different outcomes: the socio-economic profiles of Benin and
    Japan do not have an enormous amount in common.
12. There is truth in Fukuyama's evaluation, as a number of scholars have
    commented on the 'civic desert' in France that can be partly traced to
    the spirit of the French Revolution, which aimed to:

    > ... suppress all intermediary bodies between individuals and the state, out of fear that
    > the reconstitution of the Ancien Regime's guilds and the development of factions
    > might distort the general will ... For more than a century all governments perceived
    > associations as a threat to the social and political order, and they repressed their
    > development. (Mayer, 2003, p. 47)

    However, Fukuyama's judgement is unbalanced: in his analysis France
    has always been centralised and lacking in social capital and therefore
    should always have been anarchic and backward. Conversely, one
    could argue that for the previous thousand years France has either
    been 'top nation' or one of the leading nations, as well as being a con-
    sistent beacon of Western civilisation. One could further speculate that
    Fukuyama's beliefs, in favour of the benign nature of Pax-America
    and globalisation led him to be exasperated with the Gallic reluctance
    to abandon its heritage and embrace these nostrums.

13. Economic statistics from this time are limited and unreliable but the Interregnum has not been associated with an economic boom.

CHAPTER 4

1. The ecology fallacy refers to data from one level of analysis being interpreted as if it were drawn from another level of analysis (Rousseau, 1985).
2. Symbolic interaction has been criticised for being '... non-economic, ahistorical, culturally limited, and ideologically biased, has a limited view of social power, and paints an odd view of social reality' (Meltzer, 1975, p. 99).
3. Denizen offers an example of an interview with a marijuana user as an example which links conceptions of self and social reference groups (Denzin, 1970).
4. Ethnography involves studying lived experiences and with a 'Quest for Intimate Familiarity' (Prus, 1996, pp. 18−27): ethnos is the Greek root referring to peoples and ethnic cultures.
5. See Blundel and Smith (2001), and Shaw and Conway (2000, pp. 367−383) for a discussion of different SME networks.
6. See Chell (2008), 'The Search for Entrepreneurial Traits: 'The Big Three': 81−110. And Chapter 5: 'New Entrepreneurial Traits' (pp. 111−141).
7. Shibutani defines reference groups as, '... a group which serves as the point of reference in making comparisons or contrasts, especially in forming judgements about one's self' (1955, p. 109).

CHAPTER 5

1. For an overview of network theory see Nitin (1990) and for networks and entrepreneurship see Blundel and Smith (2001); and Casson and Della Guista (2007, pp. 222−228).
2. 'IT Solutions' won a national training award in 2006.
3. For a review of the literature on the importance of network to entrepreneurs and owner-managers, see De Carolis and Sparito (2006, pp. 41−42); and Lee and Jones (2008, pp. 559−561).

4. *Dunbar's number* is a theoretical cognitive limit to the number of people with whom one can maintain stable social relationships. No precise value has been proposed for this number, but a commonly cited approximation is 150.

CHAPTER 6

1. For a summary of the literature on opportunity recognition see Chell (2008).
2. For a discussion of the profit-seeking paradox see Kay (2010).

CHAPTER 7

1. Only one of the owner-managers had studied ethical theory – David of 'R-Ices', who had studied morality and ethics in an earlier career as a religious minister.
2. In Putnam's view social capital can exacerbate social divisiveness '... the central normative issue raised by communitarianism' (*ibid.*, p. 361).
3. Danielle Sered (1996) defines Edward Said's influential theory as follows: 'The Orient signifies a system of representations framed by political forces that brought the Orient into Western learning, Western consciousness, and Western empire'. Retrieved from www.english. emory.edu/.../Orientalism.html
4. See Chapter 4.
5. The chapter concludes: 'The problem that modern capitalist societies pose for moral relationships does not therefore lie in the nature of economic exchange itself. The problem, rather, lies in technology and technological change. Capitalism is so dynamic, such a source of creative destruction, that it is constantly altering the terms of exchange that go on within human communities' (2000, p. 262).
6. The limited literature examining ethics includes Fukuyama's cautions on the drawbacks of: 'Networks, understood as informal ethical relationships, are therefore associated with phenomena like nepotism, favouritism, intolerance, in-breeding, and non-transparent, personalistic arrangements' (1992, 2000). He illustrates these observations with the example of 'Barings Bank' which he characterises as a network structure that allowed Nick Leason to 'bet the firm' (2002, p. 225). Anderson and

Smith (2007) have also argued that to be entrepreneurial requires a degree of morality. Hence enterprising criminals should not be thought of as entrepreneurs.

7. See Gerber (1994).

CHAPTER 8

1. Social capital literature reviews include: Portes (1998), Paldam (2000), Foley and Edwards (1997), Adler and Kwon (2002), Fields (2003), and Lee (2008).
2. See Abelson for a discussion of this 'gross theoretical overreach' (1995, p. 34).
3. See Midgley (2010, p. 127) for a discussion of Ayn Rand's extreme individualism as the gospel of lasses faire capitalism.
4. Quoted in Patterson (2000, p. 39).
5. See Peters (2010).
6. 'I often say that when you can measure what you are speaking about, and express it in numbers, you know something about it; when you cannot express it in numbers, you're knowledge is of a meagre and unsatisfactory kind.' Lord Kelvin's lecture on 'Electrical Units of Measurement' 1883 in Kelvin (1891). Quoted in: Kay (2010).
7. See Kay (2010, p. 157) for a discussion of economic rationality from the oblique perspective.
8. Quoted in Commin (2008, p. 647).

REFERENCES

Abelson, R. P. (1995). The secret existence of expressive behaviour. In J. Friedman (Ed.), *The rational choice controversy.* Yale, CT: Yale University Press.

Adam, F., & Roncevic, B. (2003). Social capital: Recent debates and research trends. *Social Science Information, 42*(2), 155–183.

Adler, P. S., & Kwon, S. (2000). Social capital: The good, the bad and the ugly. In E. L. Lesser (Ed.), *Knowledge and social capital* (pp. 89–115). Oxford: Butterworth-Heinemann.

Adler, P. S., & Kwon, S. (2002). Social capital: Prospects for a new concept. *Academy of Management Review, 27*(1), 17–40.

Ahn, T. K., & Ostrom, E. (2008). Social capital and collective action. In D. Castiglione, J. W. Van Deth, & G. Wolleb (Eds.), *The handbook of social capital* (pp. 70–100). Oxford: Oxford University Press.

Aldridge, S., Halpern, D., & Fitzpatrick, S. (2002, April 26). *Social capital.* Discussion paper. Performance and Innovation Unit. Background paper prepared for a conference for strategic thinkers. Retrieved from www.social-capital.net/docs/PIU%20Paper%20by%20S%20Aldridge

Anderson, A. R., & Jack, S. L. (2002). The articulation of entrepreneurial social capital. *Entrepreneurship and Regional Development, 14*(3), 193–210.

Anderson, A., & Jack, S. L. (2008). Role typologies for enterprising education: The professional artisan. *Journal of Small Business and Enterprise Development, 15*(2), 259–273.

Anderson, A., & Smith, R. (2007). The moral space in entrepreneurship: An exploration of ethical imperatives and the moral legitimacy of being enterprising. *Entrepreneurship & Regional Development: An International Journal, 19*(6), 479–497.

Anderson, A. R. (1998). Cultivating the Garden of Eden: Entrepreneurial entrepreneuring. *Journal of Organizational Change Management, 11*(2), 245–272.

Anderson, A. (2010). Foreword. In D. P. Soetanto & S. L. Jack (Eds.), (2011), *Networks and networking activities of innovative firms in incubators.* International Journal of Entrepreneurship and Innovation, *12*(2), 127–136.

Anderson, A., Park, J., & Jack, S. (2007). Entrepreneurial social capital: Conceptualising social capital in new high-tech firms. *International Small Business Journal, 25*(3), 245–272.

Aristotle. (1994). *The Nicomachean Ethics.* London: Penguin.

Banfield, E. (1958/1967). *The moral basis of a backward society.* New York, NY: Free Press.

Baron, R. A., & Markman, G. D. (2003). Beyond social capital: The role of entrepreneurs' social competence in their financial success. *Journal of Business Venturing, 18*, 41–61.

Baron, S. (2004). Social capital and British policy making. In J. Franklin (Ed.), *Politics, trust and networks: Social capital in critical perspective* (pp. 5–17). Families & Social Capital ESRC Research Group Working Paper No. 7. South Bank University, London.

Baron, S., Field, J., & Schuller, T. (Eds.). (2000). *Social capital: Critical perspectives.* Oxford: Oxford University Press.

Bebbington, A., Guggenheim, S., Olson, E., & Woolcock, M. (2004). Exploring social capital debates at the world bank. *The Journal of Development Studies*, 40(5), 33–64.

Becker, G. S. (1961). *A treatise on the family*. Cambridge, MA: Harvard University Press.

Becker, G. S. (1992). *The economic way of looking at life*. Nobel lecture. Retrieved from home. uchicago.edu/~gbecker/Nobel/nobellecture. Accessed on December 9.

Becker, G. S., Grossman, M., & Murphy, K. M. (1993). Rational addiction and the effect of price on consumption. In G. Loewenstein & J. Elster (Eds.), *Choice over time* (pp. 361–370). New York, NY: Sage.

Becker, G. S., Grossman, M., & Murphy, K. M. (1993). *An empirical analysis of cigarette addiction*. Working Paper No. 3322. National Bureau of Economic Research, Cambridge.

Blanchard, A., & Horan, T. (1998). Virtual communities and social capital. *Social Science Review*, 16(3). In E. L. Lesser (Ed.), Knowledge and social capital (pp. 293–307). Oxford: Butterworth-Heinemann.

Blau, P. (1964). *Exchange and power in social life*. New York, NY: Wiley.

Bloch, M. (1961). *Feudal society*. London: Routledge and Kegan.

Blumer, H. (1962). Society as symbolic interaction. In A. M. Rose (Ed.), *Human behavior and social processes*. Boston, MA: Houghton Mifflin.

Blundel, R. K., & Smith, D. (2001). *Business networking: SMEs and inter-firm collaboration: a review of the literature*. Research Report RR003/01, Small Business Service, Sheffield. Retrieved from www.sbs.gov.uk/research

Blundel, R. K., & Smith, D. (2001). Business networking: SMEs and inter-firm collaboration: A review of the literature. Research Report RR003/01. Small Business Service, Sheffield. Retrieved from www.sbs.gov.uk/research

Bohatá, M. (1997). Business ethics in Central and Eastern Europe with special focus on the Czech Republic. *Journal of Business Ethics*, 16(14), 1571–1577.

Bohmam, J. (1992). The limits of rational choice explanation. In J. S. Coleman & T. S. Farraro (Eds.), *Rational choice theory, advocacy and critique* (pp. 207–227). London: Sage.

Bourdieu, P. (1985). The forms of capital. In J. G. Richardson (Ed.), *Handbook of theory and research for the sociology of education* (pp. 241–258). New York, NY: Greenwood.

Bourdieu, P. (1998). The essence of neoliberalism. *Le Monde diplomatique*, December.

Bourdieu, P., & Coleman, J. S. (1991). *Social theory for a changing society*. Boulder, CO: Westview Press.

Bowey, L. J., & Easton, G. (2007). Entrepreneurial social capital unplugged: An activity-based analysis. *International Small Business Journal*, 25(3), 273–306.

Brenkert, G. (2002). Entrepreneurship, ethics and the good society. In *Ethics and entrepreneurship* (Vol. 3, pp. 5–43). The Ruffin Series. Charlottesville, VA: Society for Business Ethics.

Briggs, X. d. S. (2004). Social capital: Easy beauty or meaningful resource. In J. Hutchinson & A. C. Vidal (Eds.), *Using social capital to help integrate planning theory, research and practice* (pp. 151–158). Journal of American Planning Association, 70(2), 142–192.

Bromley, D. B. (1993a). *Reputation. Image, and impression management*. West Sussex: Wiley.

Bromley, D. B. (1993b). *Reputation, image and impression management*. Chichester: Wiley.

Bryman, A., & Bell, E. (2003). *Business research methods*. Oxford: Oxford University Press.

Bryman, A. (1988). *Quantity and quality in social research*. London: Unwin Hyman.

Bueno, E., Salmador, M. P., & Rodriguez, O. (2004). The role of social capital in today's economy. *Journal of Intellectual Capital*, 5(4), 556–574.

Burrell, G., & Morgan, G. (1979). *Sociological paradigms and organisational analysis*. Hants: Heinmann.

Burrow, J. (2007). *A history of histories*. London: Allen Lane.

Burt, R. S. (1982). *Towards a structural theory of action*. New York, NY: Academic Press.

Burt, R. S. (1990). The social structure of competition. In N. Nitin & R. G. Eccles (Eds.), *Networks and organisations; Structure, form, and action* (pp. 57–91). Boston, MA: Harvard Business School Press.

Burt, R. S. (2000a). The contingent value of social capital. In E. L. Lesser (Ed.), *Knowledge and social capital* (pp. 255–286). Oxford: Butterworth-Heinemann.

Burt, R. S. (2000b). The network structure of social capital. *Research in Organizational Behaviour, 22*, 345–423.

Burt, R. S. (2004). Structural holes and good ideas. *American Journal of Sociology, 110*(2), 249–299.

Burt, R. S. (2005). *Brokerage and closure*. Oxford: Oxford University Press.

Burt, R. S. (2006). Closure and social capital.

Cairns, E., Van Til, J., & Williamson, A. (2003). *Social capital, collectivism-individualism and community background in Northern Ireland*. Coleraine, N. Ireland: Centre for Voluntary Action, University of Ulster. Retrieved from www.ofmdfmni.gov.uk/social capital.pdf

Carr, A. Z. (1994). Is business bluffing ethical. In J. Drummond & B. Bain (Eds.), *Managing business ethics* (pp. 26–38). London: Butterworth-Heinemann.

Casson, M., & Della Giusta, M. (2007). Entrepreneurship and social capital: Analysing the impact of social networks on entrepreneurial activity from a rational action perspective. *International Small Business Journal, 25*(3), 220–224.

Castiglione, D. (2008). Social capital as a research programme. In D. Castiglione, J. W. Van Deth, & G. Wolleb (Eds.), *The handbook of social capital* (pp. 177–195). Oxford: Oxford University Press.

Castiglione, D., Van Deth, J. W., & Wolleb, G. (Eds.). (2008). *The handbook of social capital*. Oxford: Oxford University Press.

Champlin, D. (1999). Social capital and the privatisation of public goods. *International Journal of Social Economics, 26*(10–11), 1302–1314.

Charon, J. M. (2009). *Symbolic interactionism: An introduction, an interpretation, an integration*. London: Pearson.

Chell, E. (2008). *The entrepreneurial personality: A social construction* (2nd ed.). East Sussex: Routledge.

Chell, E. (2010). *The entrepreneurial personality*. London: Routledge.

Chell, E., Haworth, J. M., & Brealey, S. (1991). *The entrepreneurial personality: Concepts, cases and categories*. London: Routledge.

Chomsky, N. (1999). *Profits over people*. New York, NY: Seven Stories Press.

Churchill, N. C., & Lewis, V. L. (1983). The five stages of small business growth. *Harvard Business Review, 61*(3), 30–50.

Cohen, S. S., & Fields, G. (2000). Social capital and capital gains in Silicon Valley. In E. L. Lesser (Ed.), *Knowledge and social capital: Foundations and applications* (pp. 179–200). Oxford: Butterworth-Heinemann.

Cohen, W. M., & Levinthal, D. A. (1990). Absorptive capacity: A new perspective on learning and innovation. *Administrative Science Quarterly, 35*(1), 128–152.

Cohen, D., & Prusak, L. (2001). *In good company. How social capital makes organizations work*. Boston, MA: Harvard Business School Press.

Coleman, J. S. & Fararo, T. S. (Eds.). (1992). *Rational choice theory, advocacy and critique.* London: Sage.

Coleman, J. S. (1958). Relational analysis: The study of social organization with survey methods. *Human Organization, 16,* 28–36.

Coleman, J. S. (1972). Systems of social exchange. *Journal of Mathematical Sociology, 2,* 145–163.

Coleman, J. S. (1973). *The mathematics of collective action.* Chicago, IL: Alder.

Coleman, J. S. (1988). Social capital in the creation of human capital. *American Journal of Sociology, 94,* 95–120.

Coleman, J. S. (1990). *Foundations of social theory.* Cambridge, MA: Belknap Press of Harvard University Press.

Coleman, J. S. (2000). Social capital in the creation of human capital. In E. L. Lesser (Ed.), *Knowledge and social capital: Foundations and applications* (pp. 17–41). Oxford: Butterworth-Heinemann.

Commin, F. (2008). Social capital and the capability approach. In D. Castiglione, J. W. Van Deth, & G. Wolleb (Eds.), *The handbook of social capital* (pp. 624–651). Oxford: Oxford University Press.

Cooke, P., & Clifton, N. (2002). *Social capital and the knowledge economy.* Regional Industrial Research Report No. 39. Centre for Advanced Studies, Cardiff University.

Cooke, P., & Clifton, N. (2004). Spatial variation in social capital among UK small and medium-sized enterprises. In P. Nijkamp, R. Stough, & H. de Groot (Eds.), *Entrepreneurship and regional economic development: A spatial perspective* (pp. 107–137). Cheltenham: Edward Elgar.

Cooke, P., & Willis, D. (1999). Small firms, social capital and the enhancement of business performance through innovation programmes. *Small Business Economics, 13,* 219–234.

Clifton, N., Cooke, P., & Oleaga, M. (2005). Social capital, firm embeddedness and regional development. *Regional Studies, 39*(8), 1065–1077.

Cope, J., Jack, S., & Rose, M. B. (2007). Social capital and entrepreneurship: An introduction. *International Small Business Journal, 25,* 213–219.

Crotty, M. (1998). *The Foundations of social research: Meaning and perspective in the research process.* Crows Nest: Allen & Unwin.

Curran, J., & Blackburn, R. (2001). *Researching the small enterprise.* London: Sage.

Dana, L.-P. (Ed.). (2010). *Entrepreneurship and religion.* Cheltenham: Edward Elgar.

Dasgupta, P. (2005). Economics of social capital. *The Economic Record, 81*(255), 2–21.

Davidsson, P., & Honig, B. (2003). The role of social and human capital among nascent entrepreneurs. *Journal of Business Venturing, 18,* 301–331.

de Tocqueville, A. (1835/1956). *Democracy in America.* London: Signet Classics, Penguin.

DeCarolis, D. M., & Saparito, P. (2006). Social capital, cognition, and entrepreneurial opportunities: A theoretical framework. *Entrepreneurship Theory and Practice, 30*(1), 41–56.

Denizen, N. K. (1970). *The research act in sociology.* Chicago, IL: Aldine.

Denizen, N. K., & Lincoln, Y. S. (1970). *The Sage handbook of qualitative research.* London: Sage.

Diani, M. (2004). How associations matter: An empirical assessment of the social-capital-trust-voluntary action link. In S. Prakash & P. Selle (Eds.), *Investigating social capital. Comparative perspectives on civil society, participation and government* (pp. 137–161). London: Sage.

Dodd, S. D., & Anderson, A. R. (2007). Mumpsimus and the mything of the individualistic entrepreneur. *International Small Business Journal, 25*(4), 341–360.

Dowling, G. (2001). *Creating corporate reputations. Identity, image, and performance.* Oxford: Oxford University Press.

Dudwick, N., Kuehnast, K., Jones, V. N., & Woolcock, M. (2006). *Analysing social capital in context: A guide to using qualitative methods and data.* Washington, DC: World Bank Institute.

Dunham, L. C. (2009). From rational to wise action: Recasting our theories of entrepreneurship. *Journal of Business Ethics, 46*, 99–110.

Edelman, D. C., Bresnen, L. F., Newell, S., Scarbrough, H., & Swan, J. (2004). The benefits and pitfalls of social capital: Empirical evidence from two organisations in the United Kingdom. *British Academy Journal of Management, 15*, 59–69.

Emerson, R. (1976). Social exchange theory. *Annual Review of Sociology, 2*, 335–362.

Etzioni, A. (1988). *The moral dimension: Towards a new economics.* New York, NY: The Free Press.

Etzioni, A. (1994). *The spirit of community.* New York, NY: Ouchstone.

Field, J. (2003). *Social capital.* London: Routledge.

Fine, B., & Green, F. (2000). Economics, social capital and the colonization of the social sciences. In S. Baron, J. Field, & Schuller (Eds.), *Social capital: Critical perspectives* (pp. 78–93). Oxford: Oxford University Press.

Fine, B. (2001). *Social capital versus social theory: Political economy social science at the turn of the millennium.* London: Routledge.

Fitzgerald, F. S. (1945/1960). *The crack up* (p. 69). New York, NY: New Direction Books.

Flap, H. D. (1994). No man is an island: The research program of a social capital theory. Presented at the *European consortium of political research on social capital and democracy*, 3–6 October, Milan (pp. 29–59).

Flap, H. D. (1994). No man is an Island: The research program of a social capital theory. Presented at the European Consortium of Political Research on Social Capital and Democracy, October 3–6, Milan: 29–59.

Foley, M. W., & Edwards, B. (1997). Is it time to disinvest in social capital? *Journal of Public Policy, 19*, 141–173.

Frank, R. H. (1988). *Passions within reason: The strategic role of the emotions.* New York, NY: W.W. Norton.

Friedman, M. (1970). The social responsibility of business is to increase its profits. *New York Times Magazine*, September 13.

Friedman, M. (1973). The social responsibility of business is to make profits. *New York Times.*

Friedman, J. (1995). Economic approaches to politics. In J. Friedman (Ed.), *The rational choice controversy* (pp. 1–24). London: Yale University Press.

Friedman, J. (Ed.). (1996). *The rational choice controversy.* New Haven, CT: Yale University Press.

Fukuyama, F. (1995a). Social capital and the global economy. *Foreign Affairs, 74*(5), 89–103.

Fukuyama, F. (1995b). *Trust: The social virtues and the creation of prosperity.* New York, NY: Simon Schuster & Press.

Fukuyama, F. (1999). Social capital and civil society. *IMF conference on second generation reforms*, George Mason University, October.

Fukuyama, F. (2000). *The great disruption*. New York, NY: Touchstone.

Fukuyama, F. (2001). Social capital, civil society and development. *Third World Quarterly*, *22*(1), 7–20.

Fuxman, L. (1997). Ethical dilemmas of doing business in post-Soviet Ukraine. *Journal of Business Ethics*, *16*, 1273–1282.

Gambetta, D. (1998). Can we trust trust? In D. Gambetta (Ed.), *Trust: Making and breaking cooperative relations* (pp. 213–238). Oxford: Blackwell.

Gerber, M. (1994). *The e-myth re-visited: Why most small businesses don't work and what to do about it*. New York, NY: Topeka Binding.

Ghoshal, S. (2005). Bad management theories are destroying good management practices. *Academy of Management Learning and Education*, *1*(4), 75–91.

Gladwell, M. (2000). *The tipping point*. London: Abacus.

Granovetter, M. (1973). The strength of weak ties. *American Journal of Sociology*, *78*, 1360–1380.

Granovetter, M. (1985). Economic action and social structure: The problem of embeddedness. *American Journal of Sociology*, *91*(3), 481–510.

Granovetter, M. (1992). Problems of explanation in economic sociology. In N. Nitin & R. G. Eccles (Eds.), *Networks and organisations; Structure, form, and action* (pp. 25–56). Boston, MA: Harvard Business School Press.

Granovetter, M. (2005). The impact of social structure on economic outcomes. *Journal of Economic Perspectives*, *19*(1), 33–55.

Gray, J. (1998). *False dawn: The delusions of global capitalism*. London: Granta.

Green, S. L. (2002). *Rational choice theory: An overview*. Baylor University seminar on rational choice theory, May. Retrieved from business.baylor.edu/steve_green/green1

Grootaert, C., & Bastelaer, T. V. (2002). *Understanding and measuring social capital*. Washington, DC: The World Bank.

Halpern, D. (2005). *Social capital*. Cambridge: Polity Press.

Hannafey, F. T. (2003). Entrepreneurship and ethics. *Journal of Business Ethics*, *46*, 99–110.

Harris, J. (2002). *On trust, and trust in Indian business: Ethnographic explorations*. Development Studies Institute Working Paper Series No. 02-35, London School of Economics, London.

Hayek, F. A. (1944/2001). *The road to serfdom*. London: Routledge.

Hedstrom, P., & Stern, C. (2008). Rational choice and sociology. In S. N. Durlauf & L. E. Blume (Eds.), *The new Palgrave dictionary of economics*. London: Palgrave Macmillan.

Hirsch, P. M., & Levin, Z. (1999). Umbrella advocates versus validity police: A life-cycle model. *Organization Science: A Journal of the Institute of Management Sciences*, *10*(2), 199–212.

Hoang, H., & Antoncic, B. (2003). Network-based research in entrepreneurship. *A Critical Review Journal of Business Venturing*, *18*, 165–187.

Hoffman, J. J., Hoelscher, M. L., & Sherif, K. (2005). Social capital, knowledge management, and sustained superior performance. *Journal of Knowledge Management*, *9*(3), 93–100.

Holliday, R. (1995). *Investigating small firms*. London: Routledge.

Homans, G. C. (1958). Social behavior as exchange. *American Journal of Sociology*, *63*(6), 597–606.

Homas, G. (1961). *Social behaviour: Its elementary forms*. London: Routledge.

Hooghe, M., & Stolle, D. (Eds.). (2003). *Generating social capital: Civil society and institutions in a comparative perspective.* New York, NY: Palgrave–Macmillan.

Hospers, J. (1956). *An introduction to philosophical analysis.* London: Routledge.

Huysseune, M. (2003). The case of Italy. In M. Hooghe & D. Stolle (Eds.), *Generating social capital. Civil society and institutions in comparative perspective* (pp. 211–230). New York, NY: Palgrave Macmillan.

Inkpen, A. C., & Tsang, E. W. K. (2005). Social capital, networks and knowledge transfer. *Academy of Management Review, 30*(1), 145–165.

Jack, S., & Anderson, A. R. (1999). Entrepreneurship education within the enterprise culture: Producing reflective practitioners. *International Journal of Entrepreneurial Behaviour and Research, 5*(3), 110–125.

Jack, S., & Anderson, A. R. (2000, November). *The effects of embeddedness on the entrepreneurial process.* Working Paper No. 3. Department of Management Studies, University of Aberdeen.

Jacobes, J. (1961). *The death and life of Great American cities.* New York, NY: Random House.

Jane, J. (1961). *The death and life of great American cities.* New York, NY: Random House.

Jenssen, I. J., & Greve, A. (2002). Does the degree of redundancy in social networks influence the success of business start-ups? *International Journal of Entrepreneurial Behaviour and Research, 8*(5), 254–267.

Joad, C. E. M. (1924). *Introduction to modern philosophy.* Oxford: University Press.

Johnson, S. (1999). *Who moved my cheese? An amazing way to change in your work and your life.* New York, NY: Vermillon.

Jones, B. D. (1999). Bounded rationality. *Annual Review of Political Sciences, 2,* 297–321.

Jordon, B. (2008). Social capital and welfare policy. In D. Castiglione, J. W. Van Deth, & G. Wolleb (Eds.), *The handbook of social capital* (pp. 652–676). Oxford: Oxford University Press.

Jung, C. J. (1983). *The essential Jung.* Princeton, NJ: Princeton University Press.

Kay, J. (2010). *Obliquity.* London: Profile Books.

Kelly, S. (1995). The promise and limitations of rational choice theory. In J. Friendman (Ed.), *The rational choice controversy* (pp. 95–106). New Haven, CT: Yale University Press.

Kelvin, L. (1891). *Popular lectures and addresses* (Vol. 1), London: Macmillan.

Korsgaard, S., & Anderson, A. R. (2011). Enacting entrepreneurship as social value creation. *International Small Business Journal, 29*(2), 135–151.

Lane, R. E. (1995). What rational choice explains. In J. Friedman (Ed.), *The rational choice controversy* (pp. 107–126). New Haven, CT: Yale University Press.

Lappe, F. M., & Du Bois, P. M. (1997). Building social capital without looking backward. *National Civic Review, 86,* 119–128.

Lave, J., & Wenger, E. (1991). *Situated learning. Legitimate peripheral participation.* Cambridge: Cambridge University Press.

Lee, R., & Jones, O. (2008). Networks, communication and learning during business start-up: The creation of cognitive social capital. *International Small Business Journal, 26,* 559–594.

Lee, R. (2008). Social capital and business and management: Setting a research agenda. *International Journal of Management Reviews, 10*(3), 1–27.

Lesser, E. L. (Ed.). (2000). *Knowledge and social capital.* Oxford: Butterworth-Heinemann.

Levitas, R. (2004). Let's hear it for Humpty: Social exclusion, the third way and cultural capital. *Cultural Trends, 133*(2), No. 50, 44–56.

Lewis, M. (1989). *Liar's poker*. London: Hodder and Stoughton.

Liao, J., & Welsch, H. (2005). Roles of social capital in venture creation: Key dimensions and research implications. *Journal of Small Business Management, 43*(4), 345–362.

Lin, N. (1999). Social networks and status attainment. *Annual Review of Sociology, 25*, 467–487.

Lin, N. (2001). *Social capital, A theory of social structure and action.* Cambridge: Cambridge University Press.

Lindblom, C. (1959). The science of 'muddling through'. *Public Administrative Review, 39*(6), 79–88.

Maak, T. (2007). Responsible business leadership, stakeholder engagement, and the emergence of social capital. *Journal of Business Ethics, 74*, 329–343.

Mackey, C. (1841/1980). *Extraordinary popular delusions and madness of crowds.* New York, NY: Hedley.

Manis, J. G., & Meltzer, B. N. (Eds.). (1978). *Symbolic interaction: A reader in social psychology* (3rd ed.). Boston, MA: Allyn and Bacon.

Manning, P. (2009). The entrepreneurial personality: A social construction, by E. Chell (2nd ed.). Reviewed in The International Journal of Entrepreneurial Behaviour and Research (2010), **15**(6).

Manning, P. (2010a). Explaining and developing social capital for knowledge management purposes. *The Journal of Knowledge Management, 14*(1), 83–99.

Manning, P. (2010b). Putnam and radical socio-economic theory. Special issue on Radical Economics of the International Journal of Social Economics, *37*(3), 254–269.

Manning, P. (2010c). The dark side of social capital: Lessons from the Madoff case. In W. Sun, J. Stewart, & D. Pollard (Eds.), *Reframing corporate social responsibility: Lessons from the global financial crisis* (pp. 207–228). Critical Studies on Corporate Responsibility, Governance and Sustainability. Bingley, UK: Emerald Group Publishing Limited.

Marshall, C., & Rossman, G. B. (1995). *Designing qualitative research* (2nd ed.), Thousand Oaks, CA: Sage.

Martin, C., & Hartley, J. (2006). SME intangible assets (pp. 1–79). Research Report No. 93. Certified Accountants Educational Trust, London.

Marwick, A. (1970). *The nature of history.* London: Macmillan.

Maslow, A. H. (1954). *Motivation and personality.* New York, NY: Harper & Row.

Mayer, N. (2003). Democracy in France: Do associations matter? In M. Hooghe & D. Stolle (Eds.), *Generating social capital. Civil society and institutions in comparative perspective.* New York, NY: Palgrave Macmillan.

McClelland, D. C. (1961). *The achieving society.* Princeton, NJ: Princeton University Press.

McElroy, M. W., Jorna, R. J., & Engelen, J. V. (2006). Rethinking social capital theory: A knowledge management perspective. *Journal of Knowledge Management, 10*(5), 124–136.

Meltzer, B. N., Petras, J. W., & Reynolds, L. T. (1975). *Symbolic interaction, genesis, varieties and criticism.* New York, NY: Routledge.

Midgley, M. (2010). *The solitary self: Darwin and the selfish gene.* Durham, NC: Acumen.

Murphy, J. B. (1995). Rational choice theory as social physics. In J. Friedman (Ed.), *The rational choice controversy.* Yale: Yale University Press.

Nahapiet, J., & Ghoshal, S. (1998). Social capital, intellectual capital and the organizational advantage. *Academy of Management Review, 23*(2), 242–266.

Nitin, N., & Eccles, R. G. (Eds.). (1990). *Networks and organisations; structure, form, and action* (pp. 57–91). Boston, MA: Harvard Business School Press.

O'Donnel, A., & Cummins, D. (1999). The use of qualitative methods to research networking in SMEs. *Qualitative Market Research: An International Journal, 2*, 82–91.

Ostrom, E., & Hess., C. (2007). *Understanding knowledge as a commons: From theory to practice.* Cambridge MA: MIT Press.

Ostrom, E. (1990). *Governing the commons: The evolutions of institutions for collective action (political economy of institutions and decisions).* Cambridge: Cambridge University Press.

Paldam, M. (2000). Social capital: One or many? Definition and measurement. *Journal of Economic Surveys, 14*(5), 629–653.

Passmore, J. (1957). *A hundred years of philosophy.* London: Penguin.

Pastoriza, D., Arino, M. A., & Ricart, J. E. (2008). Ethical managerial behaviour as an antecedent of organisational social capital. *Journal of Business Ethics, 78*, 329–341.

Patterson, L. (2000). Civil society and democratic renewal. In S. Baron, J. Field, & T. Schuller (Eds.), *Social capital: Critical perspectives* (pp. 39–55). Oxford: Oxford University Press.

Patulny, R. V., & Svendsen, G. L. H. (2007). Exploring the social capital grid: Bonding, bridging, qualitative, quantitative. *International Journal of Sociology and Social Policy, 27*(1–2), 2–51.

Paxton, P. (1999). Is social capital declining in the United States? A multiple indicator assessment. *American Journal of Sociology, 105*(1), 88–127.

Peters, T. (2010). Kindness can be the hardest word of all. *Financial Times.* Retrieved from cachef.ft.com/cms/s/0/f5472b94-aee1-11df-8e45-00144feabdc0.html. Accessed on August 23, 2010.

Polanyi, K. (1944/2001). *The great transformation* (2nd ed.). Boston, MA: Beacon Press.

Polanyi, M. (1958). *Personal knowledge. Towards a post-critical philosophy.* London: Routledge and Kegan Paul.

Portes, A., & Sensenbrenner. (1993). Embeddedness and immigration: Notes on the social determinants of economic action. *American Journal of Sociology, 98*(May), 1320–1350.

Portes, A. (1998). Social capital: Its origins and applications in modern sociology. *Annual Review of Sociology, 24*, 1–24.

Postan, M. M. (1972). *The medieval economy and society.* London: Penguin.

Preuss, L. (2004). Aristotle in your local garage: Enlarging social capital with an ethics test. In L. J. Spence, A. Habisch, & R. Schmidpeter (Eds.), *Responsibility and social capital: The world of small and medium enterprises* (pp. 154–164). New York, NY: Palgrave Macmillan.

Prus, R. (1996). *Symbolic interaction and ethnographic research.* Albany, NY: State University of New York Press.

Prusak, L., & Cohen, D. (2001). How to invest in social capital. *Harvard Business Review, 79*(6), 86–93.

Putnam, R. D. (1973). *The beliefs of politicians. Ideology, conflict, and democracy in Britain and Italy.* New Haven, CT: Yale University Press.

Putnam, R. D. (1993). *Making democracy work. Civic traditions in modern Italy.* Princeton, NJ: Princeton University Press.

Putnam, R. D. (1995a). Bowling alone: America's declining social capital. *Journal of Democracy, 6*, 66–78.

Putnam, R. D. (1995b). The strange disappearance of civic America. *The American Prospect, 7*(24), 34–48.

Putnam, R. D. (2000). *Bowling alone.* New York, NY: Simon Schuster.

Putnam, R. D. (2004). Preface. In J. Hutchinson & A. C.Vidal (Eds.), *Using social capital to help integrate planning theory, research and practice.* Journal of American Planning Association, 70(2), 142–192.

Quince, T. (2001). *Entrepreneurial collaboration: Terms of endearment or rules of engagement.* ESRC Centre for Business Research, University of Cambridge Working Paper No. 207. Retrieved from www.cbr.cam.ac.uk/pdf/WP207.pdf

Rae, D. (2005). Entrepreneurial learning: A narrative-based conceptual model. *International Journal of Entrepreneurial Behaviour and Research, 12*(3), 323–335.

Remenyi, D., Williams, B., Money, A., & Swartz, E. (1998). *Doing research in business and management: An introduction to process and method.* London: Sage.

Ridley, M. (1996). *The origins of virtue.* London: Penguin.

Rousseau, D. M. (1985). Issues of level in organizational research: Multi-level and cross-level perspectives. In L. L. Cummings & B. M. Staw (Eds.), *Research in organizational behavior.* Greenwich, CT: JAI Press.

Sandefur, R. L., & Laumann, E. D. (1988). A paradigm for social capital. *Rationality and Society, 10*(4), 481–501. In E. L. Lesser (Ed.) (2000), *Knowledge and social capital* (pp. 69–88). Oxford: Butterworth-Heinemann.

Schonsheck, J. (2000). Business friends: Aristotle, Kant and other management theorists on the practice of networking. *Business Ethics Quarterly, 10*(4), 897–910.

Schumpeter, J. A. (1912/1934). *The theory of economic development: An inquiry into profits, capital, credit, interest, and the business cycle.* London: Transaction Publishers.

Schumpeter, J. A. (1947). The creative response in economic history. *Journal of Economic History, 7*, 149–159.

Schwandt, T. (2000). Three epistemological stances for qualitative inquiry. interpretivism, hermeneutics and social constructionism. In N. K. Denzin & Y. S. Lincoln (Eds.), *Handbook of qualitative research* (2nd ed., pp. 189–213). London: Sage.

Scott, J. (2000). Rational choice theory. In G. Browning, A. Halcli, & F. Webster (Eds.), *Understanding contemporary society: Theories of the present.* London: Sage. Retrieved from privatewww.essex.ac.uk/~scottj/socscot7.htm

Semplar, R. (1993). *Maverick!: The success story behind the world's most unusual workplace.* New York, NY: Warner Books.

Sered, D. (1996). *Orientalism.* Retrieved from www.english.emory.edu/.../Orientalism.html

Shaw, E., & Conway, S. (2000). Networking and the small firm. In S. Carter & D. Jones-Evans (Eds.), *Enterprise and small business: Principles, practice and policy* (pp. 367–383). *Financial Times.* Harow: Prentice Hall.

Shibutani, T. (1955). Reference groups as perspectives. *American Journal of Sociology, 60.* In J. G.Manis & B. N. Meltzer (Eds.), *Symbolic* interaction: *A reader in social psychology* (3rd ed., pp. 105–115). Boston, MA: Allyn and Bacon.

Silverman, D. (1985). *Qualitative methodology and sociology: Describing the social world.* Aldershot: Ashgate Publishing.

Silverman, D. (2005). *Doing qualitative research.* London: Sage.

Simmel, G. (1950). *The sociology of Georg Simmel.* In K. Wolff (Trans. & Ed.). Glencoe, IL: The Free Press.

Simon, H. A. (1979). Rational decision making in business organisation. *American Economic Review, 69*, 495–501.

Simon, H. A. (1986). Organisation decision making and problem solving. In M. Zey (Ed.), *Decision making: Alternative to rational choice models*. Newbury Park, CA: Sage.

Skocpol, T. (1996). Unravelling from above. *American Prospect, 25*, 20–25.

Smedlund, A. (2008). The knowledge system of a firm: Social capital for explicit, tacit and potential knowledge. *Journal of Knowledge Management, 12*(1), 66–77.

Smelser, N. J., & Swedberg, R. (2005). The sociological perspective on the economy. In N. Smelser & R. Swedberg (Eds.), *Handbook of economic sociology* (pp. 3–26). New York, NY: Russell Sage Foundation.

Smith, A. (1759). *Theory of moral sentiments*. London: Penguin.

Smith, A. (1776/1999). *The wealth of nations*. London: Penguin.

Sobel, J. (2002). Can we trust social capital? *Journal of Economic Literature, 40*(1), 139–154.

Solow, R. (1999). Notes on social capital and economic performance. In P. Dasgupta & I. Serageldin (Eds.), *Social capital. A multifaceted perspective*. Washington, DC: The World Bank Publications.

Soule, E. (1998). Trust and managerial responsibility. *Business Ethics Quarterly, 8*(2), 249–272.

Spence, L. J., & Schmidpeter, R. (2003). SMEs, social capital and the common good. *Journal of Business Ethics, 45*, 93–108.

Spence, L. J. (1999). Does size matter? The state of the art in small business ethics. *Business Ethics: A European Review, 8*(3), 163–174.

Spence, L. (2004). *Forever friends? Friendship, dynamic relationships and small firm social responsibility*. Working Papers No. 8. BRESE, Brunel University. Retrieved from www://www.brunel.ac.uk/research/brese/pub/work.htm

Spence, L. J., Habisch, A., & Schmidpeter, R. (2004). *Responsibility and social capital. The world of small and medium enterprises*. New York, NY: Palgrave Macmillan.

Stake, R. E. (2000). Case studies. In N. K. Denzin & Y. S. Lincoln (Eds.), *Handbook of qualitative research* (pp. 435–454). Thousand Oaks, CA: Sage.

Svendsen, G. L. H., & Svendsen, G. T. (2004). *The creation and destruction of social capital*. Cheltenham: Edward Elgar.

Szreter, S. (2000). Social capital, the economy, and education in historical perspective. In S. Baron, J. Field, & Schuller (Eds.), *Social capital: Critical perspectives* (pp. 56–76). Oxford: Oxford University Press.

Taleb, N. N. (2007). *The black swan*. London: Penguin Books.

Thorpe, R., Holt, R., Macpherson, A., & Pittaway, L. (2006). *Studying the evolution of knowledge within small and medium-sized firms*. London: Advanced Institute of Management Research.

Tonkiss, F., & Passey, A. (Eds.). (2000). *Trust and civil society*. London: Macmillan Press.

Tonkiss, F. (2000). Trust, social capital and the economy. In F. Tonkiss & A. Passey (Eds.), *Trust and civil society*. London: Macmillan.

Tymon, W. G., & Stumpf., S. A. (2003). Social capital in the success of knowledge worker. *Career Development International, 8*, 12–20.

Uzzi, B. (1996). The sources and consequences of economic embeddedness for the economic performance of organizations: The network effect. *American Sociological Review, 61*(4), 674–698.

Vyakarnam, S., Bailey, A., Myers, A., & Burnett, D. (1997). Towards an understanding of ethical behaviour in small firms. *Journal of Business Ethics, 16*(15), 1625–1636.

Webb, J., Schirato, T., & Danaher, G. (2002). *Understanding Bourdieu*. London: Sage.

Weber, M. (1902/1992). *The protestant ethic and the spirit of capitalism*. London: Routledge.

Wenger, E., McDermott, R., & Snyder, W. (2002). *Cultivating communities of practice: A guide to managing knowledge*. Cambridge, MA: Harvard University Press.

Westerlund, M., & Savhn, S. (2008). Social capital in networks of software SMEs: A relationship value perspective. *Helsinki School of Economics Research Papers*, *37*(5), 492–501.

Wheen, F. (2004). *How mumbo jumbo conquered the world*. London: Fourth Estate.

Widen-Wulff, G., & Ginman, M. (2004). Explaining knowledge sharing in organizations through the dimensions of social capital. *Journal of Information Sciences*, *30*(5), 448–458.

Williamson, O. E. (1985). *The economic institutions of capitalism*. New York, NY: Free Press.

Williamson, O. E. (1993). Calculativeness, trust and economic organization. *Journal of Law and Economics*, *36*(2), 453–486.

Wittgenstein, L. (1968). *Philosophical investigations*. Oxford: Basil Blackwell.

Woolcock, M., & Radin, E. (2008). A relational approach to the theory and practices of development aid. In J. W. Van Deth & G. Wolleb (Eds.), *The handbook of social capital* (pp. 411–437). Oxford: Oxford University Press.

Woolcock, M. (1998). Social capital and economic development: Towards a theoretical synthesis and policy framework. *Theory and Society*, *27*(1), 151–208.

Woolcock, M. (2001). Microenterprise and social capital: A framework for theory, research, and policy. *Journal of Socio-Economics*, *30*, 193–198.

Yin, R. K. (1994). *Case study research: Design and methods* (2nd ed.). Thousand Oaks, CA: Sage.

Yu, T., & Lester, R. H. (2008). Moving beyond boundaries: A social network perspective on reputation spillover. *Corporate Reputation Review*, *11*(1), 94–108. Retrieved from reputationinstitute.com/crr/V11/Yu_Lester_Vol11.N1.pdf

APPENDICES

APPENDIX A: RELATED THEORIES

Earlier and/or Related Theory	Key Scholars	Social Capital Research Examples/Focus of Similar Phenomena	Social Capital Scholars	Commentary
Business clusters (1897)	Alfred Marshall	Silicon Valley contrasted with Boston's 'Route 28' (Cohen & Fields, 2000, pp. 179–200). Putnam puts the case that social capital leads to economic prosperity and links the concept with Alfred Marshall's 'industrial districts', '… which allow for information flows, mutual learning, and economies of scale' (2000, p. 325).	Putnam (2000, pp. 324–325), Cohen and Fields (2000, pp. 179–200) in favour of social capital process for the success of the Silicon Valley.	There is an extensive theoretical debate on the significance of social capital for the development of Silicon Valley (Cohen & Fields, 2000).
Transaction cost theory and	Williamson, (1985, 1993)	The 'Strength of Weak Ties' (Granovetter, 1973)	Granovetter (1973), Fukuyama (2000), Putnam	The economic advantages of social capital in facilitating

Appendix A. *(Continued)*

Earlier and/or Related Theory	Key Scholars	Social Capital Research Examples/Focus of Similar Phenomena	Social Capital Scholars	Commentary
exchange economics	Nobel economics prize winner 2009	Radius of Trust (Fukuyama, 2000, pp. 88–91) Homophily principle (Lin, 2001, pp. 46–52) Putnam's bonding capital (2000, pp. 22–24) Network closure for increasing trust in economic exchange (Burt, 2005)	(2000), Lin (2001), Burt (2005)	economic interaction based on closure in networks creating trust are a recurring theme in theoretical literature.
Communities of practice	Lave and Wenger (1991) Wenger et al. (2002)	Ongoing interaction to develop learning	Burt on self-managing teams (2005)	Burt quotes approvingly of Apple's CEO, Steve Jobs, on work teams: 'The greatest people are self-managing. They don't need to be managed. Once they know what to do, they'll go out and figure how to do it' (2005, p. 149).
Absorptive capacity	Cohen and Levinthal (1990)	Brokerage and entrepreneurship Social capital and knowledge management	Burt (2005) Bueno, Salmador, and Rodriguez (2004, p. 557)	'Absorptive capacity' describes the ability of organisations to recognise, assimilate and commercially exploit knowledge

2nd generation theories of collective action	Ostrom and Hess (2007) Nobel economics prize winner 2009	Economic governance and the organisation of cooperation	Coleman (1988, 1990), Putnam (1993, 2000) and Fukuyama (1995b)	All discuss community norms
Trust	Simmel (1950) Soule (1998) Tonkiss (2000)	Both can be understood as taking a 'soft', uncritical view of contemporary capitalism	Burt (2005) Fukuyama (1995a, 1995b)	Social capital and trust are used as interchangeable terms.
Reputation theory	Bromley (1993)	Achieving identity and relational intangibles	Coleman (1990, 2000), Lin (2001), Fukuyama (1995a, 1995b, p. 359), Burt (2005, pp. 100–101), Nahapiet and Ghoshal (1998, p. 252) and Putnam (2000, p. 136)	For example Burt proposes a 'bandwidth hypothesis', in which the actors own their reputation in the sense that they define their behaviour which in turn defines their reputation. Second, under the 'echo hypothesis', reputation is not owned by the individual, but rather is owned by, '… the people in whose conversations it is built, and the goal of those conversations is not accuracy so much as bonding between the speakers' (2005, p. 196).
Tacit knowledge	Polanyi (1958)	Developing the social fabric of organisations	Cohen and Prusak (2001)	Concerned with expert and insider knowledge that is hard to codify
Embeddedness	Karl Polanyi (1944/2001)	The importance of ingrained ethical habit (Fukuyama, 1995a, 1995b)	Granovetter (1985) Coleman (1990, 2000), Putnam (1993, 2000)	The idea that the economy is embedded in broader society

Appendix A. (*Continued*)

Earlier and/or Related Theory	Key Scholars	Social Capital Research Examples/Focus of Similar Phenomena	Social Capital Scholars	Commentary
		The socio-economic approach Putnam's Italian civicness (1993)	Fukuyama (1995a, 1995b)	is at the core of socio-economics
Mutual aid	Peter Kropotkin: Mutual aid: A factor in evolution (1902)	Mutual interdependence	Putnam and reciprocity (2000, pp. 134–147) Coleman states that social capital declines as people need each other less (1990, p. 321)	Putnam defines social capital with reference to reciprocity
Social exchange theories	Commentary by Fine (2001)	Commoditisation of social interaction	Coleman (1988, 1990)	Social interaction conceptualised as a market
Communitarianism	de Tocqueville (1835/1956), Etzioni 1988	American exceptionalism: 'self-interest rightly understood'	Putnam (1993, 2000)	Putnam claims to be a neo-Tocquevillian (Manning, 2010b)
Humanist understanding of the workplace	Maslow (1954)	Stress on the human factor in organisations and the economic significance of social interaction	Cohen and Prusak (2001) Fukuyama (2001, p. 10)	Lean manufacturing techniques, '… often lead to great gains in efficiency, but are totally dependent on the social capital of the workforce' (Fukuyama, 2001, p. 10).

Source: This author.

APPENDIX B: RATIONAL CHOICE THEORY AND SOCIAL CAPITAL

Scholar	Rational Choice Understanding of Social Capital	Commentary
James Coleman	'… aspects of social structure that enhance opportunities of actors within that structure' (1994).	Sociological and egocentric Communitarian-political/sociological understanding Both internal and external
Robert Putnam	'… social contacts affect the productivity of individuals and groups' (2000, p. 19). In terms of generalised reciprocity quotes approvingly of de Tocqueville's: 'Self interest rightly understood' (2000, p. 135).	Political approach that understands social capital as a property of a group, either as regions in Italy (1993) or at the level of the nation state (2000) Socio-centric, whole network, internal
Nan Lin	'… the notion of social capital-capital captured through social relations. In this approach, capital is seen as a social asset by virtue of actors' connections and access to resources in the network or group of which they are members' (2001, p. 19). Investment in social relations with expected returns in the market-place' (*ibid.*, p. 19). '… investment by individuals in interpersonal relations useful in the markets' (*ibid.*, p. 25). Moreover according to Lin, '… an elementary exchange, evoking a relationship between two actors and a transaction of resource (s), contains both social and economic elements' (*ibid.*, p. 144).	Sociological and egocentric External
Ron Burt	To provide, 'access, timing and referrals' (1990, p. 62). 'The advantage created by a person's location in a structure of relationships is known as social capital … Social capital is the contextual complement to human capital in explaining advantage … social structure defines a kind of capital that can create for individuals or groups an advantage in pursuing their end. People and groups who do better are somehow better connected' (2005, pp. 4–5).	Egocentric External

Appendix B. (Continued)

Scholar	Rational Choice Understanding of Social Capital	Commentary
Additional Social Capital Observations		
Henry Flap	'... an entity consisting of all future benefits from connections with other persons' (1994).	Utility maximisation of connections External
Ben Fine	'Essentially social capital is nepotism — you have to use the ones you know, but at least you know them' (2001, p. 157).	Utility maximisation of social connections External and internal
Portes describes Coleman and Putnam's social capital treatments as	'An approach closer to the under-socialised view of human nature in modern economics sees social capital as primarily the accumulation of obligations from other according to the norms of reciprocity' (1998, pp. 48–49).	Economic notions of rationality of instrumentalising social connections for personal advantage External
Flavio Cumin	Commented on the social capital focus on the, 'instrumentalisation of social relations' (2008, p. 629)	Sociological and egocentric, instrumentalises social interactions and relations
The Socio-Economic Approach		
Mark Granovetter	'Insofar as rational choice arguments are narrowly construed as referring to atomised individual and economic goals, they are inconsistent with the embeddedness position presented here. In a broader formulation of rational choice, however, the two views have much in common ... while the assumptions of rational choice must always be problematic; it is a good working hypothesis that should not easily be abandoned. What looks to the analyst non-rationalist behaviour may be quite sensible when situational constraints, especially those of embeddedness, are fully appreciated' (1985, pp. 505–506).	In Granovetter's view personal relations engender trust, which in turn creates vulnerability and 'enhanced opportunity for malfeasance', as reflected in the saying about personal relations that 'you always hurt the one you love' (1985, p. 491). Granovetter argues that rationality needs to be considered with reference to social structure (1985, p. 506). External and internal

Source: This author.

APPENDIX C: RESEARCH POPULATION

Number/Firm Name	Size	Sector	Research Data	Name
1. Cogs (IT services)	Micro	IT/Consultancy	Int x PP ID ED	Kevin
2. IT Solutions (IT services)	Medium	IT/Consultancy	Int x PP x ID ED	Neal
3. Easy Tech (IT services)	Micro	IT/Consultancy	Int x ID	Aftab
4. R Ices (confectionary)	Micro	Leisure and hospitality	Int x PP x ID ED	David
5. S.L. (cottages/chalets)	Micro	Leisure and hospitality/ Accommodation	Int x ED	Nick
6. H.P. (retail)	Small	Services	Int ID	Charlotte
7. S.I. Property (student flats)	Small	Accommodation Services	Int ID ED	Paul
8. A.T. (equipment company)	Medium	Services	Int x ID ED	Neil
9. S.W. (wedding planner)	Micro	Leisure and hospitality	Int x PP, ID	Sarah
10. East (cosmetic dental services)	Micro	Health services	Int ID ED	Roberta
11. A.L. (dental practice)	Medium	Health services	Int ED	Carolyn
12. A.G. (IT Skills Led Delivery)	Small	IT/Consultancy	Int x ID	Steve
13. P.X. Applications (website development, E-learning)	Micro	IT/Consultancy	Int ID ED	Darren
14. J.R. (Internet services)	Micro	IT and religious/social	Int ED	Charles
15. P.B. (party products and services)	Micro	Leisure and hospitality	Int PP ID	Phil

Appendix C. *(Continued)*

Number/Firm Name	Size	Sector	Research Data	Name
16. C.W. Promotions (nightclub promotions)	Micro	Leisure and hospitality	Int x ED	George W
17. D.G. (glass products)	Medium	Leisure and hospitality	Int ID	Matthew
18. L.S. (restaurant chain)	Medium	Leisure and hospitality	Int	George
19. W.Y. (body art supplier)	Micro	Leisure	Int ED	Lee
20. F.B. (hotels)	Small	Leisure and hospitality/ Accommodation	Int	Rob
21. P.G. (educational services)	Micro	Education services	Int	Clare
22. A.C. Coaching (education training)	Micro	Education services	Int	Terry
23. Int (HRM training)	Micro	Education services	Int ID	Maria
24. H.T.S. (Haulage)	Medium	Education services	Int ID	Julia
25. P.S, (book-keeping tools for self-employed)	Micro	Services	Int ID	Steve
26. S.V. (car wrapping service)	Micro	Services	Int x PP ID ED	Tom
27. S.D. (discount retailer)	Micro	Retail	Int x	Tony
28. T.W. (wedding cars and funeral services)	Micro	Services	Int x	Robert
29. POGO (energy services)	Micro	Services (carbon credits)	Int ID	Nils
30. K.T (management consultancy)	Micro	Recruitment and management consultancy	Int	Karl

Note: All firms have been annonymised. All names are pseudonyms.
Glossary:
Int = Interview
ID = Internal documents
ED = External documents
PP = PowerPoint
Source: This author.